Princess

PRINCESS
The Early Life of Queen Elizabeth II

JANE DISMORE

Guilford, Connecticut

An imprint of The Rowman & Littlefield Publishing Group, Inc.
4501 Forbes Blvd., Ste. 200
Lanham, MD 20706
www.rowman.com

Distributed by NATIONAL BOOK NETWORK

British Library Cataloguing in Publication Information available

Library of Congress Cataloging-in-Publication Data

Names: Dismore, Jane, author.
Title: Princess: The early life of Queen Elizabeth II / Jane Dismore.
Description: Guilford, Conn. : Lyons Press, 2018. | Includes bibliographical
    references and index.
Identifiers: LCCN 2018004753 (print) | LCCN 2018003221 (ebook) | ISBN
    9781493034635 (ebook) | ISBN 9781493034628 (hardcover)
Subjects: LCSH: Elizabeth II, Queen of Great Britain, 1926- | Queens—Great
    Britain—Biography
Classification: LCC DA590 (print) | LCC DA590 .D57 2018 (ebook) | DDC
    941.085092 [B]—dc23
LC record available at https://lccn.loc.gov/2018004753

♾™ The paper used in this publication meets the minimum requirements of American National Standard for Information Sciences—Permanence of Paper for Printed Library Materials, ANSI/NISO Z39.48-1992.

Printed in the United States of America

To my family

Contents

Introduction

Philip once met an Australian man who said: 'My wife is a doctor of philosophy and much more important than I am.' Philip said: 'Ah yes, we have that trouble in our family too.'
—QUEEN ELIZABETH II IN A SPEECH IN AUSTRALIA, 1954

When the Queen joked about her husband, the Duke of Edinburgh, she was twenty-seven, he was thirty-three, and they had been married for six years. He clearly coped with being married to the most famous woman in the world, for in November 2017 they celebrated their seventieth wedding anniversary, at the ages of ninety-one and ninety-six.

Famously she fell in love with Prince Philip of Greece, a handsome cadet in Britain's Royal Navy, when she was thirteen. They married in 1947 when Elizabeth was still a Princess, Philip was pursuing a successful naval career, and there was no indication that she would become Queen as quickly as she did. At their Golden Wedding in 1997, she said of Philip, 'He has, quite simply, been my strength and stay all these years', sustaining her through decades that in 2016 saw her become the world's longest-reigning monarch. But she had a solid foundation. With previously unpublished material and interviews from friends and relations who have known her since childhood, here is a fresh look at her life as Princess. Born in 1926 into one of the few remaining European monarchies, her early life was as stable as Philip's was turbulent, sustained by devoted parents who wanted their daughters to have as normal a life as possible. Much loved but never spoilt, despite her privileged existence, Princess Elizabeth learned the notion of duty in the difficult years after the Abdication and during the Second World War. Growing up, she often looked wistfully from castle windows and through palace gates to the world outside. Here is the rarefied world into which she was born, the people who shaped her future and the Prince who would support her through it.

Chapter I

Suddenly a Queen (1952)

I was 41 when I succeeded my father, and many thought that young. But Queen Elizabeth is only 25 – how young to assume the responsibilities of a great Throne in these precarious times – and she has the good wishes and support of us all.[1]

On 8 February 1952, the Duke of Windsor prepared to leave New York to attend the funeral of his brother, King George VI. Standing next to his black-attired wife on the deck of the *Queen Mary,* he read a prepared speech to a crowd of journalists and television cameras. Although he spoke of his sorrow at the loss of his brother and respect for his reign, the world knew it was the Duke's abandonment of that 'great Throne' that had led to his niece being placed upon it. When she became Britain's longest-reigning monarch on 9 September 2015, aged eighty-nine, the Queen said the title was 'not one to which I have ever aspired'.[2] While longevity was not an unreasonable expectation at her birth, given that her great-great-grandmother Queen Victoria had reached eighty-one, it was certainly not envisaged in 1926 that it would ever accompany the title of monarch. Even when the Abdication established her destiny at the age of ten, no one, including Edward VIII as the Duke of Windsor then was, could have imagined she would accede to the Throne so young. But as he recognised in his speech, his brother had been 'harassed by the dangers and tribulations of a second world war, and beset by more than his share of political strife'. What he did not mention was the strain that the Abdication itself had placed upon the shy, stammering Bertie, Duke of York, who had been ill-prepared for his role as King. Faced with such circumstances, a shortened life was perhaps not surprising.

How different Elizabeth's life might have been. 'We were both brought up very much as country children really, and if she hadn't had the bad luck, if you like, to become Queen, she would just have been a country lady. She loves her dogs, she's really interested in her horses – she is basically a country girl.' The Queen's first cousin, the Hon. Mrs Margaret Rhodes,[3] spent her childhood summers in Scotland with Princess Elizabeth and her younger sister and lived with them at Windsor Castle for much of the war. 'There are people who think it must be wonderful to have lots of money and live in a big house with lots of servants but you could never wake up one morning and say "What a lovely day, let's take a picnic to the seaside." You just can't. Your life is totally organised and you know from months ahead exactly what you're doing every day. And the inevitability of having to read those red boxes every day of your life, regardless of whether you're on holiday or not, and make decisions . . .'

Her life as Queen began with cruel suddenness on 6 February 1952 when her father died. At twenty-five, she was the same age as Elizabeth I had been when she came to the Throne, but unlike the Virgin Queen, she was enjoying her fifth year of married life. With two young children, and her husband pursuing the naval career he had enjoyed before they married – 'clinging [to it] with the tenacity of a barnacle to a ship's keel', as a contemporary royal chronicler observed[4] – Elizabeth had sampled the nearest she would ever come to living a normal life. As 'just another naval wife',[5] she had been spending weeks at a time with Philip in Malta, where he had command of a ship, and enjoying the luxury of a little privacy. Although they had undertaken duties that the King's poor health left him unable to fulfil, he had seemed to be recovering after a lung operation in September 1951 and was planning a trip to South Africa in the coming March. It was misplaced optimism.

The death of George VI occurred during the night as he slept on his own in his ground-floor room at Sandringham. He had enjoyed a good day's shooting, followed by a relaxed dinner with his wife and daughter, Princess Margaret, who would always remember her parents joking together that evening. He went to bed early because he was still convalescing and was seen by the night watchman opening his window. 'And then', said Princess Margaret, 'he wasn't there anymore'.[6] His long-standing servant James Macdonald found him dead in bed when he took in his early morning tea. He had died peacefully from a coronary thrombosis.

For once, the King's youngest daughter knew something before her sister did. The moment had arrived which Elizabeth had anticipated since she was ten years old but which no one expected to happen so soon. The King was only fifty-six and, as Princess Margaret said, 'He died as he was getting better.'[7] On learning of his death, his Private Secretary, 'Tommy' Lascelles, immediately informed his Assistant Private Secretary, Edward Ford, in London, using the code word they had devised for such an event: 'Hyde Park Corner'. It was Ford's task to tell the Prime Minister, Winston Churchill, and the King's mother, Queen Mary. Lascelles asked the King's widow – the Queen Mother, as she would shortly be known – to approve an announcement to be made from Sandringham, and at 11:15 a.m. the news was broadcast by the BBC.

But Elizabeth was in Kenya, and for four hours she remained blissfully unaware of the fact that she was Queen. Her lady-in-waiting, Philip's cousin, Pamela Hicks,[8] said, 'We were almost the last people in the world to know.' They had left London on 31 January to begin a six-month tour of Kenya, Ceylon and Australasia in place of the King and Queen. It was the last time Elizabeth saw her father, who, with the Queen and Princess Margaret, Churchill and other dignitaries, had waved the couple off from London Airport. Their first stop was Nairobi, where they enjoyed fishing and riding at Sagana Lodge, a wedding present from the Kenyan government, with beautiful gardens that sloped down to the River Sagan flowing through its grounds. The highlight was a night spent at Treetops, a four-bedroom observation lodge thirty-three feet up in the branches of a giant fig tree. From there they watched wild animals gathering at night at a watering hole, lured there in the absence of moonlight by artificial light. Elizabeth had excitedly filmed a cow elephant suckling her young and giving it a bath. 'It was so exciting, really wonderful', said Pamela. After a thrilling all-night sojourn they returned to Sagana Lodge. As the British public woke on 6 February to read about the Duke and Duchess of Edinburgh's walk along a quarter-mile jungle track to Treetops, the story had already been superseded.

During the afternoon, Elizabeth was writing to her father about their adventures and Philip was having a siesta. His Secretary, Mike Parker, a fellow naval officer, received a telephone call from Elizabeth's Assistant Private Secretary, Martin Charteris, who was staying a few miles away. Charteris had just been told by a journalist of a Reuters newsflash about the King's death but was unable to get through to Buckingham Palace for confirmation. Later it transpired that signals in cipher had been sent to Government House, Nairobi, but no one could read them because the cipher book had been taken by the Governor. He was already on his way to say goodbye to the royal party, who were due to leave the following day to continue their tour.

Charteris suggested that Parker find a wireless. The only portable one was in the sitting room where Elizabeth was writing her letter. Parker managed to remove it unobtrusively and switched it on; eventually he and Pamela heard the news confirmed by the BBC. When Parker told Philip, 'he looked absolutely flattened, as if the world had collapsed on him'.[9] 'This will be such a blow', Philip said,[10] covering his face with a copy of *The Times*, then composed himself and went to find Elizabeth. It was about 2:45 p.m. local time, 11:45 a.m. in London. Philip took her into the garden, where they were seen pacing up and down 'while he talked and talked and talked to her', said Parker.[11] When Elizabeth came back into the house, ever considerate, she apologised to her entourage for their trip being cut short. Pamela could not believe the King had died, for they had 'all imagined that it would be about twenty years before the princess would succeed her father to the throne'.[12]

When Charteris arrived, he found her 'very composed, absolute master of her fate', drafting telegrams of apology.[13] He was not surprised by Elizabeth's demeanour. He had worked for her since 1949 and soon he would join Michael Adeane and Edward Ford as number three in the new Queen's office: 'I fell in love with her when I met her. She was so young, beautiful, dutiful, the most impressive of women.'[14] Elizabeth's outward calm was the result of several factors. By nature she was not particularly demonstrative. Importantly, since childhood she had seen the example set by her parents and both sets of grandparents. For her grandmother, Queen Mary, in particular, stoicism and self-control were paramount.

Duty meant that emotions were to be subsumed for the sake of outward dignity. If she wanted to convey her feelings she could do so privately, to those close to her. Elizabeth replied to her cousin Margaret's letter of condolence. Of being away when he died, Elizabeth wrote, 'It really was ghastly; the feeling that I was unable to help or comfort Mummy or [Princess] Margaret, and that there was nothing one could do at all.'[15] She appreciated her cousin writing to her: 'Letters are such a comfort, and every one of them gives me further courage to go on.'

Her mother, widowed at just fifty-one, wrote to Queen Mary: 'I know that you loved [him] dearly, and he was my whole life. . . . he was such an angel to the children & me, and I cannot bear to think of Lilibet, so young to bear such a burden.'[16] Queen Mary had outlived her husband and now a third son,[17] and would soon be paying her respects to her granddaughter as the sixth monarch of her lifetime. In London, her Comptroller, Lord Claude Hamilton, made a brief announcement from her home at Marlborough House: 'Queen Mary has had a terrible shock but she is taking it remarkably well. She is staying in her rooms at present.'[18]

Everything had changed. Elizabeth's husband was now her subject and would be required in public to call her 'Ma'am' and, like other men, to bow when she entered the room. However, her name would remain the same. When Charteris asked her what she wanted to be called as Queen she replied, rather surprised, 'My own name, Elizabeth, of course.'[19] It was not a pointless question. Her father George VI was really Albert and her uncle David had become Edward VIII. Back in London, the necessary procedures that followed the King's death were being observed. An emergency Cabinet met and decided to hold an Accession Council that afternoon. Much discussion took place as to the wording of the Proclamation. It declared the new monarch as Queen Elizabeth the Second, and made her the first since George I to be proclaimed *in absentia*.

While these formalities were being observed, everything was immediately packed up at Sagana Lodge. Elizabeth changed out of her jeans into a beige dress and white hat; she had no black clothes with her. She remained completely calm as she and Philip said goodbye and thanked the staff, presenting each of them with a signed photograph. Within two hours of receiving the news, they were ready to leave. Charteris asked the Press lining the roads not to take any pictures, and as a mark of respect to the grieving new Queen, they did not. The party flew to Entebbe to pick up the royal plane, BOAC *Argonaut*; however, a severe electric storm delayed them there for two hours, extending the already long journey and thus the agony for Elizabeth, who had to make polite conversation with the Governor of Uganda. At least it gave the opportunity for a black coat, handbag and shoes to be delivered to her from SS *Gothic*, the ship on which the rest of the royal staff were travelling, so she could arrive in London suitably dressed. There was no black hat, however, so that would have to be delivered to her on board the minute they landed.

Once the plane took off, she was able to retire with Philip to their cabin while they flew through the night. She asked Charteris what would happen when they arrived in London and he realised that she did not know. Before landing, she changed into the mourning clothes, assisted by her long-serving nurse, now her dresser, 'Bobo' Macdonald. For the immediate future there was no need for the three hundred outfits that had gone with her to accommodate the diverse climates she would find during the tour, many specially designed and said to be 'the most glamorous wardrobe created in London since the war'.[20]

On 7 February, they landed. Her uncle Henry, Duke of Gloucester, came on board, with Philip's uncle, Earl Mountbatten, and Philip's Extra Equerry, who had a note for the new Queen from her grandmother. Setting in motion the protocol that would continue, Philip let his wife begin the descent of the plane's steps before he came out so that she could be photographed alone. Lady Myra Butter[21] recalls watching the news and seeing her childhood friend, now her Sovereign, coming off the plane, 'so poignant in black, being met by Churchill. I thought, she went away as Elizabeth and here she is as Queen. I knew then that her life and his were completely changed.' Churchill, who was joined by Clement Attlee, Anthony Eden and others, was so overcome with emotion that he could hardly speak.

As the world absorbed the news, the affection for the late King became touchingly apparent, even outside the Commonwealth. In New York City, the Stars and Stripes were flown at half mast, and memorial services were held in tribute to the first reigning British monarch to enter America and whose reign, overshadowed as it was by war, had seen Britain welcoming the United States as its ally. The memory of Princess Elizabeth's visit just three months earlier was still fresh too, when President Truman, clearly smitten, said, 'When I was a little boy I read about a fairy princess, and there she is.'[22]

Even though the 'fairy princess' had become a Queen, she could not yet go to Buckingham Palace. Formalities had to be concluded: her mother, suddenly swept from the main picture, was still living there; and Elizabeth and Philip would have to be moved out of their home, Clarence House, with Charles, aged three, and Anne, eighteen months. The children had been among the last to see the King. While their parents were in Kenya, they stayed with their grandparents at Sandringham. They could not know that they had moved up the ladder of succession and that Charles was now heir to the Throne. Neither could they understand that their mother was making history as the first queen regnant to succeed directly on the death of her father, and the first queen to have been brought up by the reigning sovereign as his successor. As the Archbishop of Canterbury, Dr Fisher, movingly said in a memorial service: 'We must be humbly thankful to God that for the past 15 years [the King] raised up one to be head of our family who in terrible times never failed but by his bearing in them added new power and grace to the nation, Commonwealth, and the kingship in our hearts.'[23] What the young Prince and Princess would soon find out, however, was that they would have to curtsey to their mother first thing each day before they could kiss her.

Elizabeth and Philip were taken from the plane to Clarence House, where for the first time the Royal Standard was flown. There, Queen Mary, ever the strict observer of protocol, put aside her grief and made obeisance to her granddaughter, curtseying and kissing her hand. That evening, Churchill made a broadcast. Although concerned by his new Queen's youth – 'only a child', he bemoaned privately – he spoke of 'a new Elizabethan age' and of the monarchy being 'the magic link which unites our loosely bound but strongly interwoven Commonwealth'.

As Queen, her first public appearance was the next day, at a full meeting of the Accession Council at St James's Palace. Standing before nearly two hundred 'old men in black clothes with long faces',[24] the young woman addressed them in 'a firm yet charming voice'[25]: 'My heart is too full for me to say more to you today than that I shall always work, as my father did throughout his reign, to uphold constitutional government and to advance the happiness and the prosperity of my peoples.' She prayed that God would help her 'to discharge worthily this heavy task that has been laid upon me so early in life'. Outside from the ramparts of St James's, the Garter King of Arms proclaimed her accession as 'Queen Elizabeth the Second, by the Grace of God Queen of this Realm and of all Her other Realms and Territories, Head of the Commonwealth, Defender of the Faith.' New wording appeared: 'Head of the Commonwealth' replaced 'British Dominions' and 'Emperor of India' was omitted for the first time since Queen Victoria was declared its Empress.

Afterwards, Philip led her out to the waiting car, where she broke down and cried. At Sandringham, she was reunited with her mother, her children and Princess Margaret, and saw her father's body for the first time. A few days later, it would begin its procession to Windsor Castle for the funeral on 15 February. The new Queen did not wish it to be a day of public mourning, however, only that there should be a two-minute silence. She knew that the people would remember the King 'in their hearts'.

The Duke of Windsor attended the funeral alone, as Buckingham Palace had made clear must be the case, leaving Wallis in America. He walked behind the coffin carriage with the other royal dukes: his surviving brother, the Duke of Gloucester; his nephew, the sixteen-year-old Duke of Kent; and the Duke of Edinburgh. In St George's Chapel, he 'shifted restlessly from one foot to the other and was barely still a moment'.[26] Inevitably his presence was a reminder of the events of fifteen years earlier: his reluctant brother becoming King, and his niece, now his Sovereign, who knew at the age of ten that her life's course was changed irrevocably. Yet, by abdicating, he had done the country a favour. Although charming and popular – Cosmo Lang, Archbishop of Canterbury, had spoken in 1936 of 'his most genuine care' for the needy and unemployed – some considered that he had shown, as Prince of Wales, that he would not make a good King. Lang also expressed the view, criticised for its harshness, that Edward VIII had 'sought his happiness in a manner inconsistent with the Christian principles of marriage, and within a social circle whose standards and ways of life are alien to all the best instincts and traditions of his people'. Perhaps more pertinently, the pro-German sentiments expressed by him in the years that followed demonstrated to many that it was better for the country that he had gone.

His brother turned out to be a different story. The world quickly made an icon out of his eldest daughter, a little Princess living in a glittering world, who, as part of a family that carried the country and the Commonwealth through the shock of the Abdication and the fear and deprivations of war, had come to embody hope. Now as a young Queen, she was the symbol for a post-war generation. 'Poor Elizabeth', her father had once said, 'she will be lonely all her life'. Fortunately, she found in Philip another whose life's course had been changed early on by circumstance and who took the same non-pitying, pragmatic approach to life. Despite her parents' ideas of what would make a suitable husband – 'They had selected a few nice dukes', said cousin Margaret[27] – the slightly older and more worldly Philip became her rock, and while his unstuffy, often impatient approach ruffled the feathers of conventional courtiers, 'Nobody else in the world could have done that job, nobody', says Lady Butter, 'He was perfect for it.'[28]

The 'burden' to which Elizabeth's mother had referred was not overlooked. The Dean of Westminster recognised that the public had taken advantage of her parents' devotion to duty. Deprived of any real privacy, expected 'to be on the best form on every possible occasion, the Royal Family have of late been subjected to a strain which most of us would have found intolerable', he said. 'The Queen, God bless her, is young, fresh and full of vitality. Let us give her a chance, a chance of being not only a Queen but a woman with a home to enjoy and a mother with children for whom to care.' The Queen was 'a priceless possession', which needed to be 'guarded and cherished' for the sake of the country and the world.[29]

Now everything Elizabeth had learned so far, the years of watching her parents' example, would be put into practice. They would not be an easy act to follow. She had observed her mother's strength, as well as the light and easy way she had with people: 'She was always smiling and sweet to everybody', recalls Lady Butter, 'and interested in everybody. Amusing too, very quick-witted'.[30] Of her father, Elizabeth said, 'He shirked no task, however difficult, and to the end he never faltered in his duty to his peoples.'[31] At least she would not face the fear with which he had grappled so valiantly, that of public speaking, and which her uncle David had also dreaded; he had confided to Lady Desborough: '[N]either myself or any of my brothers have had any chance of learning to speak as compared to our contemporaries who have had the advantage of speaking on political platforms or in the House of Commons. Not that any of us aspire to oratory but you will agree that we have not a hope in this direction.'[32]

Whatever doubts Elizabeth may have had about dealing with the task that lay ahead, the love and stability her parents had provided and the presence in her early life of her mother's family with their creativity and eccentricities gave her a broad and solid background from which to draw during the rapidly changing times of her long reign. Out of a little princess they made a queen.

CHAPTER 2

Into the World (1925–1926)

As 1925 arrived, King George V and Queen Mary were at their Sandringham estate in Norfolk, as they always were for Christmas and the New Year. As usual they stayed in York Cottage, and although the name was something of a misnomer, it was far smaller than the 'Big House' itself, which was still occupied by the King's widowed mother, eighty-year-old Queen Alexandra. A wedding gift in 1893 from the King's father, then the Prince of Wales (later Edward VII), York Cottage eventually accommodated George and Mary's six children,[1] but it was a tight fit. When Queen Victoria visited them, she asked: 'Do some of you sleep in the garden or on the roof?'[2] Nevertheless, the King loved it, for its small rooms reminded him of the cabins of ships on which he had served in the Royal Navy, and he could keep a closer eye on their children. Usually at this time of year the family would be together, but Prince Albert, 'Bertie', the Duke of York, was in East Africa with his wife Elizabeth.

Their visit was partly for pleasure, to include a safari, and partly official. They had arrived in late December 1924 and were having a wonderful time, as would their eldest daughter years later, familiar with her parents' tales of lion and buffalo and moonlit waterholes. The Governor of East Africa had just offered Bertie a ranch, which he was very keen to accept, but the King and his Colonial Office were against it, for various political reasons; it would also set an awkward precedent and would mean he would frequently have to go out there, which was not feasible. The King told his son that he must refuse the offer, but there was no objection to his buying a ranch if he cared to. However, as the King's Assistant Private Secretary observed, 'From what I know of him, he will not want to fork out!'[3]

Sir Alexander 'Alec' Hardinge was at Sandringham, as his position required him to be, and was privy to the King's correspondence with

Bertie. Hardinge knew the Prince well, and his wife Helen had been friends with Elizabeth since they were girls. Hardinge seldom found life at York Cottage exciting. Sometimes the only light relief provided was by a pet parrot called Charlotte, the centre of royal attention. 'The beastly parrot walks about the table round me all the time', Hardinge wrote to Helen.[4] 'I saw the Queen make a sudden dive yesterday to lift up the tablecloth . . . it turned out she had seen unmistakable signs that the parrot was going to make a mess! She was right and it went on the floor!!' At other times, it was the King's easily aroused temper that disrupted the meal, so any chance to avoid it was welcome. 'I am dining alone tonight, thank goodness',[5] Hardinge noted another day. 'Last night at dinner was exceptionally dull and at lunch today we had one of the King's tirades against the younger generation. My sympathy with his sons increases daily!'

The King's temper was not helped by the continuing effects of a serious accident he had suffered in October 1915. While inspecting his troops on the Western Front, his horse, startled by the soldiers' cheering, reared up and threw him off. It then rolled on him, breaking his pelvis and three ribs. At first his doctors thought he was just badly bruised, and it was several days before the injuries were diagnosed. For the rest of his life the King endured pain and limited mobility. Sometimes, though, his sons brought his wrath upon themselves. The King was obsessed by punctuality and at Sandringham followed the tradition started by his father of keeping the clocks set half an hour ahead of Greenwich Mean Time. Although the original purpose was to allow more daylight hours in the winter for hunting, the King could not abide being kept waiting. 'Prince George was late – apparently he is so every night and consequently got a tremendous slating', Hardinge wrote of the youngest son. 'What incredible fools they are not to humour their father in these trivial matters – the P of W was just the same when here.'[6]

Poor timekeeping was not the only thing about the King's eldest son that irked him. Known to his family by his last name, David, the Prince of Wales was still very much enjoying a bachelor lifestyle, which included affairs with married women. By contrast, Bertie had pleased his parents by marrying the lovely Lady Elizabeth Bowes Lyon. Upon their engagement in January 1923, the delighted King wrote to his son, 'I am quite certain that Elizabeth will be a splendid partner in your work & share with you & help you in all you have to do.'[7] The Queen was pleased too: 'Elizabeth is charming, so pretty & engaging & natural', she wrote. 'Bertie is supremely happy.'[8] Elizabeth was also possibly the only person whose lateness the King was prepared to overlook. When she and her parents were invited to York Cottage, she was late to dinner and apologised. The royal family were amazed to hear the King respond, 'You are not late my dear. I think we must have sat down two minutes too early.'

Bertie had married Elizabeth Bowes Lyon on 26 April 1923 at Westminster Abbey, the first time since 1383 that a royal prince had married so publicly. Usually such weddings took place in private royal chapels. The Great War had ended less than five years earlier, and the weddings of two princesses in the Abbey since then had whetted the public's appetite for glamorous occasions to lift the spirits. The bridegroom was twenty-seven, his bride twenty-two. Bertie was already a popular prince. As a Royal Navy officer he had served in the war during the Battle of Jutland and also held the rank of Wing Commander in the Royal Air Force. Like his father, he had a real interest in industry and a genuine concern for the working man, and was widely respected for his work as President of the Industrial Welfare Society. After the war, he had started the popular Duke of York Camps for boys of all backgrounds. As the Archbishop of York acknowledged in his wedding address, 'You have made yourself at home in their mines and shipyards and factories. You have brought the boys of the workshop and the public school together in free and frank companionship. You have done much to . . . increase the public sense of the honour and dignity of labour.'[9]

Upon marriage, his wife became Her Royal Highness the Duchess of York. Although she belonged to one of Scotland's oldest and most noble families, being non-royal by birth, she was a commoner. As such, their marriage was seen as a real love match, for it suggested a romantic lack of royal diktat. Elizabeth's parents, Claude and Cecilia, the 14th Earl and Countess of Strathmore, had ensured by example that their children understood the social responsibilities that accompanied the privilege they were born into. The Strathmores were deeply involved in public and charitable duties, both in Scotland, where their ancestral home, Glamis Castle, stood, and in Hertfordshire, where they spent much of the year at their estate near Hitchin, St Paul's Walden Bury. When the Great War began, Elizabeth's older brothers went off to fight, and Glamis Castle was turned into a Red Cross convalescent hospital for wounded servicemen. Still in her teens, Elizabeth was too young to help her mother and older sisters nurse the men but instead kept them company, playing cards, distributing chocolate and helping them write letters home.

Two years after Elizabeth and Bertie married they still had no children, but it was relatively early days. The King and Queen already had two young grandsons by their daughter Princess Mary and her husband Viscount Lascelles. However, as the Prince of Wales was not yet showing signs of settling down, they rather hoped the Yorks would begin a family soon. Life was already busy for the couple, who found themselves

St Paul's Walden Bury, Hitchin, childhood home of Elizabeth Bowes Lyon, latterly Queen Elizabeth the Queen Mother
AUTHOR'S PHOTO

Rear view of St Paul's Walden Bury, Hitchin, childhood home of Elizabeth Bowes Lyon, latterly Queen Elizabeth the Queen Mother
AUTHOR'S PHOTO

undertaking more royal duties than Bertie's other siblings. As heir to the Throne, David was often on tours abroad; Mary was occupied with her small children and living in Yorkshire; and Princes Henry and George, both unmarried, were serving in the armed forces. However, the Yorks' duties were not too onerous in those early days.

Behind his stern exterior, Elizabeth's father-in-law, George V, was a straightforward man, fiercely loyal to his country and friends, and with a deep devotion to duty. He loved his children, but he never understood them, and he was often harsh with them. Conscious of not having been well educated, compared to most of the men he encountered in public life, he tried to make up for it by reading widely. As a result, he was often admired by diplomats and statesmen for his knowledge and understanding of foreign affairs. However, he found it difficult to accept the social changes that resulted from the Great War and retained a deep distrust for new or foreign fashions in music, dancing and dress. His fury when something new irritated or offended him made life difficult for others. The Queen could be a little more relaxed about such matters, including the current trend for ladies' bobbed hair. However, she was concerned when her Mistress of the Robes, the Duchess of Devonshire, told her that a new lady-in-waiting had adopted the latest style. The Queen was adamant that the King should not find out and insisted that the lady should always wear a false bun when on duty.[10] Even Elizabeth did not escape the King's censure. He told her he did not like her fringe; she apologised but kept it anyway.

Yet George V was not averse to all modern thinking. At a dinner that January, Hardinge was surprised to hear him 'busy talking' to a female guest 'about birth control! Of which I gathered that he was much in favour!'[11] On this subject at least, the King was ahead of his time, for it was still a contentious issue. At the heart of the rancorous debate was the Scottish scientist, Marie Stopes, whose controversial book, *Married Love*, was published in 1921; since then, she had seldom been out of the newspapers. She had opened the world's first family planning clinic in North London and was to shortly open another. They offered free service to married women, providing access to birth control for the poor and gathering scientific information about contraception. She believed married women should be able to enjoy sex for its own sake, and that by birth control, the social problems caused by poverty and overpopulation could be eliminated. Stopes was vehemently opposed by the Church, both Anglican and Catholic, as well as the medical community.

But however enlightened the King's view was in 1925, he was unlikely to think Stopes's creed applied to his own married children. In July that year Elizabeth fell pregnant, news that was at first kept from, and then strictly within, the family and did not appear in the Press until three months before the birth. Princess Elizabeth, the first royal granddaughter, would melt the King's gruff heart and delight the Queen. But falling pregnant had not been easy, probably not helped by the four-month visit to East Africa which proved to be exhausting. After their return to Britain in April 1925, the Prince of Wales had left for a tour of South Africa and Rhodesia, so the summer was a demanding one for them.

Still newly weds in the eyes of the public, the Duke and Duchess of York were already hugely popular: he good-looking, with an attractive shyness and the glamour (albeit less obvious than David's) that went with being a royal prince; she petite and blue-eyed with a wonderful complexion, who knew even then how to embrace the people with a smile and a sympathetic tilt of the head.

In June they toured the 'Black Country', as the industrial heart of England was called, driving past 'slag mounds, colliery shafts, huge chimneys belching forth smoke',[12] to visit factories and glassworks, all the time showing interest in everything. A journey south followed, to the Royal Caledonian School at Bushey; the Duke was Chief of the Scottish Clans Association of London. Then it was back up north to York, to stay with their friend Cosmo Lang, the Archbishop of York. During the Great War the Duchess had lost a brother, and in a special service conducted by the Archbishop at York Minster, she unveiled windows dedicated to the women of the British Empire who had died.

In early July, the Duke and Duchess officially visited the vast British Empire Exhibition at Wembley Stadium, opened for a second year, during which he was President. The Exhibition was a reminder to the rest of the world that post-war Britain was more than ever a force to be reckoned with. It was first opened by George V in 1924 when, thanks to the accessibility of new wireless transmission, ten million listeners heard a monarch's voice broadcast for the first time in history. In a significant moment, the King spoke directly to his people, telling them of his great hopes for the Exhibition, which 'may bring lasting benefits not to the Empire only but to mankind in general'.[13]

Now his son inspected the Exhibition, which covered over two hundred acres. Dozens of pavilions depicted the glories of the Empire, encouraging friendship and trade. The great centre was India, in the middle of which towered a replica of the Taj Mahal, with carpet-weavers busy at work in its courtyards. Visitors could discover the diamond mines of South Africa, admire the pagodas of Burma, travel on a miniature train and watch impressive displays and bands, while buying exotic merchandise. Here, Lutyens's exquisite dolls' house, so loved by Queen Mary, was first displayed, with its library containing tiny books handwritten by contemporary authors like Arthur Conan Doyle and the King's good friend, Rudyard Kipling.

The Canadian pavilion had drawn the crowds when it opened with a life-size statue of the Prince of Wales made out of butter: an impressive feat, but he complained it made his legs look too fat. Now it was his brother's turn to grumble. In 'Newfoundland' the Duke was shown a stamp bearing his portrait and exclaimed, 'What a ghastly thing! That portrait was taken in 1908. I seem to have changed pretty considerably since then', only to be told it was an issue from 1911.[14] In 'Cyprus' he was shown an ancient wine valued at £30 a bottle and the Duchess ordered some brightly coloured towels, after being reassured that the colours would not run.

Elizabeth's pleasure in domestic matters was sometimes at odds with the changing world of her sex. Women were at last making progress with suffrage and since 1918, women aged thirty and over could vote. The Great War had also opened their eyes to the types of work they might do outside the home. At the Exhibition, Elizabeth opened the International Conference of Women in Science, Industry and Commerce, the first of its kind to be held in Britain. Flanked by some of the country's ground-breaking women, the Duchess spoke of 'the importance of women's activities in so many spheres of our national life', a sentiment that had become more widely acknowledged since the war. Yet, she herself had not embraced the idea of women doing what was traditionally men's work: to her, their proper role lay in looking after the family. It is unlikely she agreed with speaker Lady Rhondda, a suffragette and now company director, who said there would never be many women in the higher ranks of commerce until businessmen were persuaded to take their daughters to work as they did their sons.

Given her position, Elizabeth's most important trait was her unfailing interest in everything she saw, or at least a flawless pretence of it, as summed up that day by the MP Nancy Astor: 'I am perfectly certain that there is no woman here who does not realise what Her Royal Highness is doing, and what an effort it must be. I am amazed how she can always appear smiling, fresh and cheerful on the most boring occasions . . . it cannot be that she is always interested, and yet she has that faculty of never looking bored.'[15]

More leisurely activities that the couple attended were also under the public gaze. The Duke, a polo player like many princes, watched enthusiastically with the Duchess and his parents as Britain played America in the first of a series of international polo matches for the Army Championship, and disguised their disappointment (in public at least) at Britain's defeat. At Wembley Stadium, the Yorks and Princess Mary attended the first night of the world's biggest circus, with five hundred performers and seven circus rings, and watched chariot races, mock stag hunts and motor polo. As they watched amid a crowd of tens of thousands, Bertie and Elizabeth could not dream of the extent to which, in just over a decade's time, their status would change and their public exposure increase.

Although very happy and content with each other's company, the Yorks enjoyed socialising with close friends, although they were not the racy 'in-crowd' who surrounded the Prince of Wales. They liked entertaining at home, which at that time was White Lodge, Richmond, where they had lived since June 1923. It was a wedding present from the King and once a favourite house of Queen Caroline, wife of George II. Just weeks before they married, the house was still lit by gas, so electricity was rapidly installed and the kitchen was updated, but little else. It was not central enough for formal entertaining, so in mid-July 1925, the King allowed them to use St James's Palace to host their first official party: six hundred guests, mostly from the Dominions, including Prime Minister Stanley Baldwin. A week later, they attended the Garden Party at Buckingham Palace, mingling among more than a thousand guests. It must have been with some relief that they motored off to Sussex at the end of July to stay with the Earl and Countess of March for the racing season at Goodwood, followed by relaxation during August at Elizabeth's family home, Glamis Castle.

During her pregnancy, Elizabeth was under the care of gynaecologist and obstetrician Sir Henry Simson, who had been knighted for his services to Princess Mary. Although throughout her life Elizabeth never spoke publicly about personal matters, it has been authoritatively suggested that artificial insemination was necessary. It was not unusual for wealthy women at the time who had trouble conceiving to see a specialist for that purpose: Simson's late colleague, Dr Jervois Aarons, an acclaimed expert in infertility, claimed to have helped some well-known society women to conceive in that way.[16] It is likely Elizabeth confided early on in her mother, to whom she was very close. The Countess of Strathmore would have been sympathetic whatever her daughter's difficulties. After having ten children, she had problems herself that led to a hysterectomy in 1921. In the usual discreet fashion, however, no hint of such an intimate subject was given publicly, and the newspapers had referred only to the Countess having 'a serious operation'.

The Yorks also had other issues to confront. Since childhood Bertie had struggled with a stammer, which he attributed to his father's lack of patience when he was trying to talk as a young boy, although the causes still remain uncertain. Those who heard him speak in public were tolerant, but Elizabeth knew how her husband dreaded such occasions. He had already sought help. In February 1920, aged twenty-four, he told Ettie Desborough, society hostess and family friend, 'I am now having lessons in talking from an Italian, Signor Loria by name. Knowing that your son Ivo used to go to Mr Macmahon, and who taught me a good deal, I thought you might like to know of this gentleman. He is very good and knows his subject thoroughly.' Bertie enclosed a leaflet showing Loria's 'scheme of training', whose services included 'Production of Articulated Voice in the Deaf and Dumb' and 'Cure of Vocal and Speech Defects'. He had been attending for a month, 'and I have seen him nearly every day and I already find a marked difference in myself'.[17] Indeed, the King had received reports that his son was improving, and told him encouragingly: '[It] shows that yr Italian friend is doing you good which is a great thing, if you could only stick to it & persevere now, he will very likely cure you entirely'.[18]

The newspapers generally were kind. In April 1923, the month Bertie married, one correspondent had suggested the problem was almost cured: 'At first it was difficult ... but by degrees the stammer was successfully overcome, and now there are only pauses. They are awkward pauses at times but they grow constantly less noticeable, and will disappear.'[19] But two years later those pauses were still awkward. After speaking at the Royal Academy banquet in May 1925, listeners 'were much puzzled at the pauses he made in the middle of sentences. The explanation is that the

Duke has an impediment which frequently holds up his flow of words. The Duke . . . seemed to be less embarrassed . . . than those who were listening to him. He simply fingered his ring and waited for the delayed word to articulate itself.'[20]

Before he gave his speech at the British Exhibition he told his father, 'I do hope that I shall do it well. But I shall be very frightened, as you have never heard me speak & the loud speakers are apt to put one off as well'.[21] He kept it brief and his father noted that he managed quite well, although with some long pauses. However, the King was worried that Bertie's problem would be a serious obstacle in the way he was received abroad. David had carried out a very successful tour of Australia in 1920, and the King had plans for Bertie and Elizabeth to do the same. Eventually, speech therapist Lionel Logue would begin the programme that rescued him.

In early November 1925, when the Duchess was four months pregnant, they moved to central London for the winter season, renting Earl Howe's house, Curzon House, in Mayfair; Howe was Lord Chamberlain to Queen Alexandra and was rarely there to use it. It was far more convenient than White Lodge. When the Yorks socialised in London, they usually had to stay at Buckingham Palace. Its location also meant Elizabeth was nearer her doctors in those crucial early months. A couple of weeks after they moved in, Bertie was hunting in Leicestershire with David when the news reached them that Queen Alexandra had suffered a heart attack; by the time they got to Sandringham on 20 November, she had died. The beautiful and long-suffering Danish-born consort of Edward VII had been known for her kindness and love of animals and was very popular. As fond as all the Princes were of their grandmother, they nevertheless bridled at the rules their father imposed upon her death. Hardinge witnessed 'frightful rows' when the King told them, 'most unreasonably to my mind, that they must not hunt for a month . . . HM is frightfully busy settling all the arrangements and therefore rather tired. What a pity they will not take each other the right way.'[22]

Queen Alexandra's death also brought about reorganisation of the royal residences. Now the King and Queen could move in to the 'Big House' at Sandringham, which after a decent period they began sorting out. At last the Queen could indulge her love of interior design: Hardinge noted that 'The K and Q have been up at the Big House all day hanging pictures and pushing furniture about.'[23] 'The Queen never does anything except mess about in the big house between 10am and 6pm – It has again become an obsession!'[24] She could also turn her creative thoughts to Marlborough House in London. Alexandra had lived there when her husband was Prince of Wales and had returned to it after his death, until her own health failed in 1924. Built for Sarah, Duchess of Marlborough, and finished in 1711, it became Crown property and customarily the London house of the heir to the Throne.

Now they hoped David would move in; he was living in the much smaller York House within St James's Palace. Over recent years, little had been done to Marlborough House, and the Queen initiated and supervised a lengthy and expensive renovation programme. Many of its two hundred rooms were extensively modernised to accommodate her stylish son – and, she hoped, his wife too – and the old stables replaced by garages for around twenty cars. Plans were also in place to alter the traffic arrangement for the busy street outside. However, David did not move in, and seems never to have had any intention of doing so. The cost of the upkeep was expected to be at least £2,000 a week, a huge amount even for the heir to the Throne, and besides, he liked the bachelor pad that was York House. When he succeeded his father, he would transfer his pleasure den to Fort Belvedere at Windsor. Meanwhile, he would be on hand to play the fun-loving uncle when his sister-in-law gave birth, which was anticipated at around the end of April 1926.

In early April, the Yorks gave up the lease of Curzon House and decided that they did not want to move back to White Lodge, which was too inconvenient and expensive to run. They spent the Easter weekend with Elizabeth's parents at St Paul's Walden Bury and returned to London on 7 April. There they moved into the Strathmores' town house at 17 Bruton Street to prepare for the birth. Elizabeth had already organised the staff she wanted. There was nursing nurse Annie Beevers, known as Nannie B, who had been nurse to her sisters' babies, and Clara Cooper Knight, known as 'Alah', whose name came about when one of her young charges had difficulty pronouncing Clara. Born in 1879, she was the daughter of a tenant farmer local to the Strathmores in Hertfordshire and was first employed to look after the young Elizabeth. Then she worked for her eldest sister, Lady Mary (May) Elphinstone, looking after her children. May's youngest child, Margaret, born in 1925, remembered Alah with the Princesses when they were all growing up: 'She was lovely, a wonderful old-fashioned nanny, instilled wonderful discipline into the children. She was my nanny and she was taken away from me!'[25]

Thanking the Queen on 12 April for some exquisite baby clothes, the Duchess said she did not think the birth would be for another two or three weeks.[26] Her guess was a little out. At 2:40 a.m. on Wednesday, 21 April 1926, Princess Elizabeth was born by caesarean delivery. As royal custom dictated, the Home Secretary, William Joynston-Hicks, was present at Bruton Street in a nearby room while the birth took place. He received a certificate from Sir Henry Simson which said, 'Her Royal Highness the Duchess of York was delivered of a strong healthy female child at 2.40 am this morning.'[27] The Home Secretary then sent the certificate to the President of the Privy Council, after which an announcement could be made. As was also traditional, he notified the Lord Mayor of London, who posted the news on the gates of Mansion House.

As soon as the Princess was born, the King and Queen, at Windsor Castle, were woken and told. A Court Circular announced their 'great pleasure' at the news. The first visitor during the morning of 21 April was Princess Mary, bringing a sheaf of red carnations. She was followed in the afternoon by the King and Queen, who arrived to cheering crowds at 3:30 p.m., and stayed for half an hour. David could not visit his niece as he was on holiday in Biarritz, convalescing on his doctors' orders after a minor ear operation, but on receiving the news by telegram he sent his congratulations. The Princess was third in line to the Throne after her uncle David and her father. The Act of Settlement 1701 gave her precedence over her father's younger brothers, but the possibility of her succession was nevertheless quite remote. David was not yet thirty-two and could still marry and produce heirs, and even if he did not, her parents had plenty of time to have a boy.

An official bulletin was published that day, signed by Simson and the Duchess's personal doctor, Walter Jagger, saying that the Duchess and her daughter were making 'very satisfactory progress'. It also said, 'previous to the confinement a consultation took place, at which Sir George Blacker was present, and a certain line of treatment was successfully adopted.' Blacker was an esteemed obstetrician who was Dean of University College Hospital, London. The following day, 22 April, an update from Simson and Jagger said that the mother and baby had passed an 'excellent night' and that their progress was 'normal and satisfactory'.

The phrase 'a certain line of treatment' would have been understood to mean a caesarean. However, the Press were soon at pains to correct this, presumably at the request of the royal family. Newspapers said that those words had 'given rise to some misunderstanding and natural, but absolutely unnecessary anxiety. It is authoritatively stated that the phrase used, "a certain line of treatment", was not intended to imply that an operation was performed, and no operation was in fact performed. The word "normal" in yesterday's bulletin was deliberately chosen with reassuring intent. The health of the Duchess of York has been excellent throughout and her condition happily caused nor justified any unusual anxiety.'[28]

Whatever the reason for this statement – whether distaste for the disclosure, albeit indirect, of personal details concerning the Duchess, or genuine concern that the public might be worried – the official statements about the Princess's birth were intended to be uncontroversial and reassuring, as her life would continue to be presented.

Bertie had been anxious that his parents would be disappointed at the sex of their first child. He wrote to his mother telling her of the 'tremendous joy' that she had brought. 'We always wanted a child to make our happiness complete, & now that it has at last happened, it seems so wonderful and strange. . . . I do hope that you & Papa are as delighted as we are, to have a grand-daughter, or would you have sooner had another grandson. I know Elizabeth wanted a daughter.'[29] The Queen was clearly thrilled, writing that the baby was 'a little darling with a lovely complexion & pretty fair hair', while the King soon became the doting grandfather.

Although the Princess was born into peacetime Britain, much of Europe was unsettled. The Great War had seen empires crumble and monarchies abolished. Shortly before meeting their new granddaughter, the King and Queen had lunched at Windsor Castle with three guests, one of

Prince Philip with his sisters and parents, Prince and Princess Andrew of Greece, Corfu, 1922
UNIVERSITY OF SOUTHAMPTON

whom was Princess Alice of Greece. Her husband was Prince Andrea, son of Danish-born King George I of Greece who was assassinated in 1913. Prince Andrea was also a first cousin of George V. Following a military coup in 1922, he had been living in exile with Alice and their five children; their youngest child and only son was five-year-old Prince Philip. George V would never know of the coincidence of his granddaughter's choice of husband, but fortunately his Foreign Office had helped Philip's family, otherwise the outcome could have been very different.

When Philip was a baby, his father commanded a corps of the Greek army which was defeated in the Greco-Turkish War of 1919–1922. In the revolution that followed, Philip's uncle, King Constantine of Greece, was forced to abdicate. Six prominent pro-royals were court-martialled and executed on trumped-up charges of high treason for their part in what was seen as Greece's shameful defeat. In the hunt for scapegoats, Prince Andrea was also to be court-martialled. A guilty verdict would have meant death.

Secret talks initiated by Britain's Foreign Office took place between the rebel leaders and British Commander Gerald Talbot, who obtained a promise that, if found guilty, Andrea would not be executed but allowed to leave the country quietly in Talbot's charge. Andrea was found guilty and sentenced to degradation of rank and banishment from Greece for life. He and his family were secretly escorted to a British ship, which carried them to safety, eighteen-month-old Philip sleeping in a crib made out of fruit crates. Prince Andrea conveyed 'to His Majesty's Government' via a messenger 'his deep gratitude' for their help.[30] Eventually they went to France, living there as a family for a short time before other traumas disrupted them.

Princess Alice was no stranger to Windsor Castle; she was a great-granddaughter of Queen Victoria and was born there in 1885. With her at the luncheon were her sister Louise, who by marriage was Crown Princess of Sweden, and their widowed mother, Victoria, a granddaughter of Queen Victoria. Princess Victoria had married the German Prince Louis of Battenberg, Britain's First Sea Lord, but sensitivities during the Great War led to their name being changed to Mountbatten; he also had to relinquish his position and title. In recognition of his loyalty, he was created Marquess of Milford Haven. When he died in 1921, Victoria became Dowager Marchioness and moved into Kensington Palace.

Alice's brothers, George and Louis Mountbatten, would come to play an important part in her son's upbringing. Meanwhile, as the guests congratulated the King and Queen on their granddaughter's birth, none of them imagined that in years to come they would be joining Queen Mary to celebrate the marriage of that little Princess to Philip Mountbatten.

CHAPTER 3

A Hertfordshire Haven (1926)

The birth of the golden-haired, blue-eyed Princess excited the public far more than had the arrival of the King's grandsons, her Lascelles cousins. It was not as though the Empire looked to her as their future sovereign, for in 1926 there was no inkling of that. However, her arrival was a warm glow in dark times, for the period of hope that had followed peace after the Great War had turned to disillusionment. The Home Secretary, who just days earlier had been on standby for the royal birth, was now standing by for a different reason. Britain's miners were unhappy, for the subsidy that had protected their wages since 1925 had ended and negotiations between their union and the mine owners' union broke down. On 1 May 1926, the miners' strike began, followed on 4 May by the General Strike, with an estimated two million workers supporting the miners.

Fortunately, Stanley Baldwin's Conservative government had already prepared contingency plans. Crucially, volunteers did their bit, thousands of men and women carrying out work previously done by strikers. The royal household was reduced to a minimum to allow the lords-in-waiting and many equerries to take up duties as special constables. Food was transported in convoys of trucks from the docks to central London by stevedores, while soldiers patrolled the streets with bayonets. Office workers and students ran the buses. Those from the upper classes, for whom hunting was a way of life, acted as mounted police to patrol crowds, while others drove trains. Nancy Astor led a group of female volunteers to deliver the Royal Mail and Lady Curzon organised a car pool on Horse Guards Parade.

With the Duke of York's interest in industrial matters, he spent less time than he had anticipated with his wife and daughter during the first days in order to attend debates in the House of Commons. He probably missed baby's first outing, which took place when she was ten days' old, when Alah wheeled her into her grandparents' garden in Bruton Street. The General Strike was over in nine days but the miners' strike would continue until November, the army and volunteers keeping industries and essential transport functioning. Although he could not be seen to be partisan, the King had demonstrated his sympathy with the miners in previous years by setting up a distress fund for their families. During this strike, when a major coal-owner denounced the miners as 'a damned lot of revolutionaries', the King retorted furiously, 'Try living on their wages before you judge them.'[1]

But for now there were important matters to decide closer to home: the Princess's name. The newspapers, eager to find something lighter to discuss than the strike, were happy to speculate. They were mostly right: Elizabeth Alexandra Mary, which the King pronounced 'a pretty name'. Her initials were the same as those of her mother's name, Elizabeth Angela Marguerite. A few days before the christening, the Queen's friend and lady-in-waiting, the Dowager Countess Mabell Airlie, delivered to Bruton Street the holy water from the River Jordan and found such a crowd gathered outside the door 'that the baby had to be smuggled out by a back door when she went for her airing'.[2]

The Princess was christened on 29 May in the Private Chapel at Buckingham Palace. Wearing a long christening gown made of dark cream silk with a Honiton lace overlay, she was carried to the silver Lily Font, its flowers representing purity and new life, while hymns were sung by the male choir of the Chapel Royal, dressed in crimson and gold. The Archbishop of York conducted the service, during which the baby cried heartily, the only time in her life, it has been said, that she ever made a fuss in public. Lady Airlie noted that 'her old-fashioned nurse dosed her well from a bottle of dill water – to the surprise of the modern mothers present, and to the amusement of her uncle, the Prince of Wales'.[3]

Her godparents were the King and Queen; her aunt Princess Mary; her great-uncle the Duke of Connaught; her grandfather Claude, Earl of Strathmore and Kinghorne; and her mother's eldest sister, Lady Elphinstone. Other immediate family members who were present included her grandmother Cecilia and her aunt Rose Leveson-Gower.

Christening of Princess Elizabeth of York, 29 May 1926

Queen Victoria's daughter, the accomplished artist Princess Louise, Dowager Duchess of Argyll, attended too, still active at seventy-eight. The Princess's royal uncles, David and Henry, were there but Prince George was away at sea. Lady Airlie wrote of the occasion, 'I little thought then that I was paying homage to the future Queen of England, for in those days there was every expectation that the Prince of Wales would marry within the next year or two.' However, two years later he would still be single, a journalist noting, 'Whenever any eligible Royal lady "puts up her hair", HRH, in the language of the Brigade of Guards, is "for it".'[4]

The beautiful christening cake weighed an impressive 150 lb. and carried as its centrepiece a miniature silver cradle decorated with the baby's initials and coronet, the Rose and Thistle, and was padded and lined with satin. Hundreds of people waited outside Buckingham Palace's gates to see the family leave after the ceremony and broke through the police cordon, crowding the Duke and Duchess's car. The Duchess smiled and waved and allowed Alah to hold the baby up high in her arms for a lucky few to see. In those early days it was a rare view, for the Duchess was determined that her daughter should be kept out of the spotlight as much as possible.

Princess Elizabeth with her grandmother the Countess of Strathmore, her mother the Duchess of York and her uncle David Bowes Lyon (by Rachel Bowes Lyon)
RACHEL BOWES LYON

The Yorks stayed in London until 1 June, then took the Princess for her first visit to her grandparents' estate at St Paul's Walden Bury. Bertie returned to London to fulfil engagements, leaving his wife and daughter to enjoy the peace and quiet of the Hertfordshire countryside. On 11 June, *The Scotsman* newspaper confidently announced that the Yorks were leaving London at the weekend to take the Princess on her first visit to Scotland, staying at Glamis Castle. It was a visit the Scots anticipated eagerly, given her mother's ancestry. The Duchess of York was born the Hon. Elizabeth Angela Marguerite Bowes Lyon in August 1900, the ninth of ten children, when her parents were still Lord and Lady Glamis. The family's association with Glamis began in 1372 when the Scottish king, Robert II, made his favourite courtier, Sir John Lyon, the Thane of Glamis. When Lyon married the King's daughter, he received as a gift Glamis Castle. The Lyons were created Earls of Kinghorne in 1606 and of Strathmore in 1677. In 1767, the Lyon name was joined to Bowes through marriage. When Elizabeth's grandfather died in 1904, her father Claude became 14th Earl of Strathmore and Kinghorne, and she became a Lady.

A last-minute change of plan meant the Yorks' visit to Scotland did not happen; no new date was given and there was only speculation that they may go in the autumn. The London Correspondent for one newspaper, commenting on the Scots' disappointment, sniffed that 'the people of the Duchess's Scotch home still contend they have something akin to a prescriptive right to her Royal Highness'.[5] They had good reason to postpone their visit. During the General Strike, the *Flying Scotsman*, the train that took passengers from London to Edinburgh along the East Coast Line, was being manned by volunteers when it was derailed by angry miners. Although no one was injured, the incident must have been fresh in the Yorks' minds; also, train availability was affected by the strike and would have made the journey unpredictable for mother and baby.[6]

While the history and mystery of Glamis Castle captured the imagination, it was St Paul's Walden Bury that the Strathmores regarded as home. Owned by the family since 1725, it was Elizabeth Bowes Lyon's childhood home, in whose gardens she had finally accepted Bertie's proposal of marriage in January 1923. The house itself, called The Bury, was comfortable rather than luxurious. Still occupied in 2017 by Sir Simon Bowes Lyon, it retains reminders of childhoods past. On a wall in a hallway are the height markings of three generations, including Lady Elizabeth in 1905 and 1906; then 'Lilibet'; on to 'The Queen, July 1952'; and 'Charles in shoes 1964'. Nearby, a rocking horse, given by George V to Princess Elizabeth on her first birthday, and ridden many miles by her and Princess Margaret, stands ready to be enjoyed again.

The family's ownership of St Paul's Walden Bury began with Edward Gilbert in the early eighteenth century. He also began the layout of the famed gardens and provided the ornate chancel in the parish church. In 1743, Gilbert's only child, Mary, married George Bowes. The Bowes family were from the north of England and made their money from mining. They owned estates in County Durham, mainly Gibside and Streatlam Castle.

When Edward Gilbert died, Mary inherited St Paul's Walden Bury. She and her husband had a daughter, Mary Eleanor Bowes. In 1767, she married John Lyon, 9th Earl of Strathmore and Kinghorne, of Glamis Castle. Mary Eleanor Bowes was already one of the wealthiest women in the country. Her father died when she was just eleven, leaving her the Bowes estates. His will stipulated that her husband should take the additional name of Bowes, so the family name became Lyon Bowes, until the 13th Earl reversed it.

Princess Elizabeth never saw Streatlam Castle, for in 1922 her grandfather sold the estate which had been in the Bowes family since the fourteenth century.[7] In the 1930s, the house was demolished, like many others which had become unsustainable.[8] However, St Paul's Walden Bury remained in the family and found its way into the Princess's heart as she grew up. Her grandmother Cecilia is bound to have told her its tales. For much of the nineteenth century, it was run by Princess Elizabeth's formidable great-great-grandmother, Charlotte,[9] wife of Thomas, Lord Glamis. He died prematurely in 1834 before becoming Earl, leaving Charlotte, aged thirty-seven, with five children.

The widowed Lady Glamis had little time for the law. In 1863, one of her servants was sued by another woman for the return of a sum of money. Lady Glamis was called to St Albans County Court to confirm her servant's account of how much her wages were. She did so but refused to do it under oath, telling the judge, 'I shall not take an oath on such a frivolous matter.' She responded to protests: 'My word is as good as my oath. I think it would be a desecration, and taking God's name in vain in such a case.' The judge pronounced himself 'not only surprised but grieved that your ladyship refuses to do what the law requires of you. You set a sad example to those in more humble stations in society, and I must beg of you to leave this court'.[10]

Charlotte was back again in 1867, in *The Queen v Lady Glamis*. This time she was prosecuted for obstructing a lawful right of way to the parish church near The Bury by installing a swing gate. She was ordered to adjust the width of the gate but deliberately failed to do so in the way the court intended. Summoned to court again, she was given a final opportunity to put it right before further action was taken against her.

In 1880, the year before Charlotte's death, her grandson Claude George Bowes Lyon married Cecilia Nina Cavendish Bentinck, and they moved into The Bury. When the fifth of their ten children, Alexander (Alec), was born in 1887, Claude enlarged the redbrick house. The Bury became a substantial home, with around fourteen principal bedrooms and another fifteen for children and servants. Inconveniently, however, there were only two bathrooms, one at the front of the house, one at the back. When Claude became 14th Earl in 1904, he asked his agent to install another bath as cheaply as possible while he and Cecilia were in Scotland. On their return he was rather surprised to find a second bath installed next to the first one in the same room.[11] Claude continued to develop the garden, which his daughter and granddaughter so loved, although it would be his youngest son David and wife Rachael who greatly improved and extended it.

Princess Elizabeth's grandfather was tall, thin and rangy, and said to be 'a quiet, courteous, religious man, conscientious to a degree',[12] as well as a keen cricketer and good shot. He was deeply fond of his family and popular with the tenants on his estates and involved himself in many charitable and public works. His granddaughter, the Hon. Mrs Margaret Rhodes, remembered: 'Grandfather had quite a big moustache and he also smoked, so as children it was always rather fascinating. I always thought his moustache might catch fire.'[13] He was not without his eccentricities. He ate plum pudding every day. At The Bury, he had stairs built into the corner of his study from which he could escape into the cellar and into the garden if he saw anyone arriving whom he did not wish to talk to.[14] The Earl loved forestry and paid little heed to his appearance, which led to a wandering tramp striking up an acquaintance with him.

By the time Princess Elizabeth was born, the Earl was rather deaf. A close friend of her mother's since childhood was Helen Hardinge, née Cecil. Helen was a granddaughter of Robert Gascoyne-Cecil, who was Prime Minister when Elizabeth Bowes Lyon was born; their family seat was Hatfield House, just a few miles from St Paul's Walden Bury. In 1920, Helen was invited by the Earl and Countess of Strathmore to stay at Glamis Castle while Lady Elizabeth was there. She wrote to her fiancé, Alec Hardinge: 'Last night I was terribly sleepy & had to sit next [to] Lord Strathmore who is charming but very deaf which meant rather hard work & a silence always fell just as one was shouting any platitude that came into one's head! It was awful & half way through dinner he seized me by the arm to ask me to pass something, thinking that I was Elizabeth & I nearly got the giggles.'[15]

The Princess's grandmother Cecilia was the driving force of the family – vivacious, wise, musical, creative and religious. She had a tremendous sense of fun and was a natural storyteller. Life for her children was unfettered, but she ensured they were widely educated. Born in 1862 into the Cavendish-Bentinck family, Cecilia was a great-granddaughter of the 3rd Duke of Portland who had twice been Prime Minister and, had she been a boy, she would have succeeded to the dukedom. Her father, the Reverend Charles William Frederick Cavendish-Bentinck, died when Cecilia was not quite three and her twin sisters still babies. Their mother Louisa remarried five years later, becoming Mrs Harry Warren Scott: Cecilia and her children would sometimes stay with Louisa in Italy, latterly at her villa in Bordighera.

Every July the Strathmores went north, returning south in October or November. Occasionally they stayed in London, but much of their time was spent at St Paul's Walden Bury. Religion was fundamental to their lives and the family said prayers daily. The couple needed that strength to endure their tragedies, for by the time Princess Elizabeth was born they had lost three of their ten children. Their eldest, Violet, contracted diphtheria and died aged eleven, a few weeks after the birth of their eighth child, Michael, in 1893. Alec developed a brain tumour and died in 1911 aged twenty-four; and Fergus, twenty-six, was killed in 1915 in the Great War.

After Michael's birth, there was a seven-year gap until Elizabeth was born in August 1900, when Cecilia was thirty-eight. Her idyllic childhood was spent largely at St Paul's Walden Bury, and she retained a deep affection for Hertfordshire all her life. When Princess Elizabeth first visited, The Bury had changed very little. The nursery where her mother had learned to walk still had its 'high fender, the faded carpet, the toy cupboard, the favourite story-pictures framed and hung up by the gardener fifty years ago'.[16] The Princess came to love the beautiful garden with its mulberry trees, yew hedges and lawns, its ponds, temples and statues, but she especially loved the 'starfish-shaped little wood that, with its converging green alleys, to her appears an illimitable forest'; her mother named it 'the Enchanted Wood'.[17]

Elizabeth Bowes Lyon and her younger brother David were inseparable. As children they shared St Paul's Walden Bury with two black Berkshire pigs called Lucifer and Emma, goats, rabbits, a tortoise and a Shetland pony called Bobs. The Countess won prizes for her Arab ponies, and when Princess Elizabeth was born, she still kept a stud of polo ponies comprising four mares, four yearlings, three foals and a stallion called Basuto Chief. It was also at The Bury where the Princess made her first acquaintance with dogs, as her grandparents had two large chows, one black and one brown.

In July, the Duchess had to return to London to fulfil engagements, staying again at Bruton Street while the Strathmores left for Glamis. Soon the Yorks would join them, although it would not be long before the Princess herself was back in Hertfordshire while her parents were away on their Commonwealth tour.

CHAPTER 4

Family Mysteries

The histories of many aristocratic families abound with rumour and strange stories, and the Bowes Lyon family are no exception. A mystery still shrouds the Princess's mother's birthplace, about which much has been written and merits updated consideration. Elizabeth Bowes Lyon's birth certificate clearly states that she was born at St Paul's Walden Bury on 4 August 1900. The census return for 1901, relying on information provided by the head of the household (her father, then Lord Glamis) also states that she was born there. In November 1937, the year of the Coronation, she unveiled a plaque at her family's parish church, All Saints at St Paul's Walden Bury, where she was christened; it too said she was born in the parish. However, as the country prepared to celebrate her eightieth birthday in 1980, the Queen Mother, as she had become by then, declared that she was not born in Hertfordshire but in London.

The mystery began when material produced for her eightieth birthday celebrations by the St Paul's Walden Bury community stated, on the advice of her London home, Clarence House,[1] that she had spent her childhood years in the parish but did not say she was born there. A journalist noticed this omission and notified a Sunday newspaper. A copy of her birth certificate was obtained, which said she was born at St Paul's Walden Bury. It also showed that her father had been late in registering her birth: six days beyond the forty-two-day limit imposed by law.[2] (It has often been said that he paid a fine for registering late but nothing in the Act provided for such a penalty.[3] Had Lord Glamis *deliberately* given the wrong details of her birthplace or any other false information, it could have led to his conviction under the Act, so that seems very unlikely.)

The Queen Mother's official biographer William Shawcross[4] found that the assertion that she was born in London had been made as early as 1921 when her passport was issued to that effect, notwithstanding the different information on her birth certificate.[5] Today, the official website of the British Monarchy avoids stating her birthplace, saying that she 'spent her early childhood at St Paul's Walden Bury in Hertfordshire'.[6] However, Shawcross says that in the 1950s, the Press Office at Buckingham Palace repeatedly confirmed she had been born in London and the Queen Mother herself, when asked for clarification in 1978 by the President of the British Astrological and Psychic Society, wrote at the top of his letter, 'I was born in London & christened in Hertfordshire.' There is apparently no record of any statement by the Queen Mother as to why St Paul's Walden was officially recorded as her birthplace or why she unveiled a plaque containing that information if it was incorrect, as she presumably would have been able to check the wording beforehand.

Shawcross tells of investigations carried out in 1980 in an attempt to find out where she was actually born, particularly by Canon Dendle French, chaplain at Glamis and formerly vicar at St Paul's Walden Bury. Canon French traced the elderly daughter of Rev. Henry Tristram Valentine, the vicar who had baptised her, and says that Miss Valentine clearly recalled being at the Vicarage in 1900 when a maid came over from The Bury to say that Lady Glamis had given birth to a baby girl. Miss Valentine apparently told Canon French that she had asked the maid if the birth had been at The Bury and the maid said that it had. Canon French also received letters from a man who said that his father-in-law, whose name Shawcross gives as Dr Bernard Thomas, was the family's doctor in Welwyn, Hertfordshire (about six miles from The Bury), and that Dr Thomas always claimed that he was present at the birth.[7] Shawcross says it seems unlikely that a Hertfordshire doctor would be required to attend a birth in London (about twenty-five miles away).

Canon French also found that there had been some gossip in the village at the time of the birth, including the rumour that Lady Glamis had been en route from London when the contractions began, and that she was taken to Dr Thomas's home at Bridge House, Welwyn, where the baby was born. The Queen Mother herself once told a lady-in-waiting that she 'might have been born in the back of a taxi'.[8]

Why does it matter where Princess Elizabeth's mother was born? It may not, except for historical accuracy, but it is curious as to why the contradiction arose and remains unresolved, thus inviting speculation. In 2012, a controversial theory was put forward by Lady Colin Campbell.[9] She asserted that the obfuscation was because the Queen Mother was born not on the fourth but on the third of August, that Lady Glamis was not her birth mother, and that by saying she was born at St Paul's Walden Bury on the third would show the world it could not have been Lady Glamis because she was not there at the time.

In summary, Campbell says that Cecilia suffered a breakdown after the death of her daughter, Violet, and when she had Michael shortly afterwards, she was advised that she should not have any more children; however, seven years later, she and Claude wanted more. Campbell's theory is that Elizabeth Bowes Lyon's real mother was the family's French cook, Marguerite Rodier. She says this explains the nickname of 'Cookie', applied to her when she was Queen Elizabeth (Consort to George VI) by a disgruntled Duke and Duchess of Windsor after the Abdication. Campbell asserts that the Duke of Windsor had been aware of his sister-in-law's background since he was the Prince of Wales. That the couple did come to use such a nickname is evidenced by respected biographers. However, where reasons are given, they tend to vary, and no one proffers the same explanation as Campbell.

Campbell says that surrogacy was not unknown among the aristocracy, who she says knew the truth about Elizabeth, and she maintains that David Bowes Lyon, born in 1902, was also born to Marguerite. She cites specific children who were technically illegitimate but were adopted by titled parents in order to give the child the 'jacket' of legitimacy, avoiding social stigma and enabling them to inherit. In those days there was no formal adoption process, so it was largely a personal arrangement between the parties. There was indeed a French cook at The Bury called Marguerite Rodier at the time of the 1901 census, which was taken seven months after Elizabeth's birth. She was a single woman aged thirty, and Elizabeth's last name was the same as hers. It is the only public record of Marguerite being with the family, although she could have started with them at any time after the previous census of 1891. Campbell's case is that Elizabeth was born slightly early to Marguerite at The Bury when Lady Glamis was in London, causing her to hurry back, stopping at Dr Thomas's in Welwyn on the way and then going on to The Bury, where she met her new daughter.

It is frequently recorded that Cecilia referred to her two youngest children as 'the two Benjamins'. Campbell says that the source of the term was biblical and referred to stories of a man lying with his wife's maidservant, with his wife's agreement, for the purposes of providing them with a child. She says as Claude and Cecilia were both religious, they would have been aware of these stories and knew that it did not mean the husband was having an affair or being unfaithful. However, the term 'my Benjamin' can simply refer to the youngest child, and it would surely be strange if they had used a nickname that outsiders may interpret. It may also be of significance that the Doctor's name was not Bernard Thomas, as stated by Shawcross and Campbell, but *Benjamin* Thomas.[10]

Relying on information given to her by a Scottish aristocrat whom she does not name, Campbell also says that when the Earl of Strathmore was dying at Glamis in 1944 (having survived Cecilia), he told his attending doctor that Elizabeth and David were not children of his wife but those of the cook, Marguerite Rodier. Campbell says the doctor's name was Ayles, but there was no such doctor registered in Britain at that time. However, the Earl's death was certified by David *Myles*,[11] a surgeon and doctor popular in the Forfar area. Dr Myles had been the Strathmores' doctor for many years, sat on nursing committees of which the Earl and Countess were patrons, and had attended Elizabeth Bowes Lyon as a child at Glamis. He may also have attended the Countess when she had a hysterectomy in 1921,[12] and he was one of the doctors present at the birth of Princess Margaret in 1930, causing the Duchess to remark, 'Good gracious, he must have started doctoring very young.'[13] Perhaps it was his passion for mountaineering that kept Dr Myles youthful: it was a subject on which he was considered a 'racy speaker',[14] but whether his fondness for talking extended to his repeating the dying Earl's words – if indeed they were imparted to him – may never be known.

It has also been speculated that the Queen Mother could have been born in a London hospital and been driven straight to Hertfordshire,[15] or even that she was born en route between London and St Paul's Walden Bury, not least because of her own statement about a taxi. Although either is possible, the hospital hypothesis is unlikely because, as others have observed, a hospital record is bound to have emerged later and women of

The Earl and Countess of Strathmore, Princess Elizabeth's maternal grandparents
FROM *THE FINAL CURTSEY* © MRS. MARGARET RHODES. REPRINTED WITH PERMISSION.

Lady Glamis's station usually had their babies at home. Also, Claude and Cecilia had no London property of their own in 1900. They usually stayed either at her mother's home, Forbes House at Ham Common, or at the London apartment which had been his parents', in Belgrave Mansions, Grosvenor Gardens.

It was to Belgrave Mansions that an invitation to Queen Victoria's garden party on 11 July 1900 was sent to Lord and Lady Glamis. Nearly six thousand invitations were issued, and there is no record of whether she and Claude accepted or attended.[16] At that date – assuming she was indeed pregnant – Cecilia would have been only three weeks away from giving birth; given the etiquette of the time, she was surely unlikely to go. If she was not pregnant, but was intending to appear shortly as a mother, it is also unlikely that she would have gone. However, if Dr Thomas did indeed attend the birth, it seems unlikely that it would have been in London, for it would have taken him much longer to get there from his surgery at Welwyn than to The Bury. An earlier biographer of the Queen Mother, Dorothy Laird, said in 1966 that she was told by David Bowes Lyon that his sister was not born at The Bury; in the end, Laird refrained from mentioning the place of birth, although she gave 4 August as the date.[17]

Much has been made of the fact that Elizabeth's father was late in registering her birth, as though that and the possibly incorrect birthplace are connected. Hugo Vickers said the theory had been mooted (and dismissed) in court circles that if Lord Glamis was late in recording the birth, he might have settled for a date nearer to the legal deadline rather than an earlier one, in order to minimise the amount of time by which he had exceeded it, and Grania Forbes suggested that it was just absentmindedness that caused him to make a mistake when he registered.[18] Vickers also says he was told privately that Lord Glamis was in Scotland when Elizabeth was born and that by the time he registered, he could remember neither the birth place nor the correct date.

In fact, Lord Glamis was not in Scotland but in Hertfordshire around the time of the birth and certainly by 7 August. On Friday, 17 August 1900, a weekly paper local to St Paul's Walden Bury reported the number of runs Lord Glamis had scored in a cricket match at nearby Whitwell on the Tuesday of the previous week, 7 August, for which it said he had provided the lunch and tea.[19] It was probably Lord Glamis, therefore, who provided the newspapers with the birth information, for on 7 August, the *Morning Post*, a London paper, and on 8 August, the *Hampshire Advertiser*, carried the announcement in their Births column: 'On August 4th, the Lady Glamis, of a daughter.'[20] At the same time this prompt announcement affords Lord Glamis less of a convincing excuse for late, and possibly inaccurate, registration. Notably, Elizabeth's birthplace was not mentioned in the newspapers, unlike the public announcements of their first three children (who, with Elizabeth, were the only children out of their ten to be publicly announced at all).[21] By the end of August, Lord Glamis was indeed in Scotland, playing more cricket.

Elizabeth's birth was not the first time Claude and Cecilia's children were registered after the forty-two-day limit. Although the father was not the only one in law who could register a birth, no one else in their household did so. Their fourth child, John 'Jock' Bowes Lyon, was born on 1 April 1886 at The Bury, but his birth was not registered until 8 October. Their sixth child, Fergus, was born on 18 April 1889 at Forbes House, Ham, but not registered until 11 April 1890, nearly eleven months after the legal limit. Time wise, this makes the delay for Elizabeth's registration seem trifling. Neither boy's birth was announced in the newspapers, although that was probably unconnected with the late registration: the births of some of their other children who were registered on time were also not announced.

As Jock's and Fergus's births were each registered more than three months late, the law required the informant (Lord Glamis) to give a solemn declaration and to sign the register before both the registrar and the superintendent registrar, with the result that their birth certificates contain, unusually, the names of two officials. These lapses were surprising considering Lord Glamis's position. Since September 1881, he had been a Justice of the Peace for Forfarshire and a magistrate, and by 1895 was doing the same in Hertfordshire; he was also prominent in other public areas.[22] The question remains as to why he was late in registering the births in the first place. Perhaps it came down to eccentricity or perhaps, like his grandmother, Charlotte, he considered the law did not apply to him.

On 23 September 1900, two days after Elizabeth's registration, she was christened in All Saints Church by the Rev. Henry Tristram Valentine. Campbell says the choice of godparents was odd, and indeed it seems contrary to the Church's practice: no godfather, just two godmothers, who themselves were unusual choices considering her parents' social circle. They were Claude's spinster sister, Lady Maude Bowes Lyon, and Cecilia's second cousin, Mrs Arthur James. As a young woman she had been part of the Prince of Wales's inner circle (the future Edward VII) until she embarrassed him and Princess Alexandra and was banished from court. Campbell says the Rev. Valentine made a hash of naming the baby, both during the ceremony and afterwards, which she attributes to his distaste for naming the child of a noble family after a servant. She says that is why he filled out the baptism certificate incorrectly. The sections where the parents' names are given are indeed messy, but it looks simply as though their titles have been amended.

The census of 1911 repeats Elizabeth's birthplace as St Paul's Walden. By then, her brother David features. Born on 2 May 1902, astonishingly he was not registered until 18 August 1904, over two years beyond the legal limit. It was so late that Claude, by then the Earl of Strathmore, needed the authority of the Registrar General. David's birthplace is stated on his birth certificate as 24 Old Queen Street, London. Campbell's assertion that Marguerite Rodier was also David's mother seems to rely on the 'two Benjamins' story and on what the dying Earl allegedly told his doctor. David must have been conceived in late July or early August 1901. After the 1901 census, a Marguerite Rodier appears in only one place in Britain's official records: on the electoral roll of 1902, in a house in a pleasant part of Pentonville Road, London. Being eligible for the electoral roll meant she must have been single and, for at least a year, a rate payer as owner or occupier of the property. If it is the same person (and no others of that name have come to light), she must have left the Bowes Lyon household sometime after 31 March 1901 (when the census was taken) and been able to afford to live in the property either as owner or as tenant. In 1903, she remains on the electoral roll in the same house, after which she disappears. Whatever the truth may be, however, what is not in doubt is the love that Cecilia had for her children and the very close relationship Elizabeth had with her mother.

With the exception of David, Elizabeth and her siblings were wide apart in age. Nevertheless, they mostly kept in close contact throughout their lives, and Princess Elizabeth often met with her aunts, uncles and cousins. There was one family member, however, whom the Princess never met and indeed, whom, it appears, the rest of the family had nothing to do with: Constance Bowes Lyon, her second cousin. Her story was picked up by the American press in July 1924, when it seized the chance to merge two of its favourite topics, the British aristocracy and Hollywood. 'REAL ROMANCE OF SCOTCH GIRL BEATS MOVIES' shouted the *Syracuse Herald*, sub-texting, 'Miss Constance Mary Lyon, Tobacconist Clerk, Is Heiress to Ancient Estate of Strathmore'. The *New York Times* got straight to the point by mentioning her close relation: 'Shopgirl-Cousin of the Duchess of York Wins Legitimacy Suit in a Scottish Court'. Britain's press was more restrained in its headlines but voluble in its column inches announcing the judgment, which restored nineteen-year-old Connie, as she was known to the people who raised her, to her rightful position in one of Scotland's oldest and most noble families.

Not aware of her parentage until she was in her teens, it was important to Connie that it be formally recognised and her birth legitimised, at a time when the alternative was still undesirable. In April 1923, as Britain celebrated the wedding of Elizabeth Bowes Lyon and the Duke of York, Connie was preparing her court case against her father, Hubert Bowes Lyon, Elizabeth's first cousin, against whom she had been forced to take legal action because of his deliberate and sustained silence.

Constance Mary Bowes Lyon was born on Christmas Eve 1904 in an apartment in Bloomsbury, London. Her parents, Hubert, aged twenty-one, and his girlfriend, Mary Agnes Smeaton, contemplated the gift their passion had brought them: a child was not on their Christmas list. Like his younger cousin Elizabeth, whose father became Earl of Strathmore earlier that year, Hubert had also benefitted from the death of their grandfather, the 13th Earl. His will included provision for Hubert and his three younger sisters, who were the surviving children of the Earl's third son, Ernest Bowes Lyon. Ernest was in the Diplomatic Service and in 1891, aged thirty-three, was killed by a fall from a horse. Hubert was eight, his youngest sister a few days old. Hubert's share of their grandfather's inheritance was £8,000, a great deal of money for a young man.

Hubert was following a promising career as an officer in the Royal Highlanders (Black Watch), the regiment favoured by the Bowes Lyons, and, although fatherless, enjoyed other advantages of an illustrious family background on both sides: his mother Isobel was from a well-known banking family, the Drummonds. Yet although Hubert married Mary just three weeks after Constance's birth, his apparent connivance in the treatment of his daughter deprived her not only of family life with her own relations but also of all the advantages she should have enjoyed as part of Scotland's nobility. In consequence, unlike the two sons Hubert subsequently fathered with Mary, Connie Bowes Lyon's prospects were reduced to the limited horizons of an ordinary working-class girl raised in humble circumstances.

Hubert met Mary in March 1904, while he was stationed in Edinburgh. Looking for entertainment, he found himself at the city's big venue, Egyptian Halls, at the annual dance for the staff of the Kardomah Cafe. He was instantly smitten by the nineteen-year-old young woman. Clearly she was impressed too, for they immediately started a sexual relationship. Within weeks, Hubert had rented and furnished a house for them in Edinburgh, although he was required to live at his regiment's barracks in Edinburgh Castle. For Mary, one of six children of a rubber warehouseman, who had worked as a servant before becoming a shop girl, her change of circumstances must have been thrilling.

After a few months, Hubert resigned his commission and moved to London, sending money to Mary so she could join him. After Constance was born, Mary wrote to her friend Elizabeth Mackie in Edinburgh, telling her in some distress about the birth and asking how the child might be disposed of. She said she did not want her parents or the Bowes Lyons to know about her. Mackie told her of a Mrs Collie in Aberdeen, and at Mary's request, Mackie wrote to her to ask if she would take the child. Mackie told Mrs Collie that she would receive six shillings a week and that the intention was to remove the child when she was five years old, as the parents wanted her to have a better education than Mrs Collie could give her. An agreement was reached.

On 14 January 1905, three weeks after Constance's birth, Hubert and Mary married in London. Despite this, shortly afterwards, Mary and Mackie went to Aberdeen to give the child to Mrs Collie. Mackie noticed that the baby's left leg was set, having been broken. Mary told Mrs Collie that she was intending to call the child Constance and that their surname was Lyon. Nothing else was mentioned about parentage. In February 1905, Mary registered Constance's birth, naming Hubert as the father and giving their surname as Lyon.

When Connie, as she was called, was six months old, Mary asked that she be taken to a house in Edinburgh for a week while she and Hubert stayed nearby. Mrs Collie's daughter and future son-in-law, Harry Bain (whom Connie would come to regard as her parents, and Mrs Collie as her grandmother), duly took the child there, and Mary and Hubert both visited her. In 1907, Hubert and Mary moved to Dorney in Buckinghamshire, a couple of miles from where his mother's family came from; Connie was again taken to stay nearby and was visited by both parents. The house in which they lived must have belonged to the Bowes Lyons, for it was called Villa Etelinda, the same as the one in Bordighera, owned by Hubert's uncle Claude, 14th Earl of Strathmore.

That same year, 1907, they had a son,[23] and in December, Hubert was declared bankrupt. He told the court he had spent his inheritance in two years and had no assets with which to repay his debts. Although his bankruptcy was discharged in 1909, the year Connie turned five, Mrs Collie was not asked, after all, to return her to her parents for schooling. Instead, Harry Bain dutifully got on with the school-entry process, ordering the requisite copy of her birth certificate.

There is no reason to suppose that Mrs Collie and the Bains were not kind to Connie. Mrs Collie lived in a pleasant, albeit modest, house close to Aberdeen University, but she could not offer Connie the advantages the Bowes Lyons could have done. Her livelihood seems to have been looking after bastard children; even the woman referred to in court as her daughter, married to Harry Bain, appears not to have been her real daughter but an illegitimate child she had taken in.[24] In 1911, Mrs Collie received a letter signed MBL, at the top of which was written 'Please burn this letter'. Apart from sending a gift for Connie and expressing hope that she was well, Mary said it had come to her attention that someone may call upon Mrs Collie to make enquiries about Connie, with a view to taking her away. She said that if it happened, Mrs Collie should deny she knew Mary's name and say that Connie was her daughter's daughter. She also asked that she bring Connie up as her own and not to let her know that she had any other mother; neither should she call her Lyon (although Mrs Collie already had). Finally, she asked Mrs Collie to send Connie's birth certificate and any other papers to her, in case Mrs Collie should be required to give them up. This was done. It seems that Mrs Collie was so worried by the possibility of someone removing Connie that she sent her to stay in a house further along the road with an elderly widow.

In 1912, Mrs Collie died, and Mary asked Mrs Bain if she would look after Connie on the same terms. Mary said that she hoped one day to be able to send the child to a convent school, but she was afraid it would not be for some time. It never happened. Mary died in Edinburgh in 1914, aged twenty-eight, leaving Hubert – by then working in the motor industry – living in Wembley with their sons; a second son was born in 1912.

Despite the death of her mother, Connie did not see her father again; she later said that she had no recollection of her parents. The payments to Mrs Bain ceased. The court considered that perhaps Mary had concealed from Hubert the fact that she had been paying for the child for years and that he thought she had been adopted and that was that. Yet he had visited Connie, at least in the early years, and clearly knew about Mrs Bain. Had Hubert been in any doubt, he could have made enquires after Mary died. Their families may have disapproved of the illegitimacy, but they had married soon after the birth. Certainly by 1909 at the latest, Hubert's family were aware of his marriage, and it was not as though illegitimate births and related scandals were unknown to the Bowes Lyons.

After Mary died, Hubert could have made his peace with his daughter, but he did not. He served in the Great War and, after relinquishing his commission in 1919 because of ill health due to war wounds, he remarried that year. He and his wife Margaret, an actress whose stage name was Madge May, lived in a flat in Vauxhall Bridge Road, London, with their daughter Sonia, Connie's half-sister, born in 1922. Had it not been for the canniness of Mrs Collie and Harry Bain, Connie may have lived and died in ignorance of her birthright.

Mrs Collie did not burn Mary's letter of 1911 but kept it for future reference; when no one tried to remove Connie, Mrs Collie could see no reason for Mary having written the letter, except for a desire to conceal the child's identity. Before returning Connie's birth certificate to Mary, Harry Bain had taken a note of its details so that he could later apply for his own copy. He did so in May 1915, and it led him to carry out an investigation. While Harry gathered evidence, Connie left school and started work in a local newsagent's.

Following Harry's enquiries, when she was eighteen, Connie contacted Hubert through his solicitors. However, he never responded, even when legal papers were served upon him. Rather than acknowledge the young woman as his daughter, thus saving her from the embarrassment of what turned into a public case, he ignored her. While her grandmother Isobel and other relations attended Elizabeth Bowes Lyon's grand wedding in Westminster Abbey in 1923, Connie applied to Scotland's Court of Session for a declaration that she was the lawful and legitimate child of Hubert and Mary Bowes Lyon; and that, as such, she was entitled to all the rights of children born in lawful wedlock as regards inheritance or succession. Ironically, Connie's aunt, also Constance Bowes Lyon, was married to one of the judges of the Court of Session, Lord Blackburn. By then at the latest, the Bowes Lyon family must have known of the situation.

Apart from the wedding, it was not a good summer for the family. In July, another cousin of the Duchess of York, Angus Patrick Bowes Lyon, twenty-four, was found dead in his car. He had shot himself through the head after his fiancée broke off their engagement.[25]

The first of several hearings for Connie's case was held in March 1924. Witnesses included Connie, Harry Bain and Elizabeth Mackie, who had to be brought to court forcibly when she failed to obey a summons. She gave evidence in support of Connie's identity and said Mary had told her that Connie's thigh was injured at birth; Connie herself gave evidence of suffering a pain in her leg when she walked. The court noted the attempt that had been made to conceal Connie's identity. After satisfying itself that she was actually the Bowes Lyons' daughter, in June 1924 the court gave the declaration that she sought. It noted not only that her parents had married shortly after her birth, but that there may also have been an exchange of matrimonial consent during the previous year when they lived together, thus legitimising her birth. Connie was back working in the newsagent after the judgement. 'Of course I shall use the name Bowes Lyon', she told reporters. 'It was my name I fought for in the first place.' Not yet twenty-one, she would be relying on a legal guardian to advise her and manage her interests, but for now, she said, she would continue in her job, which she enjoyed immensely.

That year, Hubert's mother's family bank, Drummonds, was acquired by the Royal Bank of Scotland, although it still operated independently in London. The Deputy Governor of the RBS was the 14th Earl of Strathmore. Hubert gave a brief interview to a reporter in which he gave nothing away, merely telling of his parentage and birthplace in the Hague, and saying that he was a nephew of the 14th Earl of Strathmore and a cousin of the Duchess of York.

Not only did the judgment settle Connie's birthright, the removal of the stain of illegitimacy meant she could be considered for work of a more personal nature, where parentage was still a consideration. Legitimacy also opened the marriage door wider. Connie made progress on both grounds. After the judgment, she obtained the post of companion-help to a Mrs Lawrence in Glasgow, an author of short stories married to a banker, whose son had recently been killed in an accident. In 1933, aged twenty-nine, Connie met their friend George Dow, from a Kilmarnock family. George was ten years older than Connie and home on holiday from his work as a tobacco planter in Nyasaland (now Malawi). Within a few weeks they were engaged, and on 30 July, they were married at Blantyre.

At some point before the Second World War, Hubert Bowes Lyon moved with Margaret and their daughter Sonia to Jersey. He remained there under German occupation, while Margaret and Sonia were evacuated to England, rejoining him after Liberation. His two sons, Connie's brothers, joined the RAF.

Connie and George had no children. They visited Britain from Africa over the years until George's death in 1967, eight years after Hubert's in Jersey. Connie died in 1980. She never did meet her second cousin, Queen Elizabeth II.

CHAPTER 5

Early Years (1926–1929)

The Scots did not have to wait too long after all for their first glimpse of the Princess. On 11 August 1926, the Yorks left London for Glamis, part of an exodus of other royals and members of the aristocracy going to Scotland in time for the 'glorious twelfth', the start of the grouse shooting season. Although Bertie was looking forward to some good shooting, with a party that included his brother-in-law, David, this visit was not merely for pleasure. A busy programme of engagements was planned and the Duke was to receive the freedom of the city of Edinburgh, which he had not officially visited since his marriage.

Elizabeth was looking forward to having 'a peaceful time' at Glamis, which she regarded as 'properly' in the country.[1] Glamis Castle is said to be the oldest inhabited house in the British Isles, a vast place full of tales of the dead, which needs the living to make it breathe. In a feature for *Pall Mall Magazine* in 1897, when it was still home to her father-in-law, Cecilia wrote, '*The old Castle, as it now is . . . ringing with the glad sound of grandchildren's voices, is a truly pleasant place to live in; whilst the great iron gate lies hospitably open to welcome the many guests who pass that way, who, in spite of the Castle's reputation for ghosts, seem to pass their time merrily enough.*'

When Claude inherited the earldom in 1904, the castle officially became their home. Visitors could stay in a modern wing added by his father, so that they did not have to sleep in remote, thick-walled rooms like 'The Hangman's Room', so-called from the days when the family employed their own executioner. Claude and Cecilia added their own touches to make it more comfortable and appealing, including an Italian garden, although as Mabell Airlie, herself a veteran of ancient Scottish castles, said of Glamis, 'the traces of past bloodshed can never be completely banished by any cosiness of the present'.[2] When Princess

Elizabeth was first taken to the castle, it still had no electricity,[3] which enhanced its thrillingly chilling reputation for strange phenomena arising from disturbing events within its walls. Among them was the death of King Malcolm II in 1034, fatally wounded by Kenneth V, and the tragic fate of Lady Glamis in 1537. Wrongly accused by James V of conspiring against him by witchcraft, she was dragged from the castle and burned at the stake. She is said to visit in the form of a grey lady, and those who saw her included Elizabeth's sister, May Elphinstone, who thought she was a housemaid until she disappeared. Said to be the place where Shakespeare's Lady Macbeth murdered King Duncan, the castle's unquiet atmosphere has unsettled even rational visitors, among them Sir Walter Scott. After a visit in 1794 he wrote, 'After a very hospitable reception . . . I was conducted to my apartment in a distant part of the building. I must own that when I heard door after door shut, and my conductor had retired, I began to consider myself too far from the living and somewhat too near the dead'.[4]

In 1821, Charlotte, Lady Glamis, gave birth to the first of her five children, Thomas, who is thought to have died the same day. However, some think he was the 'Monster of Glamis', the potential source of a terrifying secret about the castle which is known only to each current Earl of Strathmore and his eldest son, and one other trusted person: '*Its venerable walls enshroud a **mysterious something**'*, wrote Cecilia. Thomas is said to have had a terrible deformity but, rather than having died, was kept locked up in a secret room. Helen Hardinge, who often stayed at Glamis before she married, remembered the unease of going to bed by candlelight and of visiting maids being terrified by stories of the monster; and Stephen Tennant said he saw a footman taking a tray of hot food into a wing of the castle that Cecilia said was never used.[5] Princess Elizabeth's cousin Margaret said it became a popular game for their parents' generation to hang a white towel out of every window; allegedly, one window always remained towel-less.

Princess Elizabeth would come to spend part of every childhood summer at the castle with her grandparents and other Bowes Lyons relations. Her mother loved to meet up with her large family, doing silly things and singing along to Cecilia playing the piano. Watching an early home film of young Elizabeth Bowes Lyon playing boisterous games with them all, Prince Charles said, 'You can see where my grandmother got her sense of fun from, how she passed that on to her own family.'[6] For youngsters the castle was a vast warren of exciting places to play hide-and-seek, although the child who clambered into the Priest's Hole concealed in the thick walls might never be found; and those who found themselves at the entrance to the dimly lit Duncan's Hall were likely to be frightened off by the huge stuffed bear standing guard. Bertie also loved being there. Cousin Margaret believed 'he found the family life at Glamis wonderful, almost a revelation to him, because life in the royal family was very formal and narrow'.[7]

The death of Elizabeth's brother Fergus Bowes Lyon in 1915 had been a terrible blow to her family. A Captain in the family's regiment, the Black Watch, he was killed leading an attack on German lines at Hohenzollern Redoubt. Fergus left his widow with a two-month-old

The Princesses and cousin Margaret Elphinstone (later Rhodes) watch the game 'Are you there, Moriarty?'

FROM *THE FINAL CURTSEY* © MRS. MARGARET RHODES. REPRINTED WITH PERMISSION.

daughter, Rosemary, adding to the Princess's cousins. However, the wide age gap between her mother and her older siblings meant some cousins were too old to be playmates. Those nearest in age to the Princess were Margaret Elphinstone and David Bowes Lyon's children, Simon and Davina. Another cousin, Katherine, was also born in 1926, but she and her older sister Nerissa suffered from severe mental illness. Their father Jock died in 1930, and some time later, the girls were put into a home. Jock's first child with his wife Fenella had died in 1917 before she was a year old. They had two other daughters, Anne and Diana, whom the rest of the family often saw; Diana would be one of the Princess's bridesmaids. However, cousin Margaret does not remember either of them talking about Katherine and Nerissa: 'I think it was a taboo subject, something that was brushed under the carpet in those days.'[8] Although they were mentioned with other members of the family in newspapers in the 1930s, they seemed to fade into oblivion.[9]

As she grew up, one of Princess Elizabeth's favourite pastimes was playing cards. Cecilia enjoyed thrilling listeners with her stories, one of which concerned a lengthy card game played by an earlier Lord Glamis one Saturday night, against the head of another noble family. So intent were the men on wagering lands and money that they failed to notice that Sunday morning was approaching, until a servant reminded them. The gamblers said they did not care what day it was, and one swore an oath that they would finish their game at any cost, even if it went on until Doomsday. At midnight a stranger dressed in black appeared and said he would take them at their word, then vanished. Cecilia said the story was *that every year on that night these noblemen, or their spirits, meet and play cards in the SECRET ROOM of the Castle, and that this will go on until Doomsday . . . loud noises are heard and some of the casements of the Castle are blown open.'* [10]

Cousin Margaret said of their grandparents, 'They had a very big dining table at Glamis and they sat at opposite ends of it, and the story is that Granny would throw food and he would have to catch it on his plate!'[11] The Earl played cricket for the Glamis cricket XI and on the way to breakfast would practise his bowling along the castle corridors.[12] Bertie had already asked his own parents not to spoil Princess Elizabeth when she got older, noting that 'the King is a much more lenient grandfather than he was a father',[13] and he hoped his in-laws would not spoil her either. However, a member of his staff said the Princess was 'almost an idol to the inhabitants of Glamis Castle, and if it were possible to "spoil" so young a baby there would seem to be great risk that the petting she receives may help to nullify the beneficent effects of the bracing Scottish air. However, the Duke and Duchess are unlikely to let their pretty little daughter run too many risks of this kind.'[14]

Indeed they were not. If the rest of Scotland thought they would see much of her, they were to be disappointed, making do with a newspaper photograph of her lying quietly in Alah's arms as the family arrived at Glamis Station[15]. When the Earl and Countess held a sale of work by the Glamis Girl Guides Association, the only glimpse the crowd outside got was from one of the upper windows, where Alah held her up for a couple of minutes. Nevertheless, it was long enough to elicit three cheers.[16] Shortly afterwards, the Guides and their mothers were rewarded for their hard work by an invitation to the Princess's first public party, in the castle's drawing room, where she was carried round and introduced to the delighted company.[17]

At her parents' other engagements that summer, the Princess was not to be seen. She was not even taken to Carberry Towers, home of her aunt and uncle, Lord and Lady Elphinstone and their children, although they had seen her at Glamis. A visit to Balmoral, however, was imperative, although the Duchess tried to resist taking her on the grounds that it would mean another change of scene. They arrived there on 20 September, spending a week with the King and Queen before returning to Glamis, where they were joined by the Strathmores' guest, the Prince of Wales; Elizabeth had told her mother that he was very keen to join them but did not want to push in uninvited. The Earl may not have been too thrilled to have him there, for his granddaughter Margaret said he was not one for a smart social life and did not want his children to be caught up in the Prince's 'fast' set.

The Princess returned to London without her parents, who had further engagements, travelling overnight on 7 October with the King and Queen on the royal train. On arrival at Euston, she and Alah were driven away unobtrusively to Bruton Street, which the Yorks continued to use as their London base. On their return on the 11 they had to start preparing for what Elizabeth called the 'horrible trip',[18] their lengthy tour of Australia and New Zealand which was to start in January 1927. In readiness for the speeches he would have to make, Bertie began therapy with Lionel Logue and Elizabeth started organising work on the house that would be their home after their return. 145 Piccadilly, a five-storey house near Buckingham Palace and St James's Palace, was the first royal residence not to have its own name and came to be known simply as '145'.

Although the Princess was rarely seen in public, it did not stop the people's fascination with her. At a time when Britain was experiencing economic uncertainty, the royal family's endorsement of a product could have a particularly beneficial effect on industry. The birth provided the ideal opportunity for British craftsmen to showcase their work by sending gifts, particularly clothing, in the early days. Among the hundreds of items the Duchess received, many of which were sent to children's charities, was a charming set that she accepted from the British Angora rabbit breeders. They were providing wool to a developing industry, which was previously the province of the French. Three little angora wool coats, all white with different coloured edging, came with matching bonnets, gloves and booties. Her lady-in-waiting thanked them: 'Her Royal Highness is specially pleased to know that this growing industry is providing an extra means of income for many ex-servicemen and smallholders.'[19]

Shortly before Christmas, there was a small ceremony at Bruton Street, where the Duchess was presented with a silver porringer[20] for the baby, on behalf of Britain's silversmiths and goldsmiths. The Duchess eschewed anything that was frivolously luxurious or self-indulgent, but with its silver and ivory coronet, this was a royal piece and thus acceptable. The craftsmen hoped that it might find its way 'upon the breakfast table of the first baby in the land, and may even be banged imperiously on the table by her infant hands'.[21] It was a charmingly cheeky image, appropriate for other children, perhaps, but not for a baby in Alah's care, for whom any hint of naughtiness was dealt with before it got out of hand. Her earlier charge, Margaret, who spent time growing up with the Princesses, said Alah was not the kind of nanny to let children leave peas on their plate.[22]

The Princess's first Christmas was spent, as they almost always would be, at Sandringham, with the King and Queen and wider royal family, including her uncles, Princes Henry and George. The ritual always began on Christmas Eve with the distribution of beef to the estate workers, who collected their gifts, wrapped in white towels, from large tables decorated with holly. On Christmas morning, the family walked across to Sandringham church, which was followed by an exchange of presents in the ballroom. Each person had his or her own length of table on which the presents were laid out, separated by a line of pink tape.[23] That year, 1926, a guest recorded that the Queen gave the King a picture of the carriage procession at Ascot, and the King gave her a large brooch containing all the regimental badges of the Brigade of Guards. The Prince of Wales received twelve corks for wine bottles, each decorated with his feathers in silver. At dinner there were bowls of Christmas roses and scarlet crackers, and everyone wore paper hats, except the King; the Queen's was a mitre, David's a penguin's head, and the Duchess of York's a poke bonnet. After dinner the four Princes and the Duchess sang music hall songs in a low tone, which the King, at the other end of the room, mistook fondly for Christmas carols. He in turn played his favourite tunes on the gramophone, making them all spring to attention when they realised he was playing the *National Anthem*, and laughed loudly at his own joke.[24]

While the brothers enjoyed the opportunity to hunt together and attend the Hunt Ball with Elizabeth, the holiday was overshadowed for her and Bertie by the knowledge that soon they would be leaving on their tour. It was an important time for Australia, which was to celebrate the institution of its new capital at Canberra, and had specifically asked if the Duke of York would preside over the inauguration ceremonies for its first Parliament. The Princess was considered too young to travel halfway around the world, so on 6 January 1927 at 17 Bruton Street, she waved goodbye in Alah's arms from the drawing room window and began a six-month separation from her parents.

The crowds thronging the house saw the Duchess hold the baby to her briefly before leaving and sensed the poignancy of the parting. People lined the streets as the couple were driven to Victoria Station, where they were waved off by the King and Queen and the Strathmores. Bertie's brothers accompanied them on the train to Portsmouth, David acting in his formal capacity as Prince of Wales, dressed in full naval uniform like Bertie. More spectators greeted them at the port and finally, with much fanfare and well-practised naval ceremony, the Duke and Duchess were piped aboard HMS *Renown*.

In their absence, the Princess was shared between both sets of grandparents, beginning with the Strathmores at Bruton Street. The King and Queen returned to Sandringham for the rest of January, where mumps had broken out in the area, so it was considered best to leave the baby in London. Not that the Strathmores were there all the time: Claude had gone to Glamis and Cecilia came and went. Elizabeth knew that would be the case, and asked only that her mother visit the baby when she was in London. When the King and Queen returned from Sandringham in early February, the Princess was taken to Buckingham Palace. There she was settled into rooms well away from her grandparents' apartments, on a different floor called The Prince's Floor, previously her uncle George's.[25] Elizabeth also wanted her mother to visit the Princess at the Palace. She just had to telephone Alah, who could bring the baby out, or Cecilia could pop in, using a little door they knew, with no danger of bumping into Their Majesties.[26]

In that fast-changing first year of the baby's life, it was an unfortunate time for her parents to be away, but royal duty prevailed, as it always did; the King and Queen had left their own young family behind twenty-six years earlier. The Queen sometimes accompanied the Princess during her morning walk in the Palace's gardens, and every afternoon, Alah took her downstairs briefly to see both grandparents. Elizabeth was conscious of what she was missing and was pleased to receive regular bulletins. In March 1927, the King said their 'sweet little daughter' now had four teeth, 'which is quite good at 11 months old, she is very happy & drives in a carriage every afternoon, which amuses her'.[27] Those drives, on fine days in an open two-horse carriage, were eagerly anticipated by the public, who waved as she sat up on Alah's knee and stared out at them solemnly. Sometimes she had tea with her Lascelles cousins, George, born in 1923, and Gerald, in 1924. Already things were being named after her. When the Queen was asked to name a new carnation at a flower show,

Princess Elizabeth with a Russian doll, 1929 (Marcus Adams)
CAMERA PRESS

she suggested 'Princess Elizabeth' but was told that several flowers had already been graced in that way, including a carnation.[28]

Meanwhile her parents, on a gruelling tour during which the Duchess succumbed to tonsillitis, were a huge success, first in New Zealand, then Australia. The King followed their progress closely, and although he could be critical in letters to Bertie of the way he handled some ceremonial aspects, he was gratified to receive positive reports. The Princess was in everyone's minds, and her parents were bombarded with presents for 'Baby Betty', as she was affectionately known, ranging from dolls with clothes carefully made by schoolgirls, to gifts from states and corporations, such as an exquisite Australian silver tea set lined with gold, emblazoned with the emu and the kangaroo.

On 11 April, Alah noted in the baby's progress book that she started to crawl. As usual the Court moved to Windsor Castle for the Easter period, where the Princess stayed in the nursery suite inside the Victoria Tower, overlooking the Great Park. The Lascelles boys were there too, and their second cousin, eight-year-old Alexander Ramsay, whose parents were away in Ceylon. As her first birthday approached, the Princess was oblivious to concerns about her mother's health. Elizabeth told the Queen, as they neared Melbourne, that she was terribly tired and found the tour very strenuous. The British press were concerned by a bulletin given by her friend Mrs Ronnie Greville, who feared she may be in danger of a breakdown; it caused at least one newspaper to say, in acknowledging the demands of the tour, that 'the Duchess is inclined to be a frail little person'.[29] She would confound such condescension and live until she was 101.

The Princess spent her birthday without her grandparents, for the King and Queen had engagements in Cardiff. Greetings came by telegram from her parents and her royal uncles abroad, and presents included a rocking horse from the King and a talking doll from the Queen. In the afternoon she was taken for a carriage drive through Windsor and Eton with George and Gerald Lascelles, to the delight of onlookers, and then had a small party in the nursery, at which Alexander was allowed to cut the three-tier birthday cake. Her milestone was marked by a set of photographs by Marcus Adams, of an almost-smiling Queen with a beaming granddaughter on her knee.

Queen Mary's formal demeanour was well known. Her bearing and her unbending emphasis on royal etiquette stemmed from her defence of the dignity of kingship. Cousin Margaret remembered it well: 'She terrified me.' When she was a child, the Queen sometimes stayed with her family, the Elphinstones. 'When she first came, I was about ten and my mother gave me strict instructions – kiss, kiss, kiss hand, curtsey. I got them all in the wrong order and I remember coming up sharply after the curtsey and hitting her under the chin with the top of my head, which was not terribly well received!' She thought the Queen's grandchildren loved her, 'but to the outsider she was just a formidable figure. I remember thinking that she must have had an armour-plated breastline: it was quite formidable, her embonpoint!'[30] In fact, Queen Mary, the most intellectual and cultured member of the royal family, was shy and reserved, not helped by the failure of her loving but inhibited husband in their early married life to help her cope with his family's hostility. As a result, she could only be herself 'in moments of intimacy', as her old friend Lady Airlie said.[31]

Family friend Myra Butter, a year older than the Princess, recalls Queen Mary always looking 'very upright' but being kind to her. Myra attended a 'wonderful Christmas party' at Buckingham Palace as a child, and was invited to choose a present. 'I was looking at a table with all these things on it and I found it bewildering. I thought, "What am I going to choose?" and I remember Queen Mary pointing. She said, "What about that?" and she was dead right. I loved collecting small things and it was a miniature desk. I've still got it.'[32] Certainly the Queen liked children if they were well behaved. She approved of the fact that the Princess was brought up simply, without undue fuss or spoiling, and with appropriate punishment where necessary. As the Princess grew, the Queen frequently reminded Alah that she must 'Teach that child not to fidget',[33] and her pockets in her clothes were sewn up so that she learned to hold her hands correctly.

The Duke and Duchess left Australia in May for their month's voyage back to Britain, during which a fire broke out in a boiler room on HMS *Renown* and could have destroyed the ship. Unaware of the drama, the Strathmores looked after the Princess at St Paul's Walden Bury for the final few weeks, during which she learned to say 'Mama' and applied it to everyone she met. According to the *Melbourne Herald*, one of the last telegrams the Yorks received said that the Princess was 'quite well but becoming very naughty'. This was said to be a relief to mothers everywhere, for 'naughtiness in a one-year-old child is an excellent sign of healthiness'.[34] The notion of the angelic-looking Princess apparently misbehaving no doubt increased her appeal even further, although what 'naughty' meant was not explained.

On 27 June, the Yorks arrived at Portsmouth. On board the ship were three tons of presents given to them for their daughter and dozens of live parrots. The King was waiting to greet them at Victoria station with the Queen and the Strathmores and had warned Bertie in advance: 'We will not embrace at the station before so many people. When you kiss mama, take yr hat off.'[35] This repression of affection was contrasted by the warm reception of the people who cheered them as they drove in an open-top carriage to Buckingham Palace; despite the heavy rain, the Duchess was seen constantly smiling beneath her umbrella.

An emotional reunion took place, the Duchess repeatedly kissing her baby, although to the Princess, her parents must have been less recognisable than her nurse. Soon the crowds were rewarded with the sight of the royal family on the balcony, the Duchess beaming as she twice brought the baby forward and waved her hand. The Yorks did not stay long, for their new house was ready, and shortly they repeated the show to a different crowd outside 145 Piccadilly, holding the Princess up on its little balcony.

Their move into their first permanent home marked the start of a happy period which they hoped would last for a long time. 'They were a real little family', says Myra Butter, who remembers going to parties as a child in the garden behind 145. Once owned by the Marquess of Northampton, the house's previous tenants included one of the Bass brewing family and a Rothschild. Next door lived Viscount Allendale and his family, whose son, 'Wenty' Beaumont, was four years older than the Princess. Incredibly, by today's standards, there was no special security at 145, nothing to stop the curious from walking up the stone-flagged path and ringing one of the two bells marked 'Visitors' and 'House'. Those invited in found themselves in a large hallway decorated with flowers, where pale green columns supported a cream-coloured ceiling. Across the soft brown carpet was the large and airy morning room, whose windows looked out onto the family's garden, just large enough for the Princess to ride her tricycle later. Beyond were Hamilton Gardens, an enclosed area with a gate that opened directly into Hyde Park where her parents' Golden Labradors were exercised.

A family friend said the morning room was 'in no sense a modern room'.[36] The Duchess did not embrace the fashionable designs of the 1920s: the angular shapes, shiny fabrics, chrome and glass. Instead, chintz-covered armchairs and sofas, standing on a Persian carpet, gave the room a homely feel. Although the new glitzy glamour of Hollywood did not impact on the decor, the Yorks enjoyed music and dancing, a love of which they passed on to their daughters, and the huge gramophone in the room was often played.

In the morning room were many books and fine bronzes and family photographs displayed on occasional tables. Irresistible to the Princess was a stash of toys, among which was a large woolly black retriever with puppies, and a large glass cabinet containing minute animals, including a herd of elephants, 'each of them tiny enough to be pushed by a ladybird'. Behind a black lacquer screen were two little scarlet brushes and dustpans, with which the Princess, and later her sister, 'swept' the carpet every morning. At bedtime she was taken past her father's study, where mahogany doors led into small panelled room, simply furnished with a book case, desk and a few chairs and pictures, including one of the Duchess from his mother-in-law; the Duke's main offices were at 11 Grosvenor Crescent, not far away. Beyond was the dining room looking out onto Piccadilly, where thirty guests could dine and admire Edmond Brock's portrait of the Princess, and on to the elegant staircase, hung with Brussels tapestries, which led up to her mother's bedroom on one side, and to a drawing room and her mother's boudoir on the other, where later she would have lessons.

From there an electric lift travelled up past floors containing a ballroom, library and twenty-five bedrooms to the top floor. There, the wide well of the staircase was crowned by a large glass dome. Light streamed down onto a circular landing where the Princess's toy horses were arranged. From there opened the rooms of the nursery suite that she had to herself until she was four. There were two nurseries, for day and night, light rooms with carpets of cherry red, and a kitchen where her meals were pre-pared. A bright bathroom contained an enticing array of sponge animals. Alah's bedroom was on this floor, together with a small sitting room. By then they had a new nursery maid, Margaret Macdonald, known as Bobo.

Most exciting for the Princess in the day nursery was a tall cabinet with glass doors, filled with toys and curios from all over the British Empire: tiny, exquisitely dressed dolls; china cottages and palaces; model soldiers and ships; animals, birds and fishes in finely blown glass, many of them gifts from Queen Mary; and the miniature silver cradle from her Christening cake. But however many toys she had, restrictions were in place. Lisa Sheridan, later a royal photographer, whose mother was a friend of Margaret Macdonald, saw the Princess wearing 'miniature red slippers which were rubbed white at the toes from constant crawling'. She watched her play mid-crawl with a teddy bear but when she opened the cupboard door to get another toy, Alah told her firmly, 'One at a time', and helped her put the bear back in its place and select another.[37]

The Princess was clearly an attractive child, with very blue eyes and golden curly hair. She was described as having a 'sunny disposition', as the Duchess herself often was. At 145, Lady Cynthia Asquith found the Princess trying to walk and talk, calling herself 'Lilibet', the name her family would adopt. She was quick to smile at efforts to entertain her and exhibited a healthy childhood curiosity: 'She deftly relieved me of my handbag,' said Asquith, 'and displayed a precocious sense of the proper use of all its contents. Spectacles were popped onto the tiny nose, pennies pocketed, lozenges posted through her teeth, the mirror ogled and face powder dexterously applied.'

The Duchess established a daily routine, during which the Princess spent time with both parents in the morning and at bedtime, and some-times lunchtime too. There were games from the Duke and bedtime stories from the Duchess, who taught her to read before a governess was employed. She played with their Labradors, her father's called Jock, her mother's Glen. While her parents did not inhibit childish impetuousness, she had to behave in company, learning to shake hands and curtsey before she was two. In the first couple of years, the Prince of Wales sometimes visited, bringing a present for his niece and romping on the floor. As a joke he told her that she must always curtsey to her elders; the obedient child took it seriously, to the extent that the royal family became embarrassed by her unnecessarily frequent displays.[38]

The King's affection for his granddaughter was clear. A visitor to Sandringham in January 1928 described her sitting in a little chair between the King and himself, and 'the King chortling with little jokes with her', while giving her biscuits to eat and to feed his dog. She was learning to say 'Grandpa' and 'Granny', and to everyone's amusement had managed to address 'the very grand-looking Countess of Airlie as "Airlie"'. Even Queen Mary's young equerry, Lord Claude Hamilton, not known for his spontaneity, got down on the floor to play bricks with her, and as she was collected by her nurse she 'made a perfectly sweet little curtsey to the King and Queen and then to the company as she departed'.[39] On another occasion the King and his granddaughter were found flat on the floor searching under a sofa: 'We are looking for Lilibet's hair slide', explained the King.[40]

She had to learn to socialise with all kinds of people. At Glamis that summer, aged two, she was the focus of attention at her grandparents' garden party for around eight hundred tenants, tradespeople and friends. Appearing first in primrose yellow, then pink, she brightened up the ancient crypt, to where the party had been moved out of the rain, and supplied a running commentary on matters of interest. 'Nice man', she said, after shaking hands with a tall, handsome guest. 'Speak to pretty boy, mama', she coaxed the Duchess of a lad who was gazing at them admiringly, only to cause him to hide shyly behind his mother.[41]

For the first time she was mentioned in her own right in the Court Circular, which announced on 5 September 1928 that she had arrived at Balmoral Castle. Winston Churchill, MP, was a guest, and he wrote to his wife that the only people there were the royal family, the household and Princess Elizabeth, who was 'a character. She has an air of authority and reflectiveness astonishing in an infant'.[42] He could not have imagined that one day she would be his Queen, and he her Prime Minister.

It might be said that the first service she performed for the Empire was before she was three, during her grandfather's convalescence. In November 1928, the King became gravely ill with septicaemia arising from a lung infection and was near death. The Prince of Wales was on safari in East Africa. He was contemplating joining his brother Henry in South Africa when he heard the news from Prime Minister Stanley Baldwin, who asked him to return. David's initial reaction, expressed to his shocked Assistant Private Secretary, Alan 'Tommy' Lascelles, was that it was not true, just a political wheeze of Baldwin's. He then went out and seduced the wife of a British official, as he told Lascelles next day. When he returned to England, Bertie prepared him for the shock of seeing their father so ill, and also told him of a story doing the rounds, that the reason for David's rushing home was because Bertie was going to 'bag the Throne' in his absence, 'Just like the Middle Ages!!!!' [43]

On 11 December, an operation was carried out to drain the abscess and remove a rib. During the next few weeks, the country and the Empire waited anxiously. For the Queen, the King's illness was almost too much to bear. Hardinge told his wife on 23 December that when he had arrived at Buckingham Palace a few days earlier, the Queen 'was in a dreadfully distressed state.... She was so dreadfully pathetic about everything, didn't dare hope for his recovery & was particularly sensitive about the King's wanderings; she seemed to bring so much more romance & sentiment into her relations with the King than I ever could have thought possible.... Since Tuesday she has been far happier & appears to have got her old interests back.' [44] Christmas that year was a subdued affair. The Yorks stayed at 145 and the Princess was told that 'Grandpa England', as she called him, had a bad cold.

Even 1929 did not get off to a happy start, with her other grandfather ill with influenza for weeks, during an epidemic that felled some of the royal household and, briefly, the Duchess. February was brighter. The Duchess's younger brother, David, married Rachel Spender Clay, a niece of Viscount Astor; and their older brother Michael, and his wife Betty, had their first son, Fergus, named after their late brother.

At last the King began his convalescence and was moved by special ambulance to Bognor on the Sussex coast, after several rehearsals during which one of his staff, of similar height and weight, was repeatedly lifted out of bed and taken downstairs, put into the ambulance, driven to Craigweil House at Bognor and lifted into the King's bed, until the royal doctors were satisfied that the move would go smoothly. In March, while her parents attended a wedding in Oslo, the Princess stayed in Bognor for a week at her grandfather's request. She accompanied him on his walks in his bath chair and played on the private beach, making sandcastles with the moulds that the Queen bought her. By then accustomed to visiting her family's houses in regular rotation, the Princess came to call Bognor a 'once-place'.[45] By the end of the week, the King was able to walk through the gardens, taking an occasional rest. Although he was not allowed to resume public ceremonials until June, he was through the worst, and the Princess was credited with helping his recovery. Before leaving, she had a farewell party at Craigweil with the five children of the Duchess's close friend, Kathleen 'Kakoo' Manners, Duchess of Rutland; they were staying nearby with their aunt, Lady Diana Cooper.

That year, the Duke was appointed Lord High Commissioner to the General Assembly of the Church of Scotland. He and the Duchess had to stay at Holyrood Palace, Edinburgh, for two weeks in May, so the Princess stayed with the King and Queen at Windsor. The Lascelles boys were there, and friends' children were brought in to play, including Julian Salmond, grandson of the Queen's Lady of the Bedchamber, Ettie Desborough. Julian was the same age as the Princess, and his grandmother enjoyed their contact, watching amused as the 'tiny' Princess led Julian up to the King, and 'putting her hand on his red curls said, "Isn't he nice?"'[46]

Alah took her three-year-old charge into the castle's quadrangle in her pushchair, to listen to the band and watch the Changing of the Guard. As George Lascelles stood to attention with his toy gun, the officers approached the Princess, being the only royal present,[47] and saluted her with their swords. When the ceremony finished, she was approached again, for permission to move off, and she was seen to give a little inclination of the head. Allowed out of her pushchair, she walked back into the castle and the sentries saluted her:[48] not unusual, but a ritual of which she was becoming increasingly aware, as she was of the spectators who waved through palace and castle railings, and whom she learned to reward with a wave and a smile.

CHAPTER 6

New Playmates (1929–1932)

With the King's health improving, the summer of 1929 was calmer for the royal family. During his absence there had been a General Election, the so-called flapper election, in which women over twenty-one were allowed to vote for the first time, and which resulted in a hung Parliament led by Labour's Ramsay Macdonald. The Conservative Party was defeated in a result that stemmed from economic unrest.[1] After a further operation, the King returned to Buckingham Palace in early July. Princess Elizabeth joined the royal family and the Strathmores on the balcony, where they were greeted by a huge crowd singing the national anthem. Waving to the people remained the extent of the Princess's public appearances; responding to one invitation, a statement was issued on the Duchess's behalf saying the Princess 'is never allowed to take part in public ceremonies'.[2] Party invitations, too, were seldom accepted, for her mother did not believe in too much organised entertainment, preferring children to make their own. Her playmates were mostly the children of her parents' friends. Myra Butter remembers the Princess having tea with her and her sister Gina at their parents' house in Regents Park, and playing in its lovely garden. That year she was allowed to attend her first major horse show at the Royal Tournament, although she was taken home by Alah part-way through.

Her parents enjoyed entertaining at 145 that summer, giving dinner parties for guests who included Ramsay Macdonald and writers John Buchan, Rudyard Kipling and J. M. Barrie. In early August, the Yorks went to Glamis as usual, followed by a stay at Birkhall, a house on the Balmoral estate. Unusually, Balmoral itself stayed closed that summer, and conscious of not having their own summer residence, Bertie asked the King if they could rent a house there. He lent them Birkhall, a Stuart house set in a glorious countryside, which had been acquired by Queen

Victoria and Prince Albert for the future Edward VII. Although the decor was old-fashioned and the house still lit by oil lamps, the family loved it.

While the Yorks hosted the shooting party at Birkhall in place of the King and Queen, the Princess remained at Glamis. Her parents returned there in late August to help the Strathmores host their annual party. They were joined by the Duchess's sisters Rose and May and some of their children: Mary and James Leveson-Gower, Margaret Elphinstone and her older sisters Jean and Elizabeth. Anne and Diana Bowes Lyon were there too. The Princess needed no persuasion to join her cousins. When she was not playing with Diana and posing hand-in-hand for the camera, she was toddling off with Margaret to investigate their grandparents' huge ornamental fountain, before they were called back to listen to the piper and shake hands with the guests, many of whom had known their mothers since they were born.

On quieter days, the Countess took the Princess and Alah shopping in the local town, Forfar, to buy sweets and chocolate from its famous confectioner's, the Peter Reid Rock Shop. A visitor to Glamis that summer was Ruth Cavendish Bentinck. Married to Cecilia's cousin, Freddy, she was a suffragist who had finally seen her activism come to fruition. Ruth was amused by her meeting with the Princess. While they were having tea, the child bounded into the room saying, 'You can't think how naughty I've been. Oh *so* naughty, you don't know.' 'Well then tell me', said Lady Strathmore, 'and I *shall* know'. 'No', said Princess Elizabeth, and that was that.[3]

After Christmas at Sandringham, the Yorks joined the Strathmores at St Paul's Walden Bury. The mother-daughter bond of the Duchess and the Princess, preferably portrayed in a cosy domestic setting, was irresistible to women's journals whose focus was on the home. A feature in the January 1930 issue of the popular *Good Housekeeping* magazine talked of the Duchess 'personally' helping to make jam, at which 'she is really expert. . . . Little Princess Elizabeth was allowed down in the kitchen during the last jam making, and was given a tiny pot of her own to stir, which highly delighted her . . . HRH also made a batch of apple jelly, because the Duke is so fond of it.' How the journal would have loved to continue the maternal theme with the Duchess's recent discovery – that she was pregnant. She immediately wrote to Nannie B, asking her if she would be free in August, although she said her doctor Henry Simson thought it could be late July. She had not told anyone yet and was hoping to keep it a secret for much longer.[4]

At the same time, the Duchess had succumbed to bronchitis, to which she was prone. It could work to her advantage, as she had found in the months after her engagement to Bertie. While experiencing the hassle of press attention, she had fallen ill and told Helen Hardinge, 'This cough has been a godsend in a way, as it's given us weeks more peace & nobody <u>dares</u> come near us! So I bless it, and shall probably whoop for years to come.'[5] Now, however, was not a good time to be ill. Her brother Jock also had bronchitis. It turned into pneumonia, and on 7 February 1930 he died, aged forty-three, from an abscess on the lung. For Claude and Cecilia it was yet another example of the natural order turned upside down, the parent surviving the child. His widow Fenella was left with their four daughters and the problems of Katherine and Nerissa. In response to a sympathetic letter from the Queen, Elizabeth told her how much better Jock had been recently and how sudden the death of her 'clever and wise' brother was.[6]

Then, on 16 April, the Court Circular announced that the Duchess had cancelled further engagements and would not be undertaking any more functions during the summer: the veiled announcement of her pregnancy. As she approached her fourth birthday, Princess Elizabeth had no idea that her life would soon change. She was busy with her first pony, a Shetland called Peggy, a present from the King, and was receiving riding lessons from Owen, the groom at Buckingham Palace. Importantly, she also made her first friend by herself. One day she saw a girl of her age playing in Hamilton Gardens. Sonia Graham Hodgson was the daughter of the King's radiographer: hardly a random member of the public but it was a friendship that would last all Sonia's life. Sonia later recalled, 'I was playing there one day when this little girl came up to me and said, "Will you come and have a game with me?" We played French cricket. She was wearing a pink and white check dress. I was wearing a blue coat.' They played for about an hour, watched as always by their respective nannies. After that, 'I went on seeing her virtually every day, except for holidays, until she moved to Buckingham Palace.'[7] She was one of the few people outside the family allowed to call her Lilibet.

Sonia said she was 'a sweet child and great fun. She always had a great sense of humour and a vivid imagination.' They made up their own games, mostly involving horses, and pretended they were adults going to dances and would discuss their outfits. Although only eight months older, Sonia was much taller and admitted that she was 'the bossy one' who usually decided what to play. Sometimes the Duke of York joined in; he enjoyed playing Sardines, a version of hide-and-seek, although Sonia remembered her own 'starchy nanny saying she found it very undignified having to hide in a bush with him'.[8]

The Court always spent the Easter period at Windsor Castle, which coincided with Princess Elizabeth's birthday. Crowds would gather to watch the Changing of the Guard and hope to catch a glimpse of her. On her fourth birthday she gracefully blew kisses to the waiting crowds, then went with her Lascelles cousins for a carriage ride around Windsor. Soon she started piano lessons with the esteemed Miss Mabel Lander, whose job must have been made easier by the Princess's ready ear, thanks largely to Cecilia. After the first lesson, which consisted mostly of 'screwing the music stool up and down',[9] she became quite accomplished and developed a good singing voice, encouraged by both grandmothers to sing English ballads and Scottish airs.

In the entertainment arena, however, she would be outperformed in years to come by her sister, who arrived at Glamis Castle on the dramatically stormy night of 21 August. The likely date had been calculated as between 6 and 12 August, which meant they would be at Glamis as usual, where the Duchess's own birthday was always celebrated. However, the delay meant the Home Secretary, Mr Clynes, and the Ceremonial Secretary, Mr Boyd, present for the birth in Scotland, had to stay around far longer than expected. It caused much inconvenience, so to keep them from getting in the way but still accessible to Glamis, they were lodged by Lady Airlie at Airlie Castle. When the twelfth arrived and nothing happened, the Strathmore household tried to continue as normally as possible, while the officials became more agitated and no one dared venture far beyond the castle.

Her cousins had not yet arrived at Glamis for the summer, so the Princess was kept occupied. She was taken to see the Strathmores' long-serving head gamekeeper who was very ill (and shortly died), and cheered him by chatting about his dogs. Alah took her walking in the village, where she insisted on stopping to watch the children in the school play-ground: other children were always a source of fascination to her. Her riding lessons continued in the castle grounds, although she had to lend her pony to her grandfather when he went grouse shooting with his brother, Malcolm Bowes Lyon, and her father, on what turned out to be the day before the birth.

If Elizabeth and Bertie had hoped for a boy, the relief of a healthy baby dispelled any disappointment. The Duke 'was obviously thoroughly delighted that everything had passed off so successfully', said Mr Clynes[10]. The Queen thought the baby 'a darling'.[11] Princess Elizabeth was told by Alah early the next morning of the 'fine chubby faced little girl', as Clynes described the blonde, blue-eyed child. Beacons were lit and celebrations held for the first royal baby born in Scotland since Charles I in 1600. Nevertheless, one journalist reported local people crowding his car to ask the sex of the fourth in line to the Throne, and when the answer came, there were 'cries of mixed joy and disappointment . . . as the villagers shouted to one another, "another daughter"'.[12]

The happy event was not without its down side. The Press overstepped the mark when it indicated that morphine had been used at the birth, which annoyed Elizabeth, who told the Queen that 'The papers have been so vulgar and stupid as usual',[13] a view she would always hold. Simson had to issue a statement denying it. Bertie, too, was irritated when the King said he should have dealt better with the newspapers. Then there was disagreement about the baby's names. Elizabeth told the Queen that she would like Ann Margaret, as Ann of York sounded pretty and would go well with her eldest daughter's name. She did not want Margaret as her first name, even though many people had suggested it, because of the lack of family links on either side and because 'she will always be getting mixed up with Margaret the nursery maid'.[14] However, the King did not like Ann, and they bowed to his wishes. The final choice was Margaret Rose. Oblivious to any dissention, Princess Elizabeth seemed delighted by her new sister. Seeing the doctor, David Myles, in the corridor, she took him by the hand, saying excitedly, 'Come and see my baby, my very own baby!'[15] To a visitor she announced she was going to call her 'Bud', because 'she's not a real rose, is she, yet? She's only a bud'.[16]

The Duchess and her daughters became affectionately known as 'the Three White Roses of York'. Princess Elizabeth did not know her mother was already marking out her sister's beauty as an important asset, telling their friend Cosmo Lang, now Archbishop of Canterbury, 'that she has got large blue eyes and a will of iron, which is all the equipment that a lady needs! And as long as she can disguise her will, and use her eyes, then all will be well.'[17] It was a prophetic observation of how different from her eldest daughter this child would turn out to be. Not that there was any question of replacement of affection. Elizabeth told the Queen what a cheerful companion Princess Elizabeth was, how she missed her when they were apart and how protective she felt towards her; she was 'terrified of her travelling by road nowadays.'[18] Neither did the arrival of the baby detract from the attention Princess Elizabeth received; rather, her own attention found a new focus and fostered her protective instincts. She began to be aware of her special position as the eldest child, although she had no idea quite how significant that status would become.

She was the proud big sister at Princess Margaret's christening on 30 October, where godparents, from royalty and aristocracy, included two uncles, the Prince of Wales and David Bowes Lyon. Bobo Macdonald's sister, Ruby, was employed as nurse; cousin Margaret considered that compared to Alah, Ruby 'was not quite so successful'.[19] At 145, the sisters shared the night nursery, until Princess Elizabeth was given her own large bedroom, from whose window she could look into Hamilton Gardens and see the bronze statue of the poet Lord Byron with his favourite dog.

In 1931, when she was five, Princess Elizabeth began dance lessons under Miss Marguerite Vacani, sharing them with her cousins and other selected children, and had French lessons from a French governess. Already she was becoming a good rider and was taken to her first hunt with the Pytchly Hounds; her father asked that she undergo the ritual of being bloodied, but no fox was found that day. Swimming lessons started at the Bath Club in London, where her father had been taught as a boy:

'I remember [the old days] so well', he told Lady Desborough, 'especially when I swam the length of the bath at the Bath Club for the first time'.[20] Myra Butter learned to swim with Princess Elizabeth and Sonia: 'Our teacher was Miss Daly. We had a rope around our middles and there was a pole in front of us which we clung onto for dear life. We were pulled along to start with, then bit by bit she loosened the rope and then the whole thing slackened and we were swimming before we knew it.' Miss Daly also taught them the four swimming shapes, in the form of letters YITX. 'Princess Elizabeth was a very good swimmer,' says Myra. 'She learned to dive for towels at the bottom of the pool and life save. I bet she could have saved anybody at one point.'[21]

That year, the King granted the Yorks Royal Lodge in Windsor Great Park as their country home. Originally built around 1814 for the Prince Regent, it had been rebuilt and needed further alterations before they could move in. The year was a difficult one, with the Great Depression taking grip. In the face of potentially drastic cuts to public expenditure, the King made voluntary cuts to his civil list. In August, a crisis point was reached when the government could still not agree on the best way through the economic doldrums and the King was faced with the threatened resignations of Ramsay Macdonald and his Cabinet. The King asked Macdonald to help form a National Government and lead the country through the crisis. It was the most important intervention of his reign. Responding to Lady Desborough, he wrote, 'I am too happy to think that I may have been of some use in getting the leaders of the three parties to agree to form a National Govt, if they had not done so, there would have been a terrible disaster & they realised the situation. I must say the Prime Minister behaved splendidly & put country before party.'[22]

The Yorks had to borrow the money for their extension to Royal Lodge, preferring not to ask the King. In those harsh financial times, Elizabeth told the Queen that her father was thinking of closing Glamis because of a new 'super tax' on the very wealthy.[23] The Earl's musing came just after the happy – and expensive – occasion of his and Cecilia's Golden Wedding celebration in August. A huge affair, for which they threw a ball at Glamis and gave a garden party for over one thousand guests, it was enjoyed by much of the Scottish society. Their presents were displayed in a marquee and included a golden cup from the King and Queen and a gold cigarette case from the Prince of Wales bearing his crest. Princess Elizabeth was seen as usual with cousin Diana and made the day for Sir Harry Lauder, Scotland's popular entertainer, by naming one of his songs as her favourite.

In early 1932, Royal Lodge was ready enough for the Yorks to move into, together with their ponies, two Welsh corgis, two Shetland collies and fifteen blue budgerigars.[24] They would spend their weekends there, leaving London every Friday afternoon. As Princess Elizabeth turned six, Cynthia Asquith found her possessing 'the manners of an ambassadress, offering me food with the unpressing politeness of a perfect hostess, and showing herself a good listener as well as conversationalist. Unlike most children, she never asks a second question before the first has been answered.' Myra Butter recalls, 'We usually had horsey games, she loved anything to do with horses,'[25] and no one was immune: Lady Asquith found herself being the pony, ridden by the Princess who used a string of Woolworth pearls for reins. Cousin Margaret remembered they 'endlessly cavorted, which was her idea. We galloped round and round. We were horses of every kind: carthorses, racehorses and circus horses, and it was obligatory to neigh.'[26]

For her sixth birthday, she received a gift from the Welsh people which served as a reminder of the relationship with England, as well as demonstrating their affection for the Princess. 'The Little House with the Straw Roof' – *Y Bwthynn Bach To Gwellt* – was presented in Cardiff to the Duke and Duchess, who acknowledged the money its building had raised for those in distress in Wales. Installed in the garden of Royal Lodge, it was surely the envy of little girls everywhere. The house and contents were scaled at two-fifths of adult size. It measured twenty-four feet by eight feet in depth, with four rooms five feet high. Everything worked. There was hot and cold running water, heating, a tiled kitchen with pots and pans, a telephone and a tiny wireless that received foreign stations. A real oil painting of the Duchess hung on the wall near a bookcase from the Prince of Wales, made by disabled servicemen. Up the staircase was the bedroom, with a bed, wardrobe and a cradle containing a lifelike doll. Silver brushes on the dressing table bore the Princess's crest and monogram. Myra Butter remembers playing in the house: 'Oh, how we loved it. It was wonderful, a charming little place. Princess Margaret's great thing was running up and down the stairs and pulling the plug on the little lavatory, which worked.'[27] The house even came with its own dog, a Welsh terrier called Ianto, or Evan, which was a gift from the Welsh Terrier Association.

Unforeseen drama nearly prevented the house reaching the Princess. The ten-ton structure was being transported by road to London in a trailer attached to a steam tractor, when it caught fire near Monmouth. The straw roof was totally destroyed and one of the upper rooms damaged; fortunately the contents were travelling separately, and insurance cover paid for repairs by the original craftsmen. Willmott, the designer, told newspapers that the fire had started at the bottom of the tarpaulin, which gave him 'a very grave suspicion of foul play . . . when it was being built, about fifty men made an attempt to damage the structure, but the police intervened in time. The only reason I can give is that some misguided persons objected to the gift to the little Princess when there is so much distress about.' However, everything in the house had been given free, he said, and the enterprise had raised money for charity. On the night before the fire, a special watch was kept. It was 'very puzzling'.[28]

But in the safe and lovely garden of Royal Lodge, the little house was a jewel of childhood, for which its owner would eventually grow too big: 'How terribly the process of growing up will be brought home to Princess Elizabeth,' wrote Lady Asquith. The child, she said prophetically, would one day 'suffer the inexorable laws of change'. One positive change occurred in December 1932, when after years of reluctance, the King gave his first Christmas broadcast. It was transmitted live from Sandringham to the Empire at 3:05 p.m. on Christmas Day, a thick cloth covering the table where he sat, so that the papers he held in his shaking hands would not be heard rustling. Written by his friend Rudyard Kipling, the speech was short, sensitive and eloquent. David upset his father by going out to play golf but Princess Elizabeth listened with the others. Her grandfather's speech marked the birth of an institution that one day she would continue, making it as familiar a part of Christmas as the oldest traditions.

CHAPTER 7

Seeds of Change (1933–1934)

Changes were coming that would lay the foundations of the future. In 1933, the United States had a new president, Franklin D Roosevelt, whom the King had met in 1918 and liked very much. He would prove to be not only a great asset for his country at a time of economic crisis but a friend to Britain. On the home front, the new year of 1933 saw a photograph published of the two Princesses sweetly embracing outside The Bury, but during that year their grandparents would move out and into another Hertfordshire estate not far away, Woolmers Park. They had intended to let Jock have St Paul's Walden Bury but his death had changed that. Instead, it became home to David and Rachel Bowes Lyon, who would host the Yorks when they stayed there. The Strathmores would not exactly slum it at Woolmers; the 250-acre estate, whose previous owners included the Duke of Bridgewater, had a substantial mansion house with thirteen family bedrooms and all the usual features – gardens, farm, stables, lodges – found in an English country estate.

For Princess Elizabeth, the greatest change of 1933 was having a governess. It was not before time. Queen Mary was concerned that she should receive a more structured education. The choice was Scottish-born Marion Crawford, whose affectionate memoir *The Little Princesses* would later see her ostracised. She was twenty-four when she began working for the Yorks, having been introduced to them by the Duchess's sister Rose. Cousin Margaret liked her: 'She was a very nice person and fun. At Windsor she held her own at lunch parties. I think she did a very good job.'[1] Crawfie, as she became known, had the staunch Presbyterian attitude of the lower middle class she came from, believing that simple living and honest thinking were among the most important virtues. She was determined not to present herself as being unduly impressed by the surroundings in

77

which she worked or the lifestyles she encountered, and always stressed the homely and unpretentious nature of the Yorks' family life.

Crawfie first met Princess Elizabeth when she was ready for bed and using her dressing gown cords as reins for her toy horses; she soon discovered the Princess's obsession with them and the stable routine that had to be followed every night. Their Majesties made it their business to meet Crawfie early on. The King's only wish was that she should teach his granddaughters 'to write a decent hand . . . with some character in it', because he said none of his children could write properly and they all did it the same way. Soon Princess Elizabeth's lessons were moved from the Duchess's boudoir to a new schoolroom on the floor below. The Queen generally approved Crawfie's curriculum, but suggested some changes. She thought there was not enough history or arithmetic, and that poetry should be added, for learning by heart was good memory training.

In the mornings from Monday to Friday, Princess Elizabeth had a weekly total of four lessons of arithmetic and four of history; two of grammar; one lesson each of literature, poetry, writing and composition, geography and Bible study. Each lesson was a half-hour long, and she also had an hour of reading each day. On weekday afternoons she had music and drawing lessons; either an 'educational visit' with the Queen or a dancing class; and singing lessons or walking, depending on the weather. On Saturday mornings there was a résumé of the week's work and reading, followed by a riding lesson.

Neither parent considered that a more intellectually rigorous timetable was necessary or that Princess Elizabeth should go to school. Crawfie felt 'that the Duke and Duchess, most happy in their own married life . . . wanted most for [their daughters] a really happy childhood, with lots of pleasant memories stored up against the days that might come and, later, happy marriages'.[2] When her uncle David became King, he is thought to have vetoed the idea of her going to school because George V had not approved, as he thought it would raise difficulties for a girl in her position.

In those early days her routine was to get up at 7:30 a.m., dress and have breakfast in the nursery. At 9:00 a.m. she was taken to see her parents. Lessons began at 9:30 a.m. and were punctuated by an hour's break, when she could play in Hamilton Gardens. From 12:00 a.m. to 1:00 p.m., there was reading. Mabell Airlie said the Queen was 'very anxious for Princess

Elizabeth to read the best type of children's books, and often chose them for her'.[3]

At 1:15 p.m. she joined her parents for lunch if they were home. Her afternoon activities continued until 4:45 p.m. when both girls had tea in the schoolroom. Before bedtime they joined their parents, often playing card games which made them shout and caused Alah to fear they were getting overexcited. After a bath, one parent would read a story. Princess Elizabeth's bedtime was 7:15 p.m., half an hour later than her sister's.

Crawfie noted that Princess Elizabeth was extremely neat and sometimes got out of bed several times to straighten her shoes. She was concerned that she had never been allowed to get dirty and had spent too much time being driven around in carriages. Her mission was to encourage her to play more active games where she might get grubby, such as hide-and-seek among the shrubberies in the park. The Duke sometimes joined them; he was very sporty and a fast runner. Crawfie's view of the Princess's physical closeting was perhaps gloomier than reality. Even if she was seldom caked in mud, she already possessed impressive riding skills, not achievable without a lack of fear of horses and falling off, and she enjoyed physical games, as a homemade film of her mercilessly beating the Duchess's obliging friend, Sir Arthur Penn, in a pillow fight illustrates.[4]

Myra Butter, too, recalls rowdy games. Her parents, the Wernhers, also had a house at Thorpe Lubenham in Leicestershire, where the Duke of York used to take a hunting box. One day, Myra watched her sister playing a game with Elizabeth involving a hut, where 'the fun was to be "locked in" and having to scream and yell to be let out! I was rather shy and I remember thinking, what a noise!' They also played Kick-a-Tin, which involved just that: 'Goodness knows where we thought we were taking it to! When we got older we played games like Sardines.'[5]

The only time Crawfie said Lilibet really misbehaved was during a French lesson with her visiting tutor, when she became so bored that she 'picked up the big ornamental silver inkpot and placed it without any warning upside down on her head'. Usually Elizabeth displayed the obedient traits of a child trained early to behave, undisturbed for four years by the distractions of a sibling. By contrast, Princess Margaret cared less about being good and quickly learned that she could attract attention by entertaining. Both girls had very good singing voices but Margaret could

Princess Elizabeth (front) and Princess Margaret (middle) play tug-of-war with their cousin, Margaret Elphinstone (later Rhodes)
FROM *THE FINAL CURTSEY* © MRS. MARGARET RHODES. REPRINTED WITH PERMISSION.

sing tunes before she could talk, and soon showed the greater talent in playing the piano. She was also a very good mimic. Such precocious skills, however, caused her to be spoilt. Cousin Margaret noticed that 'She quite often got away with a lot just by being able to make a joke out of something. She had a mischievous sense of humour.' Elizabeth 'was always the more serious of the two'.[6] Princess Margaret was not popular with the courtiers: 'She was a wicked little girl,' one said. 'There were moments when I'd have given anything to have given her a hell of a slap. [Princess Elizabeth] was always the nicest, no question about it.'[7]

Perhaps it was the Countess of Strathmore's recognition of Princess Margaret's burgeoning talents that was behind the treat for her granddaughter's third birthday in 1933. She was deemed too young to go to the theatre, so Cecilia brought a children's theatre to Glamis. Watching with the Princesses and their cousins Granville and Mary Leveson Gower was Myra: 'We absolutely loved it, it was our delight.'[8] The little company sang nursery rhymes and sea shanties and performed favourite stories and new ones specially written, with something for all ages. The event became an annual fixture.

The Countess was always conscious of her public duty. After Margaret's birthday party, Cecilia, with her daughter Rose and sister-in-law Maude, took a tier of the cake, iced with miniature roses, marguerites and white heather, to the residents of the nearby Black Watch War Memorial Home. Cecilia was President of their Ladies' Committee, and she and Claude had recently donated a bed to the Home, in memory of their son Fergus. Cecilia conveyed good wishes from the Duchess, who had gone to Birkhall with the Princesses.

Cousin Margaret always joined them at Birkhall: 'The greatest fun of the whole year was my annual childhood visit to join the Princesses. The garden descended steeply to the river Muick and sometimes we would picnic on an island in the river.'[9] When they were not playing horses they played 'catching happy days', which involved catching leaves as they fell from the trees. They wrote plays and listened to the gramophone, although their records were limited; a lasting memory of Princess Margaret's was 'marching up and down to King Cotton by Souza'.[10] Margaret's bedroom was next to Princess Margaret's, and she was often kept awake by her singing 'Old MacDonald Had a Farm', which went on and on.[11] It was a gentle time: 'We used our imaginations and were easily amused.'

It was at Birkhall where Princess Elizabeth 'pulled rank' on her cousin, the only time she recalls it ever happening. They were arguing about who owned a wooden seat outside the front door. The Duchess's nickname, given to her by another niece, was Peter, and Princess Elizabeth claimed ownership of the seat, declaring, 'I'm the biggest "P" for Princess.'[12]

After staying at Birkhall the following year, 1934, Princess Elizabeth enjoyed herself so much that when they left she nearly cried, her mother told the King. However, she had something to look forward to. In November her uncle, Prince George, was marrying the beautiful Princess Marina of Greece, and she was going to be a bridesmaid. Everyone was delighted at the match, although it highlighted the continuing bachelor state of her uncle David. In June he had reached forty. The Hon. Mrs Francis Lascelles wrote a lengthy piece for *The Evening News*.[13] The heir to the Throne was, she said, 'one of the most accomplished, shrewd and most vital men in the world today . . . [with] a knowledge of life and the world which few other men possess at sixty'. As for his own motto, 'I serve', she considered no previous Prince of Wales 'had lived up to it so fully and completely' as he had done. Mrs Lascelles apparently saw no contradiction between his position as heir to the Throne and his view that 'His matrimonial future is a matter for himself and he does not see why anybody should concern themselves with it.' Rumours about his future bride persisted, particularly in America, but he 'prefers reading about his "engagement" rather than entering into one'. Ironically, she concluded, 'It is good for Britain that it has a man in the prime of his life still ready and willing to give his unstinted and incomparable services to that country and to the Empire.'

But his 'services' were already directed elsewhere. His preference for married women was well known, about which his father had spoken to him in 1932. The King told him that 'although he was still worshipped by the public . . . this would not survive the gradual revelation of his private life, in particular his liaison with Lady Furness',[14] who was then his mistress. The Prince admitted that the only person he had ever wanted to marry was Freda Dudley Ward, a married woman with two daughters, who was his mistress from 1919 to 1923.[15] His Aide de Camp, Lord Louis Mountbatten, drew up a list of European princesses but to no avail. The King began to despair, convinced that within a year of his death David would 'ruin himself', and told a courtier, 'My eldest son will never succeed me. He will abdicate.'[16]

Some of David's letters to Freda contain an outpouring of self-pity on the misery of his position as Prince of Wales: the wearisome routine, the hostile relatives and servants, his dislike of many foreigners.[17] After they stopped being lovers, he turned his attention in 1930 to Thelma Furness. She and her twin sister Gloria Vanderbilt were the daughters of an American diplomat. When she met David, Thelma was on her second marriage, to shipping magnate Viscount Furness. In early 1931, she innocently introduced the Prince to her fellow American, Wallis Simpson. In January 1934, Thelma went to the United States and asked Wallis to 'look after him' in her absence and to see 'that he doesn't get into any mischief'. When she returned she realised that Wallis 'had looked after him exceedingly well'.[18] As for Ernest Simpson, Wallis's second husband, he was 'content to bask in the reflected glory of his wife's conquest'.[19]

At least the King could be cheered by Prince George's marriage. He too had caused his family concern. He joined the Royal Navy but hated it, plagued by seasickness and insomnia. The King kept refusing his request to leave until 1929, when he realised his son's health was being seriously affected. George instead became a Factory Inspector for the Home Office, the first member of the royal family to be a Civil Servant. He loved it, feeling he was helping to improve the lot of the working man. In his personal life, however, he had been less successful. Tall, good-looking, and the most aesthetically aware of the family, George enjoyed relationships with both sexes. Probably the most damaging was with the American socialite Kiki Preston, who introduced him to hard drugs. David managed to persuade Preston to leave the country and supervised his brother's recuperation.

Earlier, there had been George's love affair with Poppy Baring, heiress to a prominent banker. In 1927, he told his parents he wanted to marry her. They seemed to accept the news, but ten days later, it was mysteriously all off. George discovered his parents' intervention, confiding in Helen Hardinge: 'I've had two more goes with my family to no avail. . . . I'm certainly going on with it & I don't care what they say. They sent Lord S to see Lady B* & told her it was all off without telling me, which wasn't

---

*Lady Baring, Poppy's mother, and probably Lord Stamfordham, the King's Principal Private Secretary.

a <u>nice</u> thing to do, was it? . . . [I] expect I'll have to go away for a bit & give them time to think it over again <u>if</u> they will! I can't bear to be at Buck House now, it makes me feel too sick!'[20] However, any future that George envisaged with Poppy never happened.

Little wonder, then, that his engagement to the beautiful and intelligent Marina, granddaughter of the late King George I of Greece, was welcomed. The Queen told Lady Desborough, 'Marina is pretty & charming & I think Georgie is very lucky to have found such a delightful bride & we are so glad to think that everyone is pleased about it.'[21] In anticipation of the union, the King created George Duke of Kent. Marina's father, Prince Nicholas of Greece, was the brother of the exiled Prince Andrea. It was hardly surprising, then, that one of the guests at the wedding on 29 November should be Prince Andrea's son, Prince Philip of Greece.

The wedding at Westminster Abbey, at which Elizabeth was one of the bride's trainbearers, was the first time she met Philip, although she has said she does not remember it. He was thirteen and had just started at Gordonstoun, a progressive boarding school in Scotland, which provided him with the stability that much of his early life had lacked. After his father's exile, the family had settled in St Cloud in the south of France, where Philip attended a private American school from 1927. Bright and with a restless energy, he enjoyed it, but cracks appeared at home. His mother Alice was showing signs of mental illness. When her own attempts to get well proved fruitless, her husband and her mother, Victoria, sought help. Alice was diagnosed with paranoid schizophrenia and on 2 May 1930 was admitted to a sanatorium in Switzerland. The children were taken out for the day, and when they got home, she was gone.

Philip's parents' marriage had been rocky for some years. Now Andrea closed up the family house and spent the next few years drifting about Europe and occasionally involving himself in Greek affairs. His daughters, aged between sixteen and twenty-five, would all be married within eighteen months.[22] However, Philip was only nine. Alice kept in touch with her children by letter and Philip was occasionally taken to see her, but for several years he neither saw her nor heard from her.

From 1930, Andrea arranged for Philip to be looked after by Alice's family in England, under the overall supervision of Victoria. It was agreed that Alice's eldest brother, George, 2nd Marquess of Milford Haven, would act as Philip's guardian. He was sent to Cheam School in Berkshire, where he stayed for three years. Uncle Georgie attended school events, and Philip spent at least part of the holidays with him and his wife, Najada or 'Nada', at their house, Lynden Manor. Nada was a Russian Countess and Myra Butter's aunt. Nada was 'frightfully eccentric and we absolutely adored her', says Myra. 'She was completely unorthodox but complete fun. She and my mother were chalk and cheese.'

Georgie was clever and charismatic. 'I was in love with him as a little girl: he was wonderful with children,' says Myra. 'To him, you were a grown-up. He took you out and talked to you, did every sort of thing . . . He had a suitcase of puzzles that he used to do, Rubic-cube-type things. He was always making things too.'[23] As an adolescent and in the Royal Navy, he showed a genius for invention. Later, he applied his technical brilliance to industry, becoming chairman of major companies. Myra thinks that Georgie's cleverness 'spurred Dickie Mountbatten on to do well'. Myra remembers Lynden Manor, with its 'tennis court and lovely swing and a garden border full of poppies'. If Philip were not staying there, he would stay with Myra's family; her brother Alex was his best friend, and with Georgie and Nada's son, David, they were a tight-knit trio. At other times, Philip visited his grandmother Victoria at Kensington Palace.

Georgie and Nada kept interesting company at Lynden Manor. Visitors included the widowed Gloria Morgan Vanderbilt, Thelma's twin, whom Philip met while he was there. Gloria was a very close friend of Nada's. A few weeks before she attended Prince George's wedding, Nada had been embroiled in a very public legal case in New York, concerning the custody of Gloria's ten-year-old daughter. In attempting to show that Gloria was not a fit mother, her late husband's family relied on hearsay evidence about her lifestyle, including an alleged lesbian relationship with Nada, whose sexuality was said to be fluid. Nada supported Gloria during the case. Myra met Gloria: 'There was definitely something going on there, [although] at that age, you never know anything.'[24] Georgie and Nada also amassed a huge collection of pornographic literature. Philip's exposure to the unorthodox nature of their lifestyles must have broadened his mind: 'He'd have taken anybody as they were,' says Myra. 'He's got a broad vision. He had a happy base.'[25]

All controversy was put out of mind as Philip attended his cousin Marina's wedding. In the Abbey, a royal watcher recognised the young Prince: 'A little flaxen-haired boy in Eton suit is moving excitedly among distinguished guests just at the altar steps.'[26] In watching the bride's procession, Philip could not have missed Elizabeth, even if she was too young for his specific attention. She was concentrating on carrying the bride's train, together with young Lady Mary Cambridge: 'They hardly moved a muscle while the service proceeded . . . [they] gave the impression of fairies with their fluffy white frocks all gleaming with silver stars.'[27] Philip might have been distracted by a fidgety Princess Margaret, who sat at her mother's feet and kept pulling at her socks and rubbing her knees so that the Duchess had to hold her hand to quieten her.[28]

The new Duke and Duchess of Kent were a glamorous couple, and the wedding caused great excitement at home and abroad. For Philip it was a chance to catch up with friends and relatives. In the years to come, Marina would be his confidante, and he would stay with her and the Duke at their house, Coppins. For now, though, he had to return to school, and Elizabeth would have to wait a little while longer to meet her Prince.

CHAPTER 8

Celebrations and Sadness (1935–1936)

The early 1930s were a happy time for the Yorks. For the Duke, it seemed 'that the pattern of his life was now firmly established. . . . He was supremely happy in his family and his home'[1], referring fondly to 'Us Four'. Their official engagements were not too demanding. Although the Duke knew his father's health was not good and David still had no heir, it seemed his own succession was unlikely to happen for a very long time, if ever.

As 1935 dawned, the Duke did not know that it would be the last year he would just be a younger son of the King and his family able to enjoy a degree of normality without being entirely under the world's microscope. For Elizabeth, it meant being able to go shopping observed only by the locals. Hertfordshire resident Valerie Dougherty remembered stopping to watch the two Princesses go into a newsagents near The Bury and was 'consumed with schoolgirl envy when [Elizabeth] emerged carrying a copy of the latest Mickey Mouse Annual'.[2]

Normality, though, is relative. Elizabeth was the only child in the world with so much named after her: hospitals, streets, flowers, territories. 'Princess, at nine you've taken/A people for your friend' wrote the poet John Drinkwater for *The Princess Elizabeth Gift Book*. Published in 1935 in aid of the eponymous children's hospital in London, it contained stories and poems specially written for children by well-known authors, including J. M. Barrie, Rudyard Kipling and Enid Bagnold, whose famous story *National Velvet* was published that year. The colour illustrations included portraits of the Princess and Mickey Mouse scenes, by permission of Walt Disney, who had created the character seven years earlier.

Despite their privileged world, on an everyday basis the Princesses were not indulged. Elizabeth's pocket money increased to a shilling a week, but she was still expected to save weekly in her Post Office account. At Christmas, their stockings were filled with small inexpensive items, and their larger presents were relatively modest. Although the Duchess liked to take them Christmas shopping in Harrods, they bought many presents from Woolworths, a popular general store, or made their own. They were always reminded of the existence of the sick and the needy and encouraged to help; one year they helped the cook to decorate cakes for blind soldiers. In clothes, the Duchess favoured prettiness but simplicity; she also ensured her daughters were dressed the same until Elizabeth was well into her teens. Elizabeth never seemed to mind what she wore, having little interest in clothes, unlike Margaret, who was particular from a very young age.

The Princesses were discouraged from thinking themselves special. One day Elizabeth was at a performance with the Queen but was wriggling in her seat. Her grandmother asked if she would prefer to go home. 'Oh no, Granny,' she said. 'We can't leave before the end. Think of all the people who'll be waiting to see us outside.' Such an exhibition of self-interest was anathema to the Queen, who told her lady-in-waiting to take the Princess out the back way, into a taxi and home.[3] Certainly their young friends were not inclined to treat the Princesses as special, except when they were told to do so. Every summer, when Myra Butter was a child, her family stayed at Downie House in Cortachy, and sometimes the Yorks joined them. At one tea party Mabell Airlie's grandson, David Ogilvy (now 13th Earl of Airlie), was driving his toy car and, in the spirit of sharing, was told to let Princess Elizabeth have a go. Even as an adult, 'He distinctly remembers being absolutely furious that he had to hand it over!'[4]

The year 1935 marked the King's Silver Jubilee, twenty-five years since his accession, and a full programme of events was planned. It was a chance to celebrate the stability of the monarchy at a time when instability was rocking Europe once more. On 6 May, the King took part in a joyful procession through London, which marked the start of a month of celebrations and launched many charitable appeals. The night before, crowds began to gather in the streets: 'The sight of thousands of people stretching along the route of the procession . . . had to be seen to be believed.'[5] Those who looked up at the Palace windows as morning broke had 'their first great thrill of the day – a liveried servant drew up the blinds in the King's breakfast room windows.'

It was Elizabeth's first royal procession and she sat proudly in the carriage with her parents and sister and waved to the crowds. They drove to St Paul's Cathedral for a service of thanksgiving, and such was the welcome the King received; he was touched: 'I am beginning to think they must really like me for myself,' he said to his nurse.[6] In a special broadcast, he thanked his people for their loyalty. He recognised that 'it is to the young that the future belongs', and hoped the Jubilee Fund that his 'dear son the Prince of Wales' had launched would help the young 'to become useful citizens'. The King also acknowledged problems to come: 'My people and I have come through great trials and difficulties together. They are not over.'[7]

Indeed they were not. In Germany, Hitler was depriving Jews of German citizenship and forbidding marital and extra-marital relations with Aryans. At home, trouble of a different kind was brewing. The King did not know that watching the procession from a prime spot in St James' Palace was the mistress of his 'dear son'. David had asked Helen Hardinge, who lived there with Sir Alec, if she might make space for two of his scullery maids to watch from an upstairs window. Helen made her bedroom available, but thought it odd that they could not watch from Buckingham Palace. She discovered later that one 'maid' was in fact Wallis Simpson.[8] The relationship had been gathering pace for a while and becoming more open. The King gave orders to the Lord Chamberlain that she was not to be invited to any Silver Jubilee function or to the Royal Enclosure at Ascot.[9] However, even the Lord Chamberlain could not have eyes inside the Hardinges' apartments.

There were far more pleasant things for the King to think about, such as the presence at the celebrations of his granddaughters: 'All the children looked so nice', he wrote, 'but none prettier than Lilibet and Margaret'.[10] At the end of July, a garden party at Buckingham Palace for twelve thousand guests was hailed as the perfect finish to the Jubilee celebrations. Elizabeth became the centre of a separate informal court, in which she 'took the keenest interest in the proceedings and greeted her friends with the charm of an experienced hostess'.[11] Prince Philip's grandmother,

Victoria, was there too, with her son Georgie and daughter-in-law Nada. It was a happy occasion, on which even the weather was glorious. The Queen was grateful that her husband had remained well enough to see the celebrations through.

Another idyllic summer followed. The Princesses stayed at Glamis while their parents joined a shooting party at Gannochy Moors with J. P. Morgan, the American banker, who took a house there every year. Fellow shots included the Duchess's brothers, David and Michael, and her brother-in-law, Lord Elphinstone, who, with her sister May, hosted the parties for Mr Morgan. Cousin Margaret remembered the food her parents provided: 'magnificent breakfasts . . . eggs, bacon, sausages, Finnan haddock or kedgeree, cold ham and grouse', and 'the shooting lunch, another enormous meal which was eaten sitting out on the heather, with the butler and a footman . . . to wait on the guests'.[12] At Glamis the Countess took Elizabeth shopping in Dundee with cousins Anne and Diana, and was photographed gamely guiding them through a large crowd waiting outside a department store. More relations and friends arrived for Princess Margaret's birthday and were delighted again by the theatre group. To Margaret's annoyance, she was still considered too young for some events. When they moved on to Birkhall, it was only Elizabeth who accompanied their parents and the King to Craithie Church and had lunch with them at Balmoral.

There was one event that year, however, from which Margaret was not excluded: the wedding in November of their uncle Henry, Duke of Gloucester, to Lady Alice Montagu-Douglas-Scott, daughter of the Duke of Buccleuch and Queensbury. Both the Princesses were bridesmaids. The King and Queen were relieved that another son was to marry. Henry had previously had an affair with the stunning and married Beryl Markham, whom he met while on safari with David in 1928. To Henry, the most reserved of the King's sons, Beryl must have been intoxicating. Born in England but raised in Kenya, her first language was Swahili, and she was the only white woman allowed to hunt with the male warriors. Her sexual conquests were legendary. The year before she met Henry, she married her second husband, Mansfield Markham, by whom she was pregnant. However, it did not deter the affair, which she described as 'a mad little gallop'.[13] After she gave birth in London in 1929 and began visiting Henry, the Queen discovered their affair, as did Markham, who threatened to sue for divorce and name Henry as co-Respondent. The Queen intervened. On condition that Beryl leave the country immediately, Henry agreed to pay £15,000 into a trust fund. She went on to marry for a third time and became the first British woman to fly solo from England to America.

Lady Alice, aged thirty-three, was an artist and accomplished horse-woman and had also travelled in Kenya. Her father was an old friend of George V and she had known Henry since childhood. She and Henry shared a dislike of pomposity and a love of riding: when he was not away with his army regiment, Princess Elizabeth sometimes rode with him in Hyde Park. Their wedding was held in the Private Chapel at Buckingham Palace, for Alice's father had recently died, and it was considered appropriate to make the event more low-key. The death of his boyhood friend was a blow to the King, whose health was again causing concern.

Around one million people gathered in London to catch a glimpse of the newly weds. After the Jubilee celebrations, the wedding was a further tangible reminder of the reassuring and continuing presence of the monarchy. Aside from health concerns, the year had so far been a positive one for the King. 'Now all the children are married but David,' he wrote in his diary.[14] He and the Queen were also delighted when Princess Marina gave birth to their third grandson, Edward, for whom Franklin D Roosevelt was appointed a godfather. The General Election saw the National Government return under Baldwin, and the King was pleased when Ramsay Macdonald accepted his request to remain in the Government. Baldwin, however, had the feeling that his monarch, now seventy, was 'packing up his luggage and getting ready to depart'.[15]

As 1935 drew to an end, its happy moments were overshadowed for the King by two events: Mussolini invaded Abyssinia, and his beloved sister, Princess Victoria, died. For once, allowing his personal feelings to come before duty, he cancelled the State Opening of Parliament. His last official act was on 23 December 1935, when he conferred the seals of office upon his new Foreign Secretary, Anthony Eden.

As the King struggled with lack of sleep and breathlessness, the Duchess of York went down with a serious bout of influenza which turned into pneumonia. She was too ill to leave Royal Lodge and had to remain there for Christmas. The Duke stayed with her while the Princesses went to Sandringham. Alah took them to see the King every morning and at teatime. The Duchess wrote to them and she reminded her 'Darling Lilibet' to be 'polite to everybody. Mind you answer nicely when you are asked questions, even though they may be silly ones!'[16] In return, Lilibet made her mother laugh with tales of Dookie, their favourite but bad-tempered corgi.

When the King made his Christmas Day broadcast, the public heard a much frailer voice. He still kept his diary and noted with pleasure, 'Saw my Kent grandson in his bath.'[17] On 15 January 1936, a small house party gathered at Sandringham. The King went for a short ride on his shooting pony, Jock, and the Queen walked with him. The next day, he complained of having a cold and stayed in his room all day. The Queen sent for Bertie to help her with the house party: the Duchess was still unwell. On the train to Sandringham, Bertie met his father's new Assistant Private Secretary, 'Tommy' Lascelles. He had been an Assistant Private Secretary to the Prince of Wales but had resigned in 1929, despairing of his future monarch. However, he had loyally accepted George V's invitation to rejoin the royal household; he did not yet know of his illness.

The Duke of York and Lascelles arrived at a snowy Sandringham in the late afternoon of 16 January, where life seemed to be going on as normal. Lascelles noted, 'I was set down to a belated tea with the Duke, the Queen presiding over us, while the rest of a large company resumed a game of "Happy Families" with the York children.' Other guests included Lady Desborough and Lady Algy Lennox-Gordon. A few weeks earlier, the King had talked to Lady Lennox-Gordon about his son's friendship with Wallis Simpson, saying passionately, 'I pray to God that my eldest son will never marry and have children, and that nothing will come between Bertie and Lilibet and the throne.'[18]

The next day, the King was worse, and his doctors were summoned. The Prince of Wales, who was shooting at Windsor, was sent for. Bulletins were issued regularly, which prepared the nation for the worst without being too specific. The Queen had been calm but 'tonight at dinner she was obviously very strained, poor woman.'[19] On 18 January, Lascelles noted that everyone was 'very cheerful outwardly' while they ate 'anxious, unreal meals which convey no hint of the fact that the King of England is dying in an upper room'.[20] He was worried about the future. 'We are all rather sad at the demeanour of Edward VIII – esp. myself, who had hoped for some alteration after 8 years'. Lascelles knew he would be expected to continue under him: 'I can't turn back now, I feel I must do it more than ever, for if the Crown is to survive the next reign, it will need honest men to hold it up if it ever did.'[21]

On 20 January, the King's strength began to ebb. Lord Dawson of Penn told the nation: 'The King's life is moving peacefully to its close.' His family kept vigil as the Archbishop of Canterbury said prayers. At 11:55 that night, he died. Queen Mary turned and kissed the hand of her eldest son, Edward VIII.[22] For the Princesses, it was the first time that death had come into their young lives. While preparations were made for the funeral, Crawfie was asked to return to Royal Lodge from her holiday and keep them occupied there. Margaret did not pay much attention to what was happening, but Elizabeth was worried that they should not play and was reassured that it was all right. The King's body lay in state for five days in the Palace of Westminster, visited by nearly one million mourners. Queen Mary took Elizabeth to see 'Grandpa England' one last time.

The next day, thousands watched in silence as the coffin was pulled on a gun carriage through the same London streets that just months earlier had been filled with joyous cheering. Margaret was too young to attend the funeral; she watched the procession from the balcony of 145, curtseying to the coffin as it passed. Elizabeth, wearing black for the first time, travelled to Windsor on the royal train with her mother. In St George's Chapel, she watched as her grandfather was lowered into the grave, then listened as her uncle David was proclaimed King. Her father was now the King's heir and she was one step closer to the Throne. However, the prospect seemed to be safely in the distant future, a far-off land to a nine-year-old girl.

CHAPTER 9

An Early Annus Horribilis (1936)

After the stability of George V's reign, his son's felt very different to those who knew him. When the American Ambassador, Robert W Bingham, spoke at a Pilgrims Society[1] dinner in London about forging stronger links between the two countries, he never envisaged that his host, then Prince of Wales, would become inextricably bound to one of his countrywomen and cause one of the biggest dramas the British monarchy had ever experienced.

Shortly after the King's funeral, Queen Mary confided her concerns to Mabell Airlie. She thought her son's conduct was more like that of a self-interested individual than a Sovereign. 'I have not liked to talk to David about this affair with Mrs Simpson, in the first place because I don't want to give the impression of interfering in his private life, and also because he is the most obstinate of all my sons. . . . At present he is utterly infatuated, but my great hope is that violent infatuations usually wear off.'[2]

The way he conducted his private life had generally been a matter of concern to senior courtiers for years. Before George V died, Admiral Halsey, a member of the Prince of Wales's Council, wanted the Prime Minister and senior ministers to confront the Prince about his excesses, which were becoming the subject of common discussion. Although the value of the work the Prince had done from 1918 to 1925 had been 'incalculable', Halsey considered that in the last six or seven years his private life had 'devalued' his public life, and 'he is not likely to be a fitting monarch.'[3] He had never been a stranger to self-pity. Replying to a party invitation from Lady Desborough, the Prince said he could not arrive in time for dinner because 'I am very hard worked nowadays'. Instead, he asked if she could hold one of her 'small & informal parties', which would be 'such a charming & delightful change & relaxation after all the strenuous engagements that are my lot in life!!!!'[4]

94

George V's death put paid to Halsey's proposal. The reign of Edward VIII was upon them. It was not as though as Prince of Wales he had been disliked. He was stylish, charming and in touch with the common man. However, he could also be unpredictable and rude. For every story of his kindness and humanity there was another which pointed to an erosion of the charm he had possessed when younger. His unconcealed boredom, unpunctuality and increasingly irrational behaviour embarrassed his staff and left them trying to smooth ruffled feathers. They were also aggrieved by his frequent lack of consideration towards them.

For the Princesses, life remained much the same at first, with Crawfie and Alah maintaining their usual routines. The Duchess felt the loss of her father-in-law keenly, telling Lord Dawson that 'he was always ready to listen and give advice on one's own silly little affairs'.[5] She was still convalescing after pneumonia, and in March she and the Princesses went to stay at the Duke of Devonshire's house, Compton House in Eastbourne, where Bertie joined them between engagements. The eighteenth-century house was warmly familiar, for the Yorks had often stayed there with the King and Queen and had a chalet on the beach. However, 'The people were rather a bore,' the Duchess told Queen Mary, 'and though they stared quite politely, they stared & <u>STARED</u>.' Nevertheless, they had spent a lovely time at the beach '& the children enjoyed themselves enormously.'[6] They attended the local church, where a churchwarden noticed Elizabeth pointing out the words in the hymn book to Margaret, the sort of gesture that typified her thoughtfulness to her younger sister, despite their spats.[7] Like ordinary children, the sisters argued and fought with each other: Elizabeth would hit, Margaret would bite.

Bertie was also concerned about his brother's private life and, like Halsey, worried about his wish to sweep away the old traditions. Edward VIII saw himself as a moderniser of the monarchy. The first change he made was to turn Sandringham time to normal time, which upset old courtiers and retainers; Helen Hardinge, whose husband was now the King's Principal Private Secretary, called it 'a jarring descent to the trivial'.[8] The King also asked Bertie to conduct an enquiry into the cost of running Sandringham, the monarch's private property. He viewed it as something of a white elephant, favouring his modernised Fort Belvedere at Windsor.

Part of his economy drive resulted from his shock of discovering he had been left out of his father's will: George V had assumed that he would have built up sums from his revenue from the Duchy of Cornwall.[9] But David knew Wallis would be greatly disappointed, given the importance she placed on wealth. Lord Wigram had heard that he had put £250,000 into a trust for her out of his Duchy revenues, which was supposed to be invested in Britain; according to a friend of Ernest Simpson, a large sum had also been sent to the United States.[10] Wigram also noted that Mrs Simpson was 'in the pocket of the German ambassador', Joachim von Ribbentrop.[11]

Bertie had shared more in common with their father than David did. George V told Bertie when he married: 'You have always been so sensible & easy to work with & . . . ready to listen to any advice . . . that I feel that we have always got on very well together (very different to dear David)'. Even so, Bertie recognised that some changes were necessary but thought they should be brought about gradually. He was therefore unhappy when David reduced costs at Sandringham by drastically reducing the staff, then carried out another costs enquiry at Balmoral.

For months he resisted moving out of York House into Buckingham Palace where, as at Windsor, he upset staff by making adverse changes to their wages and conditions. Mrs Simpson had already upset them in 1935 when she took over the role of organising their Christmas presents. The lavish gifts they had received under his previous mistresses were replaced by a meagre sum in cash. Their lives were also made difficult because of his scant attention to state affairs: as Helen Hardinge noted, 'Confusion in the King's affairs because he's so impractical.'[12]

There was increasing confusion in Europe, too. In Spain, civil war began, and on 7 March Hitler sent military forces into the Rhineland, violating the Treaty of Versailles. Three weeks later, Edward VIII took a small party to Windsor, including Wallis and Ernest Simpson. The Hardinges were there. 'I wondered then if the King might one day marry Mrs Simpson', wrote Helen, 'but . . . she was married and her husband was with us and as far as I knew, no-one had mentioned this particular possibility.'[13]

The Princesses noted a major change of routine at Easter. Instead of the Court moving to Windsor, the King stayed at Fort Belvedere. Wallis had been a frequent weekend guest for some time, without her husband. Other regulars were Duff Cooper, newly Secretary for War, and author and friend of the Duchess of York, and his wife Lady Diana Cooper. 'The house is an enchanting folly', wrote Lady Diana, 'and only needs fifty red soldiers stood between the battlements to make it into a Walt Disney coloured symphony toy.'[14] In a house where 'the social life revolves around the swimming pool', the King was a generous host and did everything to make his guests 'happy, free and unembarrassed'.[15] His focus, though, was on Wallis. Lady Diana noted during a stay in February 1936, 'Wallis tore her nail and said "Oh!" and forgot about it, but he needs must disappear and arrive back in two minutes, panting, with two little emery-boards for her to file the offending nail.'[16] That same month, Stanley Baldwin and Lord Wigram learned that Ernest Simpson was telling people that the King wanted to marry his wife.

While her son entertained his friends, Queen Mary, deprived of enjoying Easter at Windsor, moved into Royal Lodge for a few weeks. The Duchess gave up her bedroom and bathroom and made a sitting room available so she could be as independent as possible. Queen Mary was still there by the time of her granddaughter's birthday on 21 April, the first one Elizabeth had spent at Royal Lodge rather than at Windsor. Now ten, she was permitted to have breakfast with her grandmother and her parents instead of in the nursery and had a day off lessons. Presents included a doll from her sister, a new bicycle from Queen Mary and an electrically propelled miniature car from her parents. Later she went on a ride through Windsor Great Park with her father, using her new riding whip from the King. Many gifts came from strangers as usual, including a doll perfectly dressed as a sailor in the naval uniform of the royal yacht, *Victoria and Albert*, but in accordance with the royal rule about presents from strangers, it had to be returned.

Later that spring, the Yorks had a surprise visitor. The King motored over to Royal Lodge to take Bertie for a ride in his new American station wagon. He had four guests with him, one of whom was Wallis Simpson. As they walked through the gardens, Wallis talked to the Duchess about 'the merits of the garden at the Fort and that at Royal Lodge',[17] and they had tea in the drawing room. 'In a few moments the two little Princesses joined us,' Wallis recorded. 'They were both so blonde, so beautifully mannered, so brightly scrubbed, that they might have stepped straight from the pages of a picture book.'[18] After spending 'a pleasant hour', she was left with the impression that 'while the Duke of York was sold on the American station wagon, the Duchess was not sold on David's other American interest.'[19] Crawfie thought Mrs Simpson 'a smart, attractive woman, with that immediate friendliness American woman have' and said that Lilibet asked her who she was.[20]

On 25 May, Queen Mary was diverted from her worries when she made her first visit to the ocean liner named after her, the biggest ship afloat in the world, which was about to make its maiden voyage to New York. It also marked one of her first engagements since her husband died, and the King and all the adult royals went with her in support. Princess Elizabeth was there too, for her mother said she was 'madly keen' to see the ship.[21] In the on-board nursery she sampled the toys and the telephones and watched a Mickey Mouse film in the cinema, but it was the engine room which seemed to fascinate her the most. She spent nearly an hour there and was late for tea.

Two days later it was clear that her son's 'infatuation' that so worried Queen Mary was continuing. At his insistence, the Court Circular for 27 May named for the first time Mr and Mrs Ernest Simpson as his guests at a dinner party, where illustrious figures included the Mountbattens, the Baldwins and American aviator Charles Lindbergh. Queen Mary told Lady Airlie, 'He gives her the most wonderful jewels . . . I am so afraid that he may ask me to receive her.'[22] Little did she know that David had told Wallis he wanted her there because 'sooner or later my Prime Minister must meet my future wife.'[23] The dinner would be the last one at which she publically appeared with Ernest. Shortly afterwards she told him she was starting divorce proceedings.

The date of 12 May 1937 was fixed for Edward VIII's Coronation. He became bolder. In June he could not go to Ascot because of mourning but instead sent Mrs Simpson in a royal carriage. On 9 July, the Yorks were invited to dinner at York House. Presiding over a large party, which included the Churchills, was Wallis without Ernest. Helen Hardinge thought Churchill did not consider that Mrs Simpson mattered: 'Moral and social considerations apart, he considered her presence to be irrelevant to King Edward's performance as Sovereign. The King thought the exact opposite. He considered she was the only thing that mattered.'[24]

The Princesses, meanwhile, were innocent of such adult concerns, although clearly Elizabeth had her own thoughts. A feature was published about the grand houses of Piccadilly. The author caught a glimpse at 145 of Elizabeth 'at the dining room window looking very disconsolate with elbows on the sill and head in her hands as if bored by the long, drawn-out luncheon of her elders and sent to the window to keep her quiet!'[25] Queen Mary started taking the Princesses on what she called 'instructive amusements' and in July they went to Coram's Fields, the site of the hospital for foundlings. She was 'especially fond of Elizabeth and very proud of her', said Lady Airlie. Margaret was aware of this: 'She was rude to all of us, except Lilibet,' she said later.

That month the royal family had a shock. While the King was riding back after a ceremony in Hyde Park, with the Duke of York behind him, someone threw a loaded revolver which hit the King's horse. A man was arrested for attempted assassination. Messages of sympathy and relief for the King's safety were sent from monarchs and heads of state from around the world. The *New York Times* said their people rejoiced with the British because not only had the King escaped assassination, 'but has borne himself as becomes a King, true to the ancient definition that "a King is he that has no fear"'. Soon, however, that newspaper, along with others abroad, began to publish less respectful stories.

The King's private conduct became even more public. In August he embarked on a Mediterranean cruise on board the yacht *Nahlin* with Wallis and a small group of friends and staff. His absence from Balmoral meant Queen Mary could not go there as usual and instead stayed with Princess Mary at Harewood House. The King intended to visit Italy, a plan from which Foreign Secretary Anthony Eden eventually managed to dissuade him, for Britain's relations with the country were not good. In Turkey, he was well received and his meeting with its dictator, Ataturk, was said to have been positive. Even Lascelles, who was critical of him in many ways, pronounced himself pleased with the King's behaviour. But whatever the benefits of the trip, the fact that he had travelled with Mrs Simpson was noted.

Trying to forget their concerns, the Yorks enjoyed some family events that summer. The Duchess's niece, Jean Elphinstone, married John Lycett Wills, a Life Guards officer and member of a well-known tobacco family ('a cigarette maker', sniffed Diana Cooper)[26], at St Margaret's Westminster. The Princesses enjoyed themselves with cousins who formed the bride's youngest attendants: Jean's sister, Margaret, and Fergus and Davina Bowes Lyon, children of Michael and David. In early August they went to Glamis, then Birkhall, pleased that the King let them use it as George V had done.

On 14 September, the King returned from his cruise and went to Balmoral, where the Yorks were to join him. Beforehand the Duchess told Queen Mary she was 'secretly dreading next week but I haven't heard if a certain person is coming or not – I do hope not, as everything is so talked of up here.'[27] Soon they experienced a demonstration of the King's priorities. He had been asked to open a new hospital in Aberdeen but declined because he was still in official mourning. He asked the Yorks to step in (although by his reasoning, they too were in mourning) and they agreed, although the Duchess thought it was a pity he could not open it, 'as they have all worked so hard for so long & it will be one of the best in Scotland'.[28] In fact, the King was in Aberdeen himself that day, driving over personally to meet three friends at the station, one of whom was Wallis. The Scottish newspapers that reported the Duke opening the hospital also headlined: 'The King meets friends at Aberdeen Station.' In abrogating his duty, he insulted the Scots.

He took his friends to Balmoral, where a dinner party proved to be an awkward occasion. Even Churchill deprecated Wallis going 'to such a highly official place upon which the eyes of Scotland were concentrated'.[29] The Yorks did not stay long. Helen Hardinge thought that, for the Duke, 'the situation at Balmoral had been a nightmare . . . he felt that he had lost a friend and was rapidly losing a brother.'[30] Bertie did not want to believe that, if faced with the Crown or his marriage, his brother would choose marriage. It is unlikely that Elizabeth remained immune to it all. Cousin Margaret believed that 'she began to see what was going on through the eyes of people working in their house' and got her information from them.[31]

Events gathered pace. Wallis filed an undefended petition for divorce and in October newspapers in the United States started to openly speculate that she would marry the King. The rumours reached Britain. Fearing losing their royalist readers, British newspapers printed nothing adverse. However, a stream of letters started pouring in from the Dominions and British subjects in America. One lengthy and anonymous letter to *The Times* spoke of the 'avalanche of muck and slime'[32] in the American Press about the King and Mrs Simpson, which made the writer fear for the institution of the monarchy. The editor showed a shocked Hardinge, who thought it would make the desired impression on the King.

On 20 October, the Yorks arrived back in London. Hardinge told the Duke that Baldwin had that day shown the King some of the letters and begged him to persuade Mrs Simpson to withdraw the divorce proceedings. However, the King had been adamant and said he did not have the right to interfere with the affairs of an individual. The British Press reported the divorce as they would any other case, an agreement that stemmed from consultations between the King and newspaper magnate Lord Beaverbrook. The Press thought the King just wanted to protect his friend from publicity at a sensitive time.

On 27 October, the decree nisi was granted, after which a six-month period had to pass before it could be made absolute. Chaperoned by her aunt, Mrs Simpson continued to visit the King at Fort Belvedere, to the increasing concern of ministers. If he married her, she would be Queen, and both of them would be crowned by the Archbishop of Canterbury, in a ceremony that would confirm Edward VIII as head of the Church of England – a church that held that Christian marriage is for all time. That could not happen. With the agreement of Baldwin, Hardinge prepared to carry out his duty as Principal Private Secretary and warn his Sovereign of the impending crisis.

On 3 November, the King opened his first, and last, Parliament. After a successful tour of the Welsh mining villages, he returned to London on 13 November and went straight to Fort Belvedere. Hardinge's letter was waiting for him. It warned him that the British Press was not going to stay silent for much longer and that Baldwin and senior ministers were meeting that day to discuss what action should be taken to deal with the serious situation which was developing. It could either result in the resignation of the Government, said Hardinge, or a dissolution and a general election, 'in which Your Majesty's personal affairs would be the chief issue'. Even those who sympathised with him as an individual 'would deeply resent the damage which would inevitably be done to the Crown – the corner stone on which the whole Empire rests'. The only step which would avoid this 'dangerous situation', said Hardinge, was 'for Mrs Simpson to go abroad *without further delay* – and I would *beg* Your Majesty to give this proposal your earnest consideration before the position has become irretrievable.'[33]

Hardinge's letter shocked and angered the King. It also led him to make his position clear to Baldwin that evening, 16 November, telling him categorically that he intended to marry Mrs Simpson as soon as she was free to do so. He would prefer to do so as King, but if the Government irrevocably opposed his wishes, then he was prepared to abdicate. The King then told his mother, who was devastated; the following day he told Bertie, then Henry and George. Meanwhile, Baldwin sought the opinion of the Dominion governments on whether they would prefer the King to abdicate or make a morganatic marriage, one where Wallis would not become queen but take a lesser title. This latter option was the one that the King preferred, but Baldwin considered it a distasteful solution, as did the Dominions.

It was a traumatic time. Bertie tried many times to talk to his brother, but he felt the Abdication was becoming inescapable. He and the Duchess had to carry out duties as usual, including one in Edinburgh, where they stayed with the Elphinstones at Carberry Tower. The Duchess thanked her sister for her family's support: 'Bertie and I are feeling very despairing and the strain is terrific.'[34] On their return on 3 December, the Duke was 'surprised & horrified'[35] to see at Euston Station newspaper headlines shouting 'The King's marriage'; it was also the first time that Britons learned of the impending crisis. That day the King sent Wallis abroad to stay with friends at their villa in Cannes, for she had been receiving hate mail and threats.

The situation was not helped by the Duchess falling ill again with influenza and being confined to 145. Bertie chronicled the days that followed, especially his constant efforts to see his brother who kept leaving him in agonising limbo. Eventually, they met at Fort Belvedere on the evening of 7 December: 'The awful & ghastly suspense of waiting was over. . . . [David] told me his decision that he would go.'[36] After dinner, Bertie returned: 'As he is my eldest brother I had to be there to try & help him in his hour of need.'[37] The Duchess told a friend, 'Each day seems to last a week and we can only pray & hope that we may both have the health & will power to do our job for this dear country <u>whatever</u> happens.'[38]

On 9 December, he had another long talk with David, but 'his mind was made up.'[39] When Bertie told Queen Mary, 'I broke down & sobbed like a child.' On 10 December, all the brothers were present when Edward VIII signed the Abdication papers, 'a dreadful moment & one never to be forgotten by those present'.[40] The Notice of Abdication renounced the Throne for himself and his descendants. When the Duke returned to 145 that evening as King, he found a large crowd outside 'cheering madly. I was overwhelmed.'[41]

On 11 December at 2:00 p.m. it was announced to the world. Taking his father's name for continuity, Bertie was now King George VI. His first act was to create for his brother the title of Duke of Windsor. That night at Royal Lodge, the royal family had their last dinner together, which the new Queen had to miss, but in a letter to David, she said she hoped he would find happiness in his new life. In his Abdication speech, he pledged his allegiance to the new King and his loyalty to Britain and said, 'I have found it impossible to carry the heavy burden of responsibility and to discharge my duties as King as I would wish to do without the help and support of the woman I love.'[42] Afterwards, as Prince Edward, Duke of Windsor, he left for France en route to Austria, where he would stay without Wallis while she waited for her decree absolute. The Queen told the Archbishop of Canterbury that they regretted 'the loss of a dear brother . . . because one can only feel that exile from this country is death indeed.'[43]

On 12 December, George VI, looking pale and drawn, spoke to his Accession Council. With his wife by his side, he would 'take up the heavy task' that lay before him.[44] That day, Elizabeth looked out from a window in St James's Palace to see heralds proclaiming her father King, Emperor and Defender of the Faith.

In his speech, David had pointed out that his brother 'has one matchless blessing . . . not bestowed on me – a happy home with his wife and children.'[45] Now he would need them more than ever. Later he may have been amused to hear the reaction of his niece, Margaret Elphinstone, when she heard about the Abdication. Aged eleven, she was at dancing class: 'To my eternal shame I hopped around the room chanting: "My uncle Bertie is going to be King." Very soon afterwards "Uncle Bertie" became "Sir".'[46] Her aunt was now Queen Elizabeth and her cousin and playmate was Heiress Presumptive.

It had not been an automatic consequence of the Abdication that the Duke of York should become King. Before Parliament changed the Act of Settlement and named Edward VIII's successor, it would have to consult that person. Dermot Morrah said it was widely believed that the Duke, being highly conscientious and aware of duty, 'was reluctant to sentence his daughters to the lifetime of unremitting service, without hope of retirement, even in old age, which is inseparable from the highest place of all.'[47] There was serious consideration of the Duke of Kent becoming King, as he was the only one who had a son. However, everything pointed to the Duke of York, not least because of his reputation for public service and the unpretentious way his daughters had been raised, which not only made them popular but was generally felt 'to have provided the ideal early training for a future Queen'.[48]

Reluctantly but dutifully, he did not alter his place in the line of succession. Elizabeth heard her name included for the first time in prayers for the royal family. In less than a year she had passed from being third in line to the Throne to Heiress Presumptive and the most famous child in the world.

CHAPTER 10

Everything Changes (1936–1937)

The Abdication meant everyone had to make immediate changes, practical and emotional. Myra Butter says Elizabeth was very guarded about it: 'One knew what not to ask.'[1] On the day itself, Cynthia Asquith fulfilled a previous invitation to have tea with the Princesses at 145, where she found a huge crowd and many Press photographers. As Lady Asquith was leaving, Elizabeth took her to the door, where a letter lay on the table addressed to 'Her Majesty the Queen'. 'That's Mummy now,' said the Princess, with a solemn face and a slight tremor in her voice.[2] Princess Margaret later recalled that she asked her sister if it meant she would one day be queen. 'She replied, "Yes, I suppose it does." After that Princess Elizabeth did not mention it again.'[3]

The Countess of Strathmore told Mabell Airlie that her granddaughter was 'ardently praying for a brother',[4] which was still not impossible but increasingly unlikely. However, according to cousin Margaret, 'She never said anything about wanting a brother.' Elizabeth is 'a very pragmatic' person, who has often made a point about not fighting against the inevitable: 'I think even at that stage there must have been an acceptance of inevitability.'[5]

For her father, the changes were incalculable. Bertie was not born to be King, and in that way he was like their father. George V was also the second-born but his older brother, the Duke of Clarence, died in 1892 aged twenty-eight. At least his death removed the problem of the unsavoury rumours concerning his private life. On the first day of his reign, Bertie realised with horror that he would have to face daily the dispatch boxes that held government papers. He confided in Mountbatten, their cousin and former ADC to David as Prince of Wales. Distressed, he said he never wanted this and was quite unprepared for it. 'I've never even seen a state paper. I'm only a Naval Officer, it's the only thing I know about.'[6] Mountbatten reassured him, telling him that when the Duke of Clarence died, George V had worried about the same thing to his, Mountbatten's, father, who was then Admiral of the Fleet. His answer was that there was 'no more fitting preparation for a King than to have been trained in the Navy'. Nevertheless, Bertie's newly appointed Principal Private Secretary, Alec Hardinge, was astonished at how little he knew of public affairs and made sure that he did not take any important steps without his approval.

A few days later, the Strathmores lunched with their daughter and son-in-law. Cecilia told a friend, 'I still can hardly believe that my darling little daughter is the Queen of this great Empire.'[7] They found media interest in them increased, and from then on, whenever the Earl's name appeared, it was invariably followed by 'the father of the Queen'. Given their general disdain for royalty – the Countess once remarked that 'some people have to be fed royalty like sea-lions fish'[8] – their new status was somewhat ironical. The Strathmores spent that Christmas at home at Woolmers, where staff were delighted to receive presents from the Queen, as were those at St Paul's Walden Bury.

Among those joining the family for their first Christmas of the new reign were Queen Mary, now settled in Marlborough House, and the Gloucesters. One of the first things the King did was to withdraw all the notices of termination of employment that his brother had given to Sandringham's gardeners. Inevitably the family must have looked back to the previous Christmas. However, tradition was not forgotten and fun still had, and the house looked as gloriously festive as ever, with its brightly lit, thirty-foot-high Christmas tree. On Christmas Eve, the King distributed more than six hundred joints of beef and pork among the estate workers, while at Windsor a hundred poor families received quantities of coal. At midnight, long after his nieces had gone to bed, the Duke of Windsor telephoned from Vienna to wish everyone a happy Christmas but whether he received reciprocal greetings is not known.

Christmas Day brought the happy news that the Duchess of Kent had just given birth to their second child, Princess Alexandra. An event that did not happen that year was the Christmas broadcast. So much had happened so quickly, and the new King was not ready to take on that part of his father's heritage. After attending the church service, the royal family was greeted by a crowd of around five thousand, an unprecedented number. After family presents had been exchanged and lunch eaten, they enjoyed Blind Man's Bluff and Musical Chairs.

The Princesses might also have played a game they had invented the previous year, called 'Presentation at Court', in which they acted out the formalities of being presented to Queen Mary. When she asked the Princesses whom she was 'receiving', Elizabeth answered, 'Lord Bathtub and Lady Plug', names she said their uncle David had suggested. Perhaps the game reminded the new Queen, with some irony, of a time before she was engaged to Bertie. She had been a bridesmaid at the wedding of Helen Cecil and Alec Hardinge, who had just joined George V's household, and asked Helen: 'Couldn't you present me at Court?! That would be the funniest of all – "Mrs Alexander Hardinge (curtsey) presents Lady Elizabeth Lyon (curtsey), cheers & laughter."'[9] On 27 December, the Princesses' other uncle David and aunt Rachel joined the party. David always enjoyed shooting with his brother-in-law: now he was sporting with his Sovereign.

In January 1937, Wallis Simpson appeared on the cover of American magazine *TIME* as Woman of the Year: no doubt the issue did not materialise at 145, where the family was preparing to move out. As if to emphasise the many changes in their lives, it was announced that 17 Bruton Street, where Lady Elizabeth Bowes Lyon had left for her wedding in 1923 and where Princess Elizabeth was born three years later, was to be demolished with other houses and replaced by offices and shops.[10] The Strathmores would still maintain a London house at 84 Eaton Square.

In February, the royal family officially moved into Buckingham Palace. The King and Queen went first, followed a few weeks later by the Princesses. Mabell Airlie said they 'had been completely happy in the simplicity of their private life: that would be forfeited forever. The cosy house ... where they had entertained informally and got their own supper when they came in late from a theatre, had to be exchanged for the cold magnificence of Buckingham Palace.'[11] The first thing Elizabeth did as the family packed up 145 was to ensure that her favourite toy, a wooden horse called Ben, was safe, and for that she turned to her best friend, Sonia Graham-Hodgson. 'She was concerned that Ben would not like being packed away in a removal van and put in storage, so she asked me to look after him,' said Sonia. 'A couple of weeks later she wrote to me and asked me to bring him round to Buckingham Palace.'[12] Sonia had been the recipient of a story the eight-year-old Princess wrote for her in July 1934, called The Happy Farm, which was dedicated 'To Sonia, My dear little friend and lover of horses'.[13] She knew Ben would be safe in Sonia's care. Once all the horses had been re-housed in the Palace, they were lined up in a long row in the corridor outside the Princesses' rooms: Crawfie said Lilibet's were still there on her wedding day.

The Queen set about making changes to the Palace, turning it into a more comfortable family home. It was not easy. The sheer size of the place, with over three hundred rooms, plus cellars and basements, was daunting after the homeliness of 145. The Princesses' nurseries had been re-decorated and were bright and cheerful. They had a bedroom each, with Alah sharing Margaret's room and Bobo Elizabeth's. However, antiquated fittings still abounded: Crawfie's bedroom light could only be operated by a switch positioned two yards outside her doorway in the passage. Mice were not uncommon, and a special vermin catcher was employed.

The Princesses saw it all as an adventure and enjoyed playing games in the corridors. However, there was no escaping the fact that Buckingham Palace was the official headquarters of the monarchy and as such was like a small town. It even had its own post office, with letters delivered to the many rooms containing staff. At 145, visitors had been mostly personal friends, but now there was a constant stream of people coming and going. Crawfie said they found the distances wearing. 'It was a day's march to get from one end of it to the other. The food had to come all the way from the kitchens to the dining rooms. . . . The better part of half a mile, along corridors and up and down stone steps. One day when we were exploring, Lilibet said dryly, "People here need bicycles."'[14]

Soon Margaret would share lessons with Elizabeth. The existing schoolroom was very dark, so the King moved it to a small bright room overlooking the gardens. The Princesses loved the large lake into which Elizabeth fell one day while trying to find a duck nest and emerged covered in green slime. At the end of the garden was a small hill which they climbed to look out onto the road beyond the Palace walls, fascinated by ordinary people going about their business, although in that area many were nannies looking after their privileged charges. As the Princesses looked out from the garden, outside the Palace railings, people constantly gathered and looked in. Now Elizabeth had her own detective.

Aware that the generally popular ex-King was still very much in people's minds, Hardinge was determined that Their Majesties should be seen as much as possible all over the country, and their public appearances began on 13 February, with a visit to the East End. For the King, the sheer workload, the constant daily attention to paperwork, was crushing. The Queen had separate engagements, too, and their evenings were often taken up with functions. Their days still began with the Princesses, but their evening romps were often curtailed or abandoned.

During the first year, life in the Palace itself gradually became easier. The King loved to embrace technology, and he ensured that he and his secretaries had every business device to make their work more efficient. He also had new telephones installed throughout, so he could communicate direct with any room without having to go through the Palace's switchboard. In the nursery suite, a telephone was installed with a special line to the Queen's private apartments so that the Princesses could talk to their mother easily.

Meanwhile, the family was swept up in preparations for the Coronation, which was to take place on 12 May, the date originally fixed for Edward VIII's. Much of the basic preparation was completed, but there was still much to be done, including fittings for robes and crowns. Both Princesses were to attend and, to Crawfie's frustration, had to be taken out of lessons for fittings. She was worried how Margaret, not yet seven, would get through the three-hour-long ceremony, full of important and complex symbolism. Elizabeth was eleven by then and was well prepared by Crawfie, who read to her Queen Victoria's account of the day; soon she became quite an expert on the thousand-year-old tradition. Her parents asked her to write an account of the day, which she did in a very neat hand, using red pencil and a penny copy book. The account, 'To Mummy and Papa . . . from Lilibet', is vivid and unique, not least because few children had the privilege of attending, let alone having a direct connection with such a magnificent occasion.

She was woken at 5:00 a.m. by the Royal Marines striking up outside her window and 'leapt out of bed and so did Bobo. We put on dressing gowns and shoes and Bobo made me put on an eiderdown as it was so cold and we crouched in the window looking onto a cold, misty morning'.[15] Shortly they were joined by cousin Margaret. Despite being a year older than Elizabeth, she was not allowed to go to the service itself, the only one of her family who did not. Margaret remembered: 'I was put out because a girl I knew of my own age, who had a tiny drop of Royal blood, was attending in a lovely long dress.'[16] However, dressed in her 'best pink coat with a velvet collar', she was taken to the Palace to have breakfast with the Princesses, who ate little because they were too excited. While they waited to be dressed, they looked out of the window with their cousin at the gathering crowds and the Canadian Mounted Police, and Lilibet noted that 'when a policeman went by on his bicycle, everybody cheered!'[17]

The King had been particularly interested in what his daughters were wearing, and Crawfie remembered something of a scene 'when Margaret found Lilibet was to wear a little train, while she had none!'[18] Lilibet described their dresses: 'They were white silk with old cream lace and had little gold bows all the way down the middle. They had puffed sleeves with one little bow in the centre. Then there were the robes of purple velvet with gold on the edge.'[19] The King also had special coronets made for them that were very light to wear. They all went along the corridor to see the King and Queen. 'Papa was dressed in a white shirt, breeches and stockings,' wrote Lilibet, 'and over this he wore a crimson satin coat.'[20] The Queen's dress was of white satin and old lace, with a white ermine shoulder cape and purple velvet train, nearly four feet wide and eighteen feet long, everything exquisitely embroidered with symbols of Empire. 'Then a page came and said it was time to go down, so we kissed Mummy and wished her luck and went down.'[21]

The girls travelled to Westminster Abbey in a glass carriage with their royal aunts. Elizabeth was worried that her sister might fall asleep during the ceremony, but afterwards, she said she only had to nudge her a couple of times when she played too loudly with the prayer books. Meanwhile, cousin Margaret watched from Buckingham Palace 'the procession of the Indian maharajas and princes, their tunics, coats and turbans encrusted with diamonds worth a king's ransom. . . . Even the horses pulling their carriages were clad in the most gorgeous tack.'[22]

At the Abbey, the Princesses walked down the long aisle with Princess Mary and joined Queen Mary in the royal box. She was determined to break with tradition, making it the first time the widow of a king was present to see his successor crowned: she could not bear to miss Bertie going through the ritual that her eldest son had renounced. The Archbishop of Canterbury conducted the service. Lilibet 'thought it all <u>very, very</u> wonderful and I expect the Abbey did, too. The arches and beams at the top were covered with a sort of haze of wonder as Papa was crowned, at least I thought so.' When their mother was crowned, the peeresses put on their coronets, and Elizabeth thought it was 'wonderful to see arms and coronets hovering in the air and then the arms disappear as if by magic'.[23] She was deeply impressed by the music too, but thought the end of the service 'got rather boring as it was all prayers'.[24] As the service drew to a close, the anointed monarchs removed their crowns and received Holy Communion, a final moving moment in a spectacular ceremony.

Later they appeared on the balcony of Buckingham Palace, then stood for nearly an hour in front of photographers. They did not sit down for tea until nearly six o'clock, and by the time Elizabeth went to bed, she said her legs 'ached terribly', but she fell asleep immediately. Events continued with the King's live broadcast, which he had practised many times with the Queen and with Lionel Logue; fortunately, he was word perfect.

Apart from a couple of hitches, such as the chain on the Duke of Portland's collar getting hitched up with the cushion of the Queen's crown, the ceremony had gone very smoothly. Afterwards the King told Ramsay Macdonald that he had been so dazed with fear for much of it that he was unaware what was happening. Despite his anxiety, the King had supported the Archbishop's wish to have the service broadcast from the Abbey, against opposition, for he wanted his people all over the world to share the occasion.

With such positivity, they could put behind them the less pleasant fallout from the Abdication, the whispering campaign at the start of that year. Led by supporters of the ex-King, it stemmed from George VI's decision to postpone for a year his visit to India and, inadvertently, from comments the Archbishop had made about his stammer and led to the question of whether he was physically and mentally fit to be King. But the Coronation, with its emphasis on constitution and tradition, conveyed the message that Britain and its Empire were a force of goodness and strength and an example of stability to the world. Diplomacy meant inviting to the Coronation not only those with whom Britain enjoyed warm relationships but also those who were less comfortable acquaintances. While the Duke of Kent welcomed members of Europe's royal families at Victoria Station, Ambassador von Ribbentrop was there greeting his country's delegates and exchanging Nazi salutes.[25]

The Coronation process continued with two months of state balls, banquets and tours. Interest in Elizabeth increased even further, and on appropriate occasions, she was given special tasks to carry out. At a tea party at the Palace in June for four hundred disabled ex-service men, she had to cut a giant cake decorated with red, white and blue ribbon, before chatting to the men.

June was a month of 'firsts' for them all: the King's first Trooping of the Colour; the first Buckingham Palace Garden Party of the reign; and for the first time in twenty-three years, the revival of the service of the Order of the Knights of the Garter at St George's Chapel, founded by Edward III in 1348 to honour his most trusted supporters. With their royal aunts and grandmother Cecilia, the Princesses watched the symbolic and moving ceremony. Their parents, wearing their rich Garter robes, sat under a canopy of Garter blue, velvet and gold, and prayed with their knights: among them were the newly knighted Stanley Baldwin, who had just retired as Prime Minister, and their grandfather, the Earl of Strathmore. It was a wonderfully vivid way for Elizabeth to experience history first-hand.

A less welcome event took place that month. In France on 3 June, his late father's birthday, the Duke of Windsor married Wallis Warfield, the name to which she had reverted. They had learned that she would not be granted the title of Her Royal Highness, and the choice of date was like an act of revenge. Lord Wigram advised that any member of the royal family attending the wedding 'would be a firm nail in the coffin of monarchy'.[26] It was a blow to David, who thought that at least Henry and George would act as his 'supporters', although the Kents sent messages and Henry a present. David had also assumed that they could return to Britain and he could perform some role as the King's brother. He had underestimated the effect of his actions. In 1938, in response to his request to clarify her position, Queen Mary would spell it out. Reminding David that she had implored him not to abdicate for the sake of the royal family and of Britain, she said, 'It seemed so inconceivable to those who made such sacrifices during the war that you, as their King, refused a lesser sacrifice.' His marriage had not changed her views, and she was sorry not to see him but, 'all my life I have put my Country before everything else, and I simply cannot change now.' If he returned there would be 'division and controversy'.[27]

Some friends who were also close to the royal family wished him well. Lady Desborough, who had known him since childhood, sent a present. Thanking her, he said, 'We have both of us had a long and trying time of waiting but it's wonderful to be together again and to have such great happiness to look forward to.'[28] After the wedding, he told her, 'We are very happy and find great peace after all we have been through during the last months.'[29] Now the Princesses seldom heard their uncle's name mentioned, although he remembered Elizabeth's eleventh birthday and from Austria sent her tennis racquets. Since the Abdication, he had frequently telephoned her father with unwelcome advice for him in his new role and with unreasonable demands. It was George VI's unique misfortune to be King while his predecessor lived.

The family's free time became even more precious. In July they went to Balmoral earlier than usual, to visit towns and villages en route as part of their Coronation tour, and found even the most remote cottage decorated with flags or bunting. When the Queen and Princesses travelled to Glamis ahead of the King, there were so many people on the roads that their car had to slow down, and some even jumped on the running board to get a closer look. Finally able to relax, they were joined by the Queen's siblings Rose, Michael and David, and some of her nephews: Fergus and, unusually, John and Timothy, sons of her eldest brother, Patrick. On the moors the men enjoyed shooting with the Earl, while the Princesses picnicked and played in the heather with cousin Fergus.

In October, the Princesses attended the State Opening of Parliament, the first of the King's reign, at which he spoke of the friendly relations he enjoyed with foreign powers. Unbeknown to him, the ex-King and his wife were embarking on a tour of Germany, during which they would meet Adolf Hitler. The Duke of Windsor had ensured the tour was publicly announced from Paris earlier in the month, its purpose being to study housing and working conditions. The King was horrified when he heard this, angry that he had been given no notice of his brother's plans and adamant that no official support should be given to what seemed to be public and political work: after all, David had chosen to renounce his public position.

The Windsors were feted and flattered, the Germans referring to Wallis as 'Royal Highness', and were invited to dine with Göring, Hess and ultimately Hitler in his mountain resort. Behind the hospitality was a hidden agenda. Göring said the German government had hoped he would remain King, and that 'The natural opposition between British and German policy . . . could easily be set aside with the aid of such a man as the Duke.'[30] When the Duke queried a map of Germany showing Austria as part of it, he was told that Austria was bound to decide to throw in their lot with their neighbour. He was concerned that Hitler seemed to assume that he sympathised with the ideology and practices of the Third Reich, although he said nothing to justify the assumption.[31]

In November, the King and Queen visited St Paul's Walden Bury, where she unveiled the Coronation plaque in the church that many years later would add to the confusion about her birthplace. They stayed at The Bury with David and Rachel, where the King had the welcome chance to go shooting. The Princesses were in Windsor that weekend, although they would continue to visit. Rachel remembered Elizabeth as 'quick-witted and great fun, because it was a fun family. She liked the general running about here, and feeling that it was her mother's home.'[32]

At Buckingham Palace that autumn, a Girl Guide company was formed for Elizabeth, with a Brownie Group for Margaret. With their motto, 'Service for Others', the international Scout and Guide movements were at the height of their popularity. In the Coronation year jamborees were held all over the country, with a thanksgiving service in Westminster

Abbey, led by the Scouts founder, Lord Baden Powell. The vice-President of the British Girl Guides was the Princesses' great-aunt, Princess Alice, Countess of Athlone. Getting the group started was not easy, however, because the leader they wanted, Miss Violet Synge, could not see how the other girls would be able to avoid treating the Princesses differently. All Guides were supposed to treat each other as sisters, and Crawfie had to explain that there was nothing the Princesses would like better. Eventually, Miss Synge agreed. Always sartorially aware, the King insisted that the Princesses should not wear the 'hideous' regulation long black stockings, which he said reminded him of his youth, so knee-length beige stockings were introduced instead.

The 1st Buckingham Palace Guide Company with twenty Guides, and its Brownie Pack of fourteen, had their meetings in the Palace during the cooler months and in the tea house in the garden when it was warmer. Signalling practice took place in the Palace's long corridors, while other skills for their guiding badges, such as cooking over a campfire, were practised outdoors as much as possible. There were three patrols, made up of girls who were the daughters of friends and Palace employees. Among them were Elizabeth Hardinge and the Hon. Ela Beaumont, daughter of the Allendales, their old neighbours at 145. Princess Elizabeth was second in command of Kingfisher Patrol, under the command of Mountbatten's eldest daughter, Patricia. Two years older than Elizabeth, she was her third cousin and a first cousin of Prince Philip. Myra Butter was a Guide with them: 'Once a year we went from Buckingham Palace to Windsor Great Park in a bus. It was a tremendous day out, great fun, and we lit fires. I remember trying to light a fire with three matches.' Scottish dancing was introduced to their group: 'Princess Elizabeth was very good at all that.'[33] Patricia Mountbatten said Elizabeth was 'a very efficient and capable deputy' who already had an air of authority. She was also popular and easy to deal with, someone that 'you'd want as your best friend'.[34] She said Elizabeth was also aware of the way she must behave in public and knew she must not give way to tears.

Prince Philip, meanwhile, faced a trauma not so easily kept in check. In the Easter school holidays that year, 1937, he had stayed in Germany with his sister, Princess Cecile of Greece, and her husband, George Donatus, known as Don; he was a great-grandson of Queen Victoria and a member of Germany's royal house of Hesse. Philip was very fond of them and their three young children, and while he was there, they went to see their mother, whom none of them had seen in five years. Philip looked forward to seeing Cecile and Don again in November, when they were coming over to England for the wedding of Don's brother, Ludwig. By then, Don had succeeded his father as Grand Duke of Hesse and by Rhine, and Cecile, now Grand Duchess, was pregnant again. Leaving behind their daughter Johanna, who was too young, they left Frankfurt aerodrome on 16 November with their two sons aged six and four. Also with them were Don's widowed mother, a lady-in-waiting and Ludwig's best man.

They left in bright sunshine, but near Ostend, they became caught in thick fog, yet the pilot tried to land. Three rockets were fired to guide him but only the first worked. He continued to land blind, but the plane hit a brickworks chimney and broke up, part of it crashing through the building and the rest crashing onto the brickfield, where it burst into flames. Fire engines and ambulances could not get near the wreckage; soon it became clear that of the eleven people on board, there could be no survivors.[35] In the wreckage the remains of a premature infant were found, indicating to the Brussels enquiry that the pilot tried to land when Cecile went into labour.[36]

They were to have stayed with the Mountbattens at their London apartment; Pamela Mountbatten heard the terrible news as she was going home from school. After the wedding, they were going to stay with Myra's family, the Wernhers. She was twelve. 'Oh God, when I was told this! Cecile was so beautiful and her husband was so charming. They were lovely. It's unimaginable.'[37] Philip, aged sixteen, learned of the tragedy from his headmaster, Kurt Hahn, who said: 'His sorrow was that of a man.'[38] Philip attended the funeral in Germany, to which Hitler and Goebbels sent messages of sympathy and which was attended by Göring and other SS officers, including the husband of Philip's youngest sister, Sophie: shortly before their deaths, Don and Cecile had become members of the Nazi Party. Dickie Mountbatten was there, too. Later, Philip joined the Wernhers at Thorpe Lubenham for Christmas; Myra's sister Gina remembered he did not talk much about it but showed her a little piece of wood from the aeroplane, which meant a lot to him.[39] Philip found solace with their brother Alex and cousin David. 'They were like the three musketeers,' says Myra.[40]

No doubt Elizabeth heard about the tragedy from the Wernhers. But as Christmas approached, there were more pleasant things for an eleven-year-old girl to think about. As the first anniversary of the Abdication came and went, the King spent a happier birthday than his last one, helped by the presence of children. In the White Drawing Room, the Princesses were holding their Christmas party for ninety children and their parents. Among them were their fellow Guides and Brownies and their little Kent cousins. Honoured to be invited to entertain them was the Scottish Children's Theatre they had so loved at Glamis. Soon the Princesses got on with writing their Christmas cards, which were specially produced for them by a proud Messrs Valentine, a Scottish firm from Dundee. Elizabeth's design was a picture of her favourite corgi, Dookie, by Lucy Dawson, and Margaret's was from Mabel Lucy Attwell's original picture, 'There *are* fairies.'[41]

On 21 December, the girls were formally enrolled as Guides by their aunt, Princess Mary, who was a Guide Commissioner. Later that day the Queen took Elizabeth (Margaret had a cold) to the Holborn Theatre in London to see a musical play called *Where the Rainbow Ends*. Aptly, it was a patriotic tale with St George as its central character, along with the Dragon, hyenas and a wicked aunt. Elizabeth must have been surprised at the end, when the audience of fifteen hundred sang a special children's version of the National Anthem. Written by Miss Italia Conti, founder of the world-famous theatre school, and approved by the Queen, it was like a rally in response to the clouds gathering beyond that rainbow:

We who are children weak,
We for the future speak,
Rainbow we bring.
Children of Empire rise,
Hope – faith or battle cries,
Who lives if England dies?
God save the King.[42]

CHAPTER 11

Before the Storm (1938)

Christmas 1937 saw the biggest family gathering at Sandringham for years. The King made his first Christmas Day broadcast, thanking the people for their support over the last year, but he kept it very short, saying he was not sure that the people would want him to continue a tradition that was personal to his father. They did, of course, and in the coming years his messages would provide comfort to millions.

1938 started less well when both the Queen and Elizabeth had flu. Confined to their beds the Queen, with her characteristic sense of fun, sent her daughter a silly letter, addressing it to 'Gettingupforlunch, The Nursery, Sandringham', and told her that after only drinking tea, she was looking forward to eating proper food again soon: 'Irish stew, steak & kidney pudding, haricot mutton, roast beef.'[1] Then, in February, the family were saddened by the death in Athens of Princess Marina's father, Prince Nicholas of Greece, more unhappy news for his nephew, Philip.

After the rapid changes of the previous year, home life for the Princesses settled into a routine. Their parents were far busier than before, of course, but they all came together at Royal Lodge at the weekends, with church either at the Chapel Royal in the garden, or at St George's Chapel. The girls' menagerie kept them occupied, and they could swim in the outdoor pool at Royal Lodge or enjoy cycling and walking in Windsor Forest or in the grounds of Frogmore House. Elizabeth's position as Heiress Presumptive highlighted a difference between the sisters. Already the more serious of the two, she knew that one day she would be queen; Margaret, on the other hand, with a less demanding future, could continue to express her mischievous nature. Cousin Margaret said that George VI 'doted on Elizabeth, knowing she was going to follow him, and he tried to give her all sorts of advice and he loved her deeply. But Margaret was very

King George VI and Queen Elizabeth with the Princesses, 1938 (Marcus Adams)
CAMERA PRESS

close to his heart and he never really managed to criticise her because she always made him laugh.'[2] Myra Butter remembers the King's 'hot temper', which Margaret could diffuse. She says the Queen once said that she had a temper too, but Myra never saw it.[3] Elizabeth was protective towards Margaret, even though she could be annoying like all younger siblings, and she sometimes worried about her behaviour, although Crawfie thought she gave in to Margaret more than was good for her.

The Princesses enjoyed a secure and happy life, but the outside world was not ignored. Elizabeth was increasingly made aware of events which impacted on Britain; not only had her father succeeded to the Throne against his expectations and wishes, he had become King at a time of increasing unrest. In February, Hitler made himself supreme commander of the Wehrmacht and demanded that the Austrian government 'invite' German troops into Austria, effectively marking the end of Austria's independence; the chilling truth behind what the Duke of Windsor had been told was emerging. Czechoslovakia was the next to be threatened. Prime Minister Chamberlain made it clear that Britain would not risk war with Germany to defend Czechoslovakia's integrity and tried to break the alliance between Mussolini and Hitler. It led to Britain signing the Easter Accords with Italy, which had the effect of recognising Italian conquests in Africa. Foreign Secretary Anthony Eden resigned in protest and was replaced by Lord Halifax.

Elizabeth's education was also augmented by meeting many of the people her father dealt with. On 1 March 1938, the new American Ambassador, Joseph P. Kennedy, arrived in England and was presented to the King. He was soon followed by Rose and the youngest five of their nine children, aged six to eighteen; the others, studying in the United States, were to join them in the summer holidays. The Queen received Mr and Mrs Kennedy at Buckingham Palace, and the Duke of Kent hosted the Pilgrims' Society Dinner at Claridges Hotel, given in the new Ambassador's honour. For Britain, it was as though Hollywood had arrived: with their good looks and all-American breezy confidence, the Kennedys were glamour personified. Wealthy Joe Kennedy used his own money to redecorate the already impressive fifty-two room Ambassadors' residence on the edge of Hyde Park and brought over home comforts from the United States to make his family feel at home.

But if the Kennedys dazzled Britain, the royal family made a deep and lasting impression on the Kennedys, particularly Rose. In early April she and Joe were invited to spend the weekend at Windsor, a time she remembered as one of the 'most fabulous, fascinating events' of her life. She and Joe discovered Elizabeth hiding in the shrubs, and Rose was entranced by the sisters appearing together, dressed alike in rose dresses with checked blouses, red shoes with silver-coloured buckles and white socks. The King saw that Elizabeth was placed next to the Ambassador at lunch, and afterwards both girls walked with the Kennedys and their parents to Frogmore. Rose wrote, 'I lay in bed thinking that I really must be dreaming, that I, Rose Kennedy, a simple, young matron from Boston, am really here at Windsor Castle the guest of the queen and two little princesses.'[4]

Shortly afterwards, Elizabeth celebrated her twelfth birthday at Windsor. For the first time she received telegrams from the Dominions and Colonies, and in a move to give her more responsibilities, the Queen agreed she could become President of the Children's League of Princess Elizabeth of York Hospital for Children. Her parents specifically asked that celebrations be kept informal so that public bodies did not feel obliged to honour her in a specific way. The day felt special enough anyway, beginning with a peal of bells rung from Windsor Castle's Curfew Tower; and when the 3rd Battalion Grenadier Guards had finished changing the guard, they played a selection of the Princess's favourite tunes and the drum-major wore his State livery in her honour. During her birthday tea, Elizabeth acted as hostess to her parents, and afterwards, she and her guests enjoyed a cartoon show in the ballroom.

A few days later a major family event took place when the Princesses' cousin, Anne Bowes Lyon, married Viscount Anson, son of the Earl and Countess of Litchfield. The magnificent wedding was held at St Margaret's Church Westminster and conducted by the Archbishop of Canterbury. In the absence of her father, the Queen's late brother Jock, Anne was given away by the Earl of Strathmore. She had an extravagant fifteen attendants, more than a royal wedding; Simon Bowes Lyon was the only pageboy and Anne's sister, Diana, was a bridesmaid. No mention was made in the guest list of their disabled sisters. The wedding dress was a gift from their grandmother, Cecilia, whose absence was the only negative note. Although she had come to London for the wedding, she had suffered a slight heart attack after months of poor health.

Elizabeth appeared in her own special outfit a few weeks later when she wore her Guide uniform in public for the first time, to watch a parade of a thousand Girl Guides at Windsor Castle. They were going to their annual National Service in St George's Chapel, to be led by Lady Baden-Powell. Proudly wearing the proficiency badges she had achieved, Elizabeth stood to attention as the Guides marched past, with Margaret next to her in Brownie uniform. Elizabeth was seen having a little trouble with her belt buckle and beckoned her sister over, and eventually, the King had to help.

Meanwhile, their grandmother worsened, and on 23 June she died, aged seventy-six. It happened to be the Duke of Windsor's birthday but any mention of it in the Press was eclipsed by the tributes that poured in to the Countess, extolling her 'gentle, dignified and friendly influence',[5] said to be reflected in the Queen. The Queen was heartbroken, telling Cosmo Lang she was 'an Angel of goodness & fun.'[6] Crawfie said, 'Princess Margaret is too young to realise . . . but Princess Elizabeth has felt it deeply.' The funeral took place at Glamis and a service was held simultaneously in London, attended by Queen Mary and the Prime Minister and other dignitaries. The Princesses were not taken to either service – the attendance of children at funerals was not considered appropriate – and a cross of white carnations and irises was sent on their behalf.

The Countess's will distributed money and jewellery, paintings, furniture and china, among her children and some grandchildren. Her widowed daughter-in-law Fenella, and Anne and Diana, were beneficiaries, but Katherine and Nerissa were not mentioned. The Queen received her diamond snake bracelet, yellow diamond cross, half the china at 84 Eaton Square and a picture. The Countess also remembered friends and staff, including Clara Knight, 'Alah'. At St John's Church near Woolmers, a stained-glass window depicting St Cecilia holding an organ would be installed in her memory in 1939. The Earl and two of his children were present at the dedication ceremony; the Queen and the Princesses would visit on another occasion.

Even in mourning Elizabeth's parents set an example of duty. A few days after the Countess's death, they were supposed to make their first state visit to France, Britain's main democratic ally in Europe. The Queen knew the King could not go without her, yet the visit could not be cancelled, and after a three-week postponement, they fulfilled their engagement. Not wishing to wear the sombre colours of mourning when she needed to stand out, the Queen accepted the suggestion of young couturier Norman Hartnell, who pointed out that white was also a mourning colour, the one that Queen Victoria had insisted on for her funeral. Within two weeks, his team had remade her wardrobe, to stunning effect.

The visit lasted only three days but was a resounding success. President Lebrun and his wife were charming hosts, and the King and Queen were received everywhere with rapturous enthusiasm. During a crowded programme every opportunity was taken to emphasise the solidarity of Anglo-French relations and the basis of that friendship as one of peace. Lady Diana Cooper was in Paris and witnessed the euphoria, as did Churchill, who was said to be like a schoolboy, he was so delighted. On the last evening a glittering party was held at the Quai d'Orsay, the elegant French Foreign Ministry, where they were enchanted by scenes performed from the ballet and opera and strolled in lantern-lit gardens. Lady Diana said, 'Many times the King and Queen were summoned to the balconies by insistent clamouring . . . I can never forget it. To the French the Royal Visit seemed a safeguard against the dreaded war.'[7] Two years later the same mansion and gardens would be under Nazi occupation.

Extending the hand of friendship to those left at home, the children of France sent the Princesses two dolls, called France and Marianne, along with their own tiny jewels and exquisitely made trousseaux by the leading Paris fashion houses. President Lebrun would have been pleased to know Elizabeth was continuing diligently with her French lessons, although she had little choice: even when they were at Balmoral, Georgina Guérin, their tutor, came over every morning.

For their Scottish holiday that year, the family travelled by boat to Aberdeen, on the royal yacht *Victoria and Albert*. It was only the second time a reigning monarch had arrived in Aberdeen by sea: the first was Queen Victoria in 1848. Instead of cosy Birkhall, now they stayed in the baronial-style Balmoral Castle. Queen Victoria had fallen in love with the Highlands early on in her reign and bought Balmoral, turning it into almost a parody of everything Scottish, as immortalised by Sir Walter Scott. Tartan was everywhere, and the heads of stags were mounted on walls and represented in pictures by her favourite artist, Landseer. A life-size statue of Prince Albert stood in the front hall: Crawfie said he had a slightly martyred expression, as though he was getting tired of waiting around.

After finishing their French lessons, the Princesses often rode their ponies, and if the men were shooting, the Queen took her female guests and children to join them for lunch. Afterwards the girls might play their gramophones or watch the guests playing cricket. At tea, eaten in late afternoon, there would be 'shrimps, hot sausage rolls, scones, and . . . griddle cakes known in Scotland as baps and bannocks.'[8] At 7:00 p.m., Their Majesties and their guests changed for dinner. Although life was a little less formal than under George V, etiquette still had to be observed, and white tie was the dress code. That August a typical dinner was 'clear soup, fish, beef, grouse, chocolate pudding, iced pudding, cheese soufflé, peaches, plums and grapes, with several different wines'.[9] After dinner, seven pipers in their kilts played as they walked through the hall and into the dining room, a ceremony that the Princesses loved and would peep over the banisters to watch. Afterwards there was often a film for everyone. A regiment stood guard unobtrusively, and sometimes, the young men played games with the Princesses. Every Sunday the family attended Craithie Church, where the royal family had worshipped for generations.

Their visit to Glamis that year was poignant. The Queen visited the Black Watch Memorial Home, with which her mother had been so involved, and took with her a box of toys and books from the Princesses. Back at Balmoral, the family attended a special service at Craithie church. Before a congregation of farmers, ghillies and estate workers, among whom George V had worshipped, his son unveiled his gift to the church: a marble bust of the late King by Scottish sculptor, Sir William Reid Dick.

Then came the eagerly anticipated annual highlight. The Braemar Gathering at Ballater is an ancient event where teams compete in tossing the caber and throwing the hammer, and light-footed locals perform sword dancing and listen to pipe playing. The Princesses were smart in Hunting Stewart tartan with lemon jerseys, with dark blue cardigans and berets with gold thistles. The Queen's sisters May and Rose and their families joined the royal party. As the pipe bands played much-loved Scottish songs, Elizabeth and cousin Margaret 'kept time eagerly with their feet' as they sat on steps in front of the Royal box with Princess Margaret and young friends.[10] There was always a broad mix of people: landed gentry chatted with farmers and shopkeepers, Cabinet ministers cheered teams with the Archbishop of Canterbury. It was a treasured occasion, when old friendships and family ties were renewed.

Their holiday that year, however, was disrupted. In early September, Prime Minister Neville Chamberlain visited the King at Balmoral. Hitler had declared that the condition of the Sudetan Germans under Czech rule was intolerable and was beginning to clamour for their 'return' to the Reich. Britain had not found a compromise formula acceptable to the Czechs and the Sudetan Germans. The danger of German intervention was growing, and it was now accepted that if that occurred and the French acted in support of their Czech allies, Britain could not remain impassive. Chamberlain told the King that he thought peace could nevertheless still prevail.

But on 12 September came Hitler's venomous speech at Nuremberg, contemptuous of the Czechs and their state and demanding that the Sudetan Germans revolt. Chamberlain appraised the King of the situation and told him that Hitler had not yet decided on violence. There was, therefore, still a chance that war could be averted, and to that end, Chamberlain had told Hitler that he would fly to Germany to meet him.

On the fourteenth, the King telephoned his approval and Chamberlain left. That evening, the King left Balmoral and was back at Buckingham Palace the next morning; Queen Mary told him how the public took comfort in seeing the Royal Flag flying over the Palace. The King mentioned to Lord Halifax a plan of his own. He had prepared a draft personal letter to Hitler, on the basis of 'one ex-Serviceman to another', urging him to spare the youth of Britain and Germany from the slaughter of another war. The idea was Hardinge's who, although against appeasement, thought the King could make a contribution to peace from a non-political angle. Halifax was not convinced that such an approach would work but told the King the time might come when it could be of assistance.

There would never be such an opportunity. Chamberlain made three more trips to Germany over the next ten days. The Queen left the Princesses at Balmoral and travelled down to London on 21 September to join the King. Meanwhile, emergency war measures began. Hospitals were cleared and trenches and shelters dug. London's population was registered and fitted for gas masks. On the twenty-seventh, the King and Queen were expected in Glasgow to launch the *Queen Elizabeth*, the sister ship to the *Queen Mary*. Clearly the King could not go, so the Queen returned to Scotland alone and found the stations en route full of children preparing for evacuation to the country.

The Princesses were taken to Glasgow overnight on a special train and enjoyed the excitement of having their breakfast in a railway siding, guarded by local police, while they waited for their mother to arrive. At Clydeside, they watched her deliver a message on behalf of the King which was broadcast live to millions: 'He bids the people of this country to be of good cheer in spite of the dark clouds hanging over them.... He knows ... that they will keep cool heads and brave hearts'.[11]

That night Chamberlain made a broadcast in which he said the only way to keep Britain out of a war that did not directly concern it – 'a quarrel in a far away country, between people of whom we know nothing' – was to allow Hitler to occupy the Sudetenland. Hitler invited him to a Four-Power Conference at Munich the next day and told him that the territorial demands he made on Czechoslovakia were his last. Chamberlain accepted it. Hitler signed a paper to say the agreement was 'symbolic of the desire of our people's never to go to war again'. When Chamberlain returned to England with the Munich Agreement, he was hailed as a hero; later he spoke of 'peace for our time'.

The King immediately invited him to the Palace, where they stood on the balcony with the Queen and Mrs Chamberlain before tumultuous crowds. Not everyone was happy. Chamberlain's policy was criticised both by the Labour Party and by members of his own. Duff Cooper, since 1937 First Lord of the Admiralty, handed the King his resignation. Churchill spoke powerfully of what he felt would be demanded of Britain and called for rearmament. In later years the Queen regretted hers and the King's actions in appearing on the balcony, for it was unconstitutional: the monarch must always be above politics.

While the Princesses awaited their parents' return to Balmoral, they attended a thanksgiving service at Craithie Church, where the minister made reference to the heavy burdens that had fallen on their parents in the past troubled days. But soon, with lighter hearts, the King and Queen hosted the annual Ghillies' Ball for estate workers and tenants. It was always a lively event, everyone wearing Highland dress and dancing traditional Scottish reels. The King and Queen began the dancing with the oldest members, and now that Elizabeth was twelve, she was allowed to join in a few dances, something she was very good at.

An activity Elizabeth was less skilled at was knitting. She disliked it and struggled with it, but it was considered a craft that a young girl should master. Back in London, she was probably surprised to discover that her grandmother was planning to display, on a stall for the Queen Mary's London Needlework Guild, a baby's matinee coat and dress that she had managed to complete, to be sold for charity. Margaret's contribution of a green woollen scarf was less sophisticated, but she found the craft less tortuous than her sister.

As Armistice Day dawned, the King and senior royals led the laying of poppy wreaths at the Cenotaph during the ceremony which seemed to have taken on new significance since the recent threat. Soon reports came of Hitler's atrocities which made it clear he had reneged on his assurances to Britain: the destruction of Jewish property in Germany, Austria and the Sudetenland, in what became known as Kristallnacht.

Shortly afterwards, the King's aunt, Queen Maude of Norway, wife of King Haakon, died unexpectedly in London, just short of her sixty-ninth birthday. The youngest sister of George V, she had never broken her ties with England. Every autumn she stayed at Appleton House on the Sandringham estate, a wedding gift from her father: it would prove to be very useful to the family in the coming years.

As the royal family prepared for Christmas, Philip was finishing the term at Gordonstoun. This Christmas he would not be seeing his beloved uncle Georgie, for tragically he had died in April, aged just forty-five.

A few months earlier he had slipped and broken his thigh, and it was discovered he had bone cancer. His funeral was a full naval occasion, attended by the King and the Kents; they walked behind Georgie's son David, who at nineteen was now 3rd Marquess of Milford Haven. Philip would still see Nada, sometimes at her villa in the south of France, which attracted a glamorous international crowd. That summer he stayed off and on with the Mountbattens at Adsdean, their rambling house near the Sussex Downs. Pamela, eight years younger than Philip, said he was always good fun: 'He was the inspiration behind all the naughty, boisterous games we played, including vicious bicycle polo matches with my father.'[12] Now Dickie Mountbatten, vain, adventurous and ambitious, would oversee Philip's education.

The Headmaster sent Philip's estranged parents a glowing end-of-term report, telling them that he had made him Head Boy for the Easter term: 'He is universally liked, trusted and respected,' said Hahn. 'He has the greatest sense of service of all the boys in the school.'[13] How invaluable that quality would prove to be!

CHAPTER 12

Love and War (1939)

No one realised when 1939 dawned how different everything would be by the end of the year. Britain would be at war; Elizabeth would be in love. Meanwhile, she found her education taking a different course. She began lessons twice a week in constitutional history with the Vice Provost of Eton College, Henry (later Sir Henry) Marten, a subject which was essential for a future monarch to understand. Cousin Margaret said her sister was jealous: 'She was heard to say quite often that it was very unfair, that she jolly well ought to have had the lessons too.'[1] Marten was a highly experienced teacher and a writer of historical text books. Crawfie would take Elizabeth over to his rooms at Eton College near Windsor Castle and stay in the room during lessons. She remembered him as 'a charming person, learned and erudite but extremely human.'[2] He had a fondness for sweet things and kept sugar lumps in his pocket. Elizabeth was rather overawed by all the books piled up everywhere in his study: 'Crawfie, do you mean to tell me he had read them all?'

Elizabeth's history lessons became more complex as she got older, but Marten made them interesting. He divided the subjects into departments so that a whole term was devoted to 'The Colonies' and another to 'The Evolution of a Self-Governing Dominion'. She learned about India's problems and had lectures on national expenditure before and after the 1939 war.[3] They also discussed current affairs and sometimes Marten sent Elizabeth a newspaper cutting that had caught his eye. As they sat in his study his regular pupils, Eton's schoolboys, sometimes came in with a message for him and would acknowledge Crawfie and Elizabeth with a polite bow.[4] If they realised who the girl was, they did not indicate it, and in their unique uniform of top hat and tails they were a far more curious sight than she, but their presence must have reinforced the Princess's sense of separateness from young people outside her immediate circle.

From 1942, both Princesses would also have lessons in European history, as well as French language and literature, from their mother's friend Vicomtesse de Bellaigue, known as Toni. She always felt that the Queen did not take sufficient interest in her daughters' academic education. Rather, the Queen put great store on moral and spiritual education, applying her Christian principles; cousin Margaret said her aunt's faith 'was very solid and I think it helped her in being queen. She had a very strong sense of doing your duty and helping other people.'[5] In letters to the Princesses, the Queen always encouraged them to be kind and thoughtful and to keep their temper and their word. Attention was never drawn publicly to intellect; in the Queen's view, the home was where true felicity lay and formed the bedrock of society where spiritual values began. Elizabeth's supposed domestic skills were therefore often emphasised in the Press. One not untypical newspaper article said she was baking and icing a cake for her sister's birthday: 'The Princesses have both been having cookery lessons for some time past but Princess Margaret does not shine in the kitchen. She is a gay, vivacious girl, whose talents lie more in the artistic and musical direction. Princess Elizabeth is a really good cook and can prepare and serve a four-course dinner, as well as make all kinds of fancy pastries and sweets.'[6] Clearly, the Heiress Presumptive should appear to have something in common with the majority of women at the time. Her younger sister was excused.

One family who did not hide their lights were the Kennedys. In February 1939, John F Kennedy, 'Jack', graduated from Harvard and was going to work as a glorified 'office boy' in the embassies of London and Paris: his parents believed 'everyone should start low down in their profession.' Jack wrote to a friend about being presented to the King at Court Levee: 'The King stands and you go up and bow. Met Queen Mary and was at tea with Princess Elizabeth, with whom I made a great deal of time.'[7] No one imagined then what his future would hold.[8]

In March the royal family had a pleasant and infrequent opportunity to meet up with the Queen's eldest brother, Patrick, Lord Glamis; the Queen was less close to him than her other brothers, partly because Patrick's wife, Dorothy, daughter of the Duke of Leeds, was generally considered difficult and did not embrace family relations. But this was a joyous occasion, at which their daughter Cecilia was marrying Kenneth Harington, the son of a Judge, and the royal family were delighted to attend the London wedding. They sat with the widowed Earl of Strathmore, who was about to celebrate his eighty-fourth birthday, and met up with extended family. It was one of the last happy events that they would celebrate together. Within the next eight years Patrick's wife, his eldest son, his daughter and his father would all be dead.

That year, building foreign relationships was more important than ever. On 21 March, the King and Queen welcomed the President and Mme Lebrun on their reciprocal state visit. In Paris the President had been driven in a car with unbreakable glass, flanked by police on motorbikes; in London the King drove with him in an open brougham led by just five policemen on horseback. At Buckingham Palace, the President was the first foreign head of state to appear on the famous balcony. 'Here there was no fear and little ceremony,' wrote the *Daily Herald*. 'All London that could be there lined the route or went to the Palace . . . [giving] convincing proofs of the fervent friendliness that unites the two nations.'[9] As the crowd shouted 'Vive le President' and 'Three Cheers for France' Elizabeth joined in, and as they went back indoors, she turned and gave one more wave of her own. When the Lebruns left, unusually the royal family accompanied them to Victoria Station; the King placed Elizabeth in the first of the cars with him and the President.

The visit gave Chamberlain the chance to discuss with France's Minister in Attendance their countries' policies in view of the recent aggression by Hitler against Poland and Lithuania. Chamberlain told the Commons that if the Polish government considered it 'vital to resist with national forces' a threat to its independence, Britain would support it, and the French Government would do the same.[10] On 7 April, Italy invaded Albania, and Britain gave similar guarantees to Rumania and Greece. The decision of whether Britain should go to war had been placed in the hands of foreign powers. Chamberlain still wished to resolve outstanding differences by way of peaceful change, but not if it involved pressure, force or blackmail. Such changes of British policy towards Europe and the dictators caused much debate.

While her parents considered their own conflicting views, Elizabeth's thirteenth birthday arrived. Acknowledgement of her growing up was reflected in the family's presents and shouted in headlines such as 'NO MORE DOLLS AND TOYS'.[11] Along with a diamond-studded bracelet from the King and a new riding habit from the Queen was a pair of silk stockings. With a silver dressing table set from Queen Mary, she had the excuse to spend more time considering her appearance, although it would always be Margaret who expressed the greater interest in matters sartorial. From the Windsors in Paris came the latest type of cine camera and projector, and in the afternoon Elizabeth tried it out on the family, until the King took it over and filmed her riding her bicycle.

'She is especially fortunate in the fact that her parents have brought her up wisely. She has simple tastes and enjoys simple pleasures,' wrote one newspaper. 'What are treats for her and her sister Margaret would be looked upon as quite ordinary everyday happenings to the average modern child.'[12] Nothing illustrated that observation more keenly than the fact that this London-based child had never travelled on the Underground. The 'average modern child' who did such things held 'an enormous fascination, like mystic beings from another world', said Crawfie. The Princesses would smile shyly at children they liked the look of. 'They would so have loved to speak to them and make friends but this was never encouraged.'[13] In May, while their parents were in Canada, the Princesses at last went on the Underground. They were going to the headquarters of the YMCA with Crawfie and a lady-in waiting, Lady Helen Graham. At St James' Park station they put their pennies into the machine and bought tickets. Wearing green berets and coats, they looked like the ordinary children they so longed to be among. They got into a third-class smoking carriage, jostling with other passengers: only the presence of their detective at the other end reminded them they were different.

Using the escalator was part of the novelty; Elizabeth stepped on boldly, but Margaret nearly stumbled and held Crawfie's hand tightly. Even the YMCA itself was a treat. Although the visit had to be planned ahead, it was kept as unofficial as possible and few people knew who the girls were. They had to collect their own tea on trays. 'Lilibet left her teapot behind. The lady in charge bawled out to her, "If you want it, you must come and fetch it.'"[14] To drink tea out of thick cups and pay for it themselves with actual money was a new experience. By the time of their return journey, however, they had been recognised. At St James's station a crowd had gathered; the girls were distracted and forgot to give up their tickets, and the collector had to run after them. Crawfie had to call the Palace for a car to pick them up.

The Princesses eagerly told their parents about their experience when they returned from their tour. It had been proposed by Canada's Prime Minister Mackenzie King when he came over for the Coronation. The idea of a visit to the United States too had taken form during a conversation with the Kennedys in 1938; the Queen had told Joe Kennedy, 'I only know three Americans. You, Fred Astaire and J.P. Morgan.'[15] President Roosevelt encouraged them to combine their Canadian trip with a visit to the United States. He was convinced that war between Britain and Germany was inevitable, at which point Britain would be America's first line of defence, and he hoped the presence of Their Majesties would strengthen the bond between the countries. He thought that for political reasons the trip should be unofficial and informal. Roosevelt wanted to invite the Princesses too, but the King thought them too young.

The six-week trip was planned for early May 1939. By then, Hitler and Mussolini had entered into a military and political 'pact of steel' and Hitler had marched into Prague. The night before they left, they attended a dinner given in their honour by the Kennedys at the American Embassy. The Queen was seated between Joe Kennedy and William Bullitt, the American Ambassador to France. Wishing to sour the American visit, he told Roosevelt, 'the little Queen . . . is a nice girl,' 'The little King . . . remains a rather frightened little boy.'[16]

The following day they travelled in royal procession to Waterloo Station, the Princesses with them. The send-off was a major ceremonial event all the way to Portsmouth. The parting of the Princesses from their parents was an emotional one, made worse by distance and the uncertain European situation. At Portsmouth, Elizabeth was seen giving a helping hand to her sister as they walked up the steep gangway to the ship and said goodbye to their parents. The Press scrutinised the Princesses for signs of emotion when the ship pulled away: 'Their hands clasped, they seemed so overcome by emotion that they forgot to wave their hand-kerchiefs.'[17] When Margaret finally got hers out, Queen Mary sternly reminded her that it was for waving, not for crying into.

During their successful tour, the King and Queen were troubled by a couple of events elsewhere that were outside their control. The royal car carrying Queen Mary back to Marlborough House after an engagement was involved in a collision with a lorry. The car mounted the pavement and overturned, throwing Queen Mary across the feet of her equerry; the window had to be broken to get them out. At almost seventy-two, it was amazing she suffered no broken bones. Stoical as ever, she even waved to the crowd that gathered and said she just needed a cup of tea. However, she had suffered severe bruising and shock and an injury to one eye, and her doctors confined her to bed for a few days. The King and Queen received bulletins and the Princesses visited her at Marlborough House. By early June she was back to normal. The other issue, less likely to clear up quickly, was the Duke of Windsor. Shortly after leaving England they heard he had accepted an invitation to broadcast an appeal for peace to the American people direct from the First World War bat-tlefield of Verdun. It was 'troublesome of him to choose such a moment', the Queen told Queen Mary.[18] The broadcast seemed to be a gesture of appeasement and the Queen considered it was designed to upstage the King.

Their first visit to Canada since the accession was an arduous trip, with long periods of travelling and constant ceremonies. From the Queen's letters to the girls, it was clear she missed them greatly but she and the King found much to appreciate. They were delighted by their warm reception, even in traditionally Republican areas. The King's Assistant Private Secretary, Tommy Lascelles, wrote, 'I hope people at home realise what a wow this adventure is being. It is on a crescendo rather than a diminuendo.'[19]

Meanwhile, the Princesses experienced two 'firsts' of their own. On the weekend of 20 May, they went to stay with David and Rachel at St Paul's Walden Bury. It was the first time they had spent a weekend away without either of their parents and were accompanied only by their nurses. On Sunday, they were thrilled to receive a telephone call from their parents, the first royal transatlantic telephone call ever made. Just after 3:00 p.m. the local switchboard was asked if it would accept a call from Ottawa for David Bowes Lyon. The call was put through, and David talked to the Queen, then Elizabeth spoke; then the King came on and the four of them chatted for fifteen minutes. The Princesses were amused to find that it was morning in Ottawa and the King was about to unveil the Canadian War Memorial. They ended by holding Dookie up and pinching his bottom to make him bark down the phone.

On 9 June, their parents entered the United States, a historic moment, for it was the first time a reigning British monarch had ever done so. On the train, Lascelles was delighted to be knighted, the first time a knighthood had been conferred by a British sovereign on American soil. They did not know what kind of reception they would find, for in 1935 Congress had passed the Neutrality Act, designed to keep the United States out of any European war. During their brief stay in Washington, there was a tremendous heatwave with stifling humidity but they carried on uncomplainingly; it brought them sympathy and admiration from the crowds, who greeted them everywhere. When they spent the weekend at the Roosevelts' country home, their friendship was cemented; they even discovered hot dogs. The King had the chance to talk properly to the President, for the diplomatic possibilities of the relationship were significant. Mackenzie King was there too. The King told him he found the President very easy to talk to, as though he were a father giving wise advice.

Afterwards Mrs Roosevelt wrote, 'I like them both, but what a life! They are happy together however & that must make a difference in the life they have to lead.' When the Commerce Secretary, Harry Hopkins, came to England early in 1941 as Roosevelt's personal representative, he described the 1939 visit as an 'astounding success'.[20]

The Princesses eagerly anticipated their parents' return on 22 June and at Southampton were taken out on a destroyer to meet the ship so that they could spend the last two hours on board. As they ran into their parents' arms, there was none of the inhibited restraint that George V had demanded of public reunions. The crew presented the Princesses with toy pandas and there was a happy lunch party, during which the King kept throwing balloons out of the portholes and Lord Airlie kept popping them with his cigarettes. Later the King broadcast a speech about the tour, which had a profound effect on all his listeners: 'I have never heard the King – or indeed few other people – speak so effectively or so movingly,'[21] wrote Lascelles.

If 1939 so far would be remembered for the success of the tour and its significance for the future, for Elizabeth the year was about to become memorable for a different reason. On 22 July the family began their holiday on *Victoria and Albert*. Their first port of call was a weekend visit to the Royal Naval College, Dartmouth, the King's *alma mater*, where engagements included an inspection of the cadets. Among their entourage was Mountbatten, the King's Personal Naval Aide-de-Camp. The royal family were to attend a service in the chapel but were told that two cadets had developed mumps. They decided that it would be best if the Princesses did not attend and Crawfie was asked to take them instead to the house of the Captain of the College, Sir Frederick Dalrymple-Hamilton. There they were joined by his son, North, aged seventeen, and their daughter, and they all played with a clockwork railway on the nursery floor. Soon a good-looking blonde boy came along, whom Crawfie described as 'rather like a Viking, with a sharp face and piercing blue eyes', whose manner was 'rather off-hand'. He acknowledged Elizabeth, and for a while they sat playing trains, until he got bored – hardly surprising, given that he was eighteen. He suggested they go to the tennis courts and jump the nets.

The young man was HRH Prince Philip of Greece, a cadet at the College since May, who had been sent along to look after the Princesses; later North said he thought Mountbatten had 'fixed it that he should'.[22] Indeed, it is often said that Mountbatten was steering Philip towards Elizabeth as early as Dartmouth. However, given Mountbatten's position as the King's ADC and the relationship the families had, it would have been a natural move to ask his nephew to help out in an unforeseen situation. Philip was also one of the King's dinner guests that night on the royal yacht, for which the list would have been drawn up in advance, so being asked to help out earlier in the day was not unreasonable.

At the tennis court, Crawfie thought Philip 'showed off a good deal' but Lilibet kept remarking how good he was and how high he could jump. Crawfie said she never took her eyes off him. He did not pay her any special attention, although he was polite, and spent time teasing 'plump little Margaret'. Philip was on the *Victoria and Albert* when they went back for lunch and chatted and laughed with them all. Although Elizabeth was maturing, with a slim figure and lovely features, she was still very young-looking, not least because of the way she was dressed. She was also rarely allowed to stay up beyond her usual bedtime, so there was no question of her attending the formal dinner on the yacht and seeing Philip that evening.

The next day Philip was invited to lunch once more, at which Elizabeth kept asking him what he would like to eat. Crawfie said he managed several platefuls of shrimps and a banana split, while 'Lilibet sat, pink-faced, enjoying it all very much.' To the Princesses, 'a boy of any kind was always a strange creature out of another world'.[23] Afterwards, his uncle Dickie recorded, 'Philip came back aboard V&A for tea and was a great success with the children.'[24] When the royal party left Dartmouth the cadets were allowed to accompany the ship in small boats as it left the harbour, and most of them had obeyed orders and returned to shore before it became unsafe. However, one boy was still rowing away as hard as he could. Elizabeth kept him in her gaze through the binoculars, until her father exclaimed, 'The young fool! He must go back!' and Philip was shouted at through a megaphone to turn around.

For Elizabeth, Philip was not just 'a boy of any kind', he was the only boy she ever really noticed. 'She fell in love with him literally when she saw him as a cadet at Dartmouth,' says Myra Butter.[25] 'He was so good looking, a Scandinavian Adonis!' said cousin Margaret.[26] Elizabeth was not the first girl to be smitten: 'All the girls were absolutely bowled over,' remembers Myra. The previous year he had fallen in love with an American actress and model, Cobina Wright, whom he had met in Venice when staying with family. She was the same age, tall, slim, blonde and pretty, and they spent a lot of time together. Philip was said to have cried when she and her mother, a notoriously pushy socialite, left for America. According to a friend of Cobina's, Philip wanted to marry her, but in 1941 she married a wealthy American corporal; later they became alcoholics.[27] In an interview she gave in 1973 to American *Town and Country,* she said she kept a photo of the three loves of her life, one of whom was Philip.[28]

For the time being, Philip would have to remain a lovely memory for young Elizabeth. There were plenty of other things to occupy them both. As Dartmouth's summer break began, Philip went to Kensington Palace, where his mother Alice was staying with his grandmother, Victoria. Myra Butter remembers Victoria: 'She used to stay with us a lot, the most amazing woman and frightfully clever. I think she taught her children before they had any proper schooling. She had all the tragedy of the murders of the Russian royal family and had been through a lot, the awful humiliation of her German husband during the Great War. I remember her as being very old and wrinkled and always wearing black.'[29] Victoria also had the probably unique experience of having her grandmother, Queen Victoria, sitting with her as she gave birth to Alice, her first child, in 1885. The sixty-six-year-old Queen-Empress stayed with Victoria in Windsor Castle all through her labour, from 7:00 a.m. until 5:00 p.m. and said she found the experience 'strange, and indeed affecting'.[30] Alice was now much better, and in August 1939, she and Philip travelled together to Paris and on to Greece.

Meanwhile at Balmoral the King held what would be the last of his boys' camps at nearby Abergeldie Castle. The King himself acted as camp chief and took the boys out on expeditions, assisted by section leaders, one of whom was the Queen's nephew, Andrew Elphinstone. The Queen and Princesses joined them for games and songs, doing all the actions to 'Under the Spreading Chestnut Tree.' Andrew invited his royal cousins to sit on the grass by a tree trunk to listen to the King playing the ukulele, while he and another leader played the piano accordion. In view of the worries about the world, the Press could be forgiven for waxing lyrical: 'The three players were playing a merry Tyrolean melody, and for a few minutes the little picture in that woodland setting, with the three musicians and the two bonny Princesses, was one of the prettiest that any man could see. It was one of the many moments during the day when the clouds that hang over Europe seemed far away.'[31] Later, as the traditional bonfire was lit, the Balmoral pipers played Auld Lang Syne and everyone sang the National Anthem with even greater fervour than usual.

The King and Queen hoped for an untroubled summer and had invited several shooting parties to Balmoral. However, on 22 August came the news that the USSR and Germany had signed a non-aggression pact; suddenly war seemed imminent. Chamberlain recalled Parliament; the King left Balmoral and arrived at Buckingham Palace on 24 August. On the twenty-fifth, Britain formally signed a treaty of alliance with Poland, which said it would negotiate with Germany; Chamberlain informed Hitler, but with the renewed assurance that Britain and France stood by their pledges to Poland.

On 28 August, the Queen left the Princesses, now at Birkhall, and joined the King, telling Queen Mary, 'It is awful to think of being parted but one must see what happens before risking their coming south.'[32] On 1 September, Germany invaded Poland. On the second, Britain issued an ultimatum that if Hitler withdrew his troops, the British government would try to broker peace but if not, Britain and France would declare war. Britain delivered a final warning on Sunday, 3 September, giving Germany until 11:00 a.m. No such assurance was received, and thus it was formally declared that Britain was at war with Germany. That night the King made a moving broadcast, asking his people everywhere 'to stand firm and united in this time of trial'.[33]

The Queen asked her sister Rose to look after the Princesses if any-thing should happen to her and the King; Rose told her, 'I would give up everything to try & make the two darlings happy & try my very best to sooth their lives'.[34] For the time being, the Princesses remained at Birkhall, joined by cousins Diana and Margaret. Balmoral itself was closed up, as it was too much of a target for the enemy. With the girls were their French holiday governess, Georgina Guérin, who later became part of the French Resistance, and one of the Queen's ladies in waiting, Lettice Bowlby. Cousin Margaret recalled that the two women 'were not best of friends and behind her back Georgina called Lettice "la sale Bowlbee [the dirty

Bowlby]'".[35] In late September the Queen returned to Birkhall, and they visited the evacuees from Glasgow; the King opened up houses for them to live in on the Balmoral and Abergeldie estates.

Soon the Queen returned to London. Crawfie was summoned from her own holiday to get to Birkhall; Alah was with them too, together with the head of the household, Sir Basil Brooke, and a small staff. The Queen asked Crawfie to ensure people did not talk too vividly about the war in front of Margaret, who had only just celebrated her ninth birthday. Every night at 6:00 p.m. the King and Queen phoned the Princesses. Lessons resumed and a French teacher, Madame Montaudon Smith, known as 'Monty', was installed; she also sang duets with the girls, which they loved. Elizabeth continued her constitutional history lessons by post. In the afternoons they walked and rode their ponies, and after tea Crawfie read the newspapers to them, leaving out the worst details about Hitler; nevertheless, Lilibet said anxiously, 'Oh dear, Crawfie, I hope he won't come over here.' She was very shocked to hear of the sinking of the battleship *Royal Oak*, torpedoed by the Germans while at anchor, killing 810 officers and men.

Crawfie set up a weekly sewing group for the local women, at which the Princesses helped organise and serve teas and chatted to the women. They played the gramophone to keep them all entertained, and sometimes Margaret, always responsive to an audience, sang along. The Princesses joined the local Girl Guides and in between times liked to ride out to see the lumber camp at Ballater on the royal estate, worked by Canadians to harvest wartime timber.

If Scotland felt peaceful and miles away from the war, London was on constant alert. Queen Mary was persuaded to move out of Marlborough House and stay with her niece and her husband, the Duke and Duchess of Beaufort, at their house at Badminton. It was an arrangement the Duchess found trying, while Queen Mary found the country life of Badminton dull after London, but somehow they survived their co-habitation. Her sons rallied to their war duties. The Duke of Kent, who was preparing to move to Australia with his family to start his post as Governor General, was instead commanded to take up a naval appointment; under Churchill as First Lord of the Admiralty, the full mobilisation of the Royal Navy was taking place. The Duke of Gloucester, now Major General, was appointed to the British Expeditionary Force (BEF) in France as its Chief Liaison Officer.

It left the tricky question of what to do about the Duke of Windsor: after all, he should still play his part in supporting his country in wartime. The King decided it would be better if he remained abroad. The Windsors came over to England to discuss it; before they came, the Queen told the Duchess in a letter that she was sorry that she would be unable to receive her. The King and his brother met and discussed his attachment to the British Military Mission in Paris. The Queen was not at home: David's attitude to the royal family and his actions since the Abdication had hardened her view of him. She was appalled to learn that he behaved with the King as though nothing had happened, and she was not sorry when they returned to France.

The Queen's ire was soon further aroused when she heard in a BBC broadcast that David had visited the Maginot Line. Referring to it in a memo to Hardinge, she said,

> there was an account of the Duke of Windsor looking younger (&
> I suppose more beautiful) than ever, making a tour of the Maginot
> Line & chatting to Tommies & Poles, & saying how glad he was
> to find such true friendship between them etc. I don't want to sound
> super critical but it sounds so like the old stuff, & never a mention of
> the poor Duke of Gloucester or Duke of Kent. Please don't trouble to
> acknowledge this, but I am sure that we must be on the lookout for
> these advertisements. I do not trust him one inch.[36]

Again she saw him stealing centre stage, ignoring the work his brothers were doing and pushing the boundaries; and not for the first time she resented the fact that physically he looked untroubled, while the King was already looking worn by assuming responsibilities that should not have been his.

The King had other aggravations, too. In the first week of the war, Ambassador Joe Kennedy – 'a bad man', said Tommy Lascelles – had made it clear that, while he had favoured appeasement, he now questioned whether war was ever worthwhile, given that whatever the ultimate result, financial and material disaster seemed inevitable. He also was unable to understand the reason for Britain entering the struggle. Alarmed by Kennedy's views and the effect they may have in Washington, the King presented his views in a letter to him, which was unmistakably firm yet diplomatic, a skill his ministers came to value greatly.

Being apart, the Princesses and their parents missed each other greatly, a point the Queen made in her broadcast on Armistice Day: 'a message of hope and encouragement' to the women of the Empire, in response to appeals for her to give comforting words to those who were separated from their families. She now recognised that women, 'no less than men, have real and vital work to do'.[37]

At the moment it was still quiet, the period that became known as the Phoney War. The King managed to get in a weekend's shooting at St Paul's Walden Bury, before going to France to visit the BEF. Meanwhile, at Birkhall the Princesses wondered where Christmas would be spent. Being near the coast, Sandringham was considered risky. It was all rather strange for them, because they had never been in Scotland so late in the year. It was much colder than they were used to, for there was no central heating in the bedrooms at Birkhall. Often their drinking water was frozen, as were their washing flannels. Crawfie said they regarded this as an adventure and made nothing of discomforts. To keep their spirits up, she took them Christmas shopping in Aberdeen, where they bought cheap brooches and china to give as Christmas presents. Elizabeth had to wear bands on her teeth, which meant lots of visits to the dentist. Margaret started playing up Alah about bedtimes, especially when guests were there, and had to be gently hauled off by Crawfie.

As the Princesses waited to find out what they would be doing, at Dartmouth Philip was wondering the same thing about himself. The head of the College thought his uncle may have plans and wrote accordingly to Lord Mountbatten: 'The boy is anxious to know so that he can make his arrangements for this leave etc. I gather that he, being a most enterprising young man, is full of ideas as to his future movements. I am told that he has done extremely well here and is one of the most outstanding cadets of his term.'[38] Soon afterwards he won two prizes, one for best all-round cadet of his term and one for the best cadet of the college. Inevitably there was some jealousy and classmates accused him of being 'a bit of a bully' and having 'German arrogance of command'.[39] As he was classed as 'a neutral foreigner', he was barred from serving at war and his application to become a British citizen would have to wait until afterwards. His uncle Dickie had to pull strings to allow him to continue his naval career in the Royal Navy, and in February 1940 he would be posted as midshipman on a battleship, *Ramillies*.

The Princesses were happy to hear that Christmas would be at Sandringham after all. It was the first time they had seen their father for four months. His message that year would become his most famous. Important for the country's morale, it established the continuance of the custom. He ended, 'A new year is at hand. If it brings peace, how thankful we shall all be. If it brings us continued struggle, we shall remain undaunted. . . . May that Almighty hand guide and uphold us all.'

CHAPTER 13

A Symbol of the Future (1940)

As 1940 dawned, the royal family at Sandringham listened to a broadcast from the children of France, in which they thanked the Princesses for the chocolates they had sent to those who had been evacuated. The Princesses' war efforts were used as positive propaganda. A letter Elizabeth sent before Christmas to their Guide Captain in London told her what she and Margaret were doing for the war effort in Scotland. It was published in the 'Girl Guide Bulletin' and then in the Press in early 1940: 'Yesterday we went over to a meeting of the Balmoral Company which was great fun, and we taught them some of our games. They have five evacuees from Glasgow with them. We have been knitting very hard for the Red Cross, the evacuees, and the soldiers and sailors, and also gathering sphagnum moss. Please would you send me the details of the war service badge?'[1]

The evacuees on the Balmoral estate gave the Princesses a chance to mix with ordinary children. *The People* noted, 'Princess Elizabeth is still shy with them but Princess Margaret calls them by their Christian names.'[2] Apart from being seen 'doing their bit' like everyone else, they were shown projecting a cosy 'family hearth' image, a reminder of a life that was under threat and which men all over the Empire were fighting to protect. They were seen as stoical, too, in the face of separation from their parents. That was about to continue, although only during the week. Their parents decided they should not return to Birkhall because it was too far away, and 'at their age their education is too important to be neglected', the King wrote in his diary.[3] Instead, from February they would live at Royal Lodge, while the King and Queen stayed at Buckingham Palace during the week. The Princesses' whereabouts would be kept secret, described only as 'a place in the country'.

As the 'phoney war' continued, they settled back into a proper routine. Elizabeth resumed her lessons at Eton, and both Princesses joined the local Guide Company. Miss Vacani came over to continue her dance lessons, and other girls known to the family joined them. The Princesses' contact with ordinary children continued with evacuees from London's East End, who now attended the nearby village school; some remained in contact after the war ended. At the weekends, the King and Queen joined their daughters, their usual family activities curtailed, but at least they were together. Crawfie noted that the Queen never showed she was worried: 'At that time she seemed to drop her cares at the gates of Royal Lodge and became just Mummie when she was there.'

Rationing was in force, which applied to the royal family too like everyone else, although the Queen and Queen Mary had extra clothing coupons for their official clothes and for State occasions. The Princesses had the normal allowance, but the Queen had previously bought material in tweeds and cottons from British Industry fairs, so they would not go short. However, thrift was the word, with 'make do and mend'.

Meanwhile, Prince Philip sailed off in HMS *Ramillies*. To his annoyance, it was not exactly action-packed, as its job was escorting convoys of Australian and New Zealand troopships bound for Egypt, but it was a start, and far from an easy ride. He and Elizabeth began to correspond on a platonic basis. Myra Butter is 'sure it was the intention of Mountbatten that Philip should marry Elizabeth'. He saw it as a good thing, both for his own ambitions – particularly after the humiliation his father had suffered in the Great War – and for Philip himself. Philip's first captain had a meeting with him, concerning his becoming a British subject so he could one day achieve a rank higher than Acting Sub-Lieutenant. He was surprised when Philip said, 'My uncle Dickie has ideas for me: he thinks I could marry Princess Elizabeth.' His captain asked, 'Are you really fond of her?' 'Oh yes, very,' said Philip, 'and I write to her every week.'[4]

Myra says, 'Philip would never have married her if he hadn't been in love with her, I can tell you that, because I knew his other girlfriends.'[5] And these were still early days. Elizabeth was barely fourteen and Philip had a girlfriend, one his uncle Dickie was indirectly responsible for his meeting. Osla Benning was a beautiful, dark-haired Canadian, with alabaster skin and an exquisite figure. She had been presented at Court in July 1939 and was considered one of the loveliest debutantes of the season. She was a flat-mate of Mountbatten's goddaughter, Sarah Norton (later Baring), and while Philip was in London for a while, Mountbatten asked Sarah to find a 'nice girl' for him because he did not know anyone.

Osla had come to England with her mother after her parents divorced. Her mother went on to marry three times, and Osla was sent to finishing school in Austria: her lack of security gave her something in common with Philip. They met in late 1939 when she was working at an aircraft factory and sharing a cottage with Sarah and her father. Osla and Philip kept in touch, and Sarah said he rang her when he was home but she was sure that it was not a full-blown affair: 'We were brought up to what my mother used to call "behave nicely,"' said Sarah.[6] Later Osla's daughter, Janie Spring, claimed, 'I do know he was her first love. She never told me about him for years. She just said, "I fell in love with a naval officer."' Then Janie found a 'wonderful' picture of a young Philip.[7]

In April, events took a turn for the worst. Hitler had invaded Denmark and Norway. Norway declared war on Germany but British naval and expeditionary forces, with the French, were unable to protect their ally. By 4 May almost all of Norway was in German hands. On 10 May, the Wehrmacht marched into Holland, Belgium, Luxembourg and France. In Britain, a vote of no confidence led to Chamberlain's resignation. Lord Halifax advised the King that the best person to invite to form the next government was the First Lord of the Admiralty, Winston Churchill. Although the King was not entirely convinced of Churchill at that stage, he called for him and he accepted. Chamberlain's resignation speech was very moving. Elizabeth told her mother, 'I cried, mummy.'[8]

Given the new threat, on 11 May the Princesses were moved into the impregnable fortress of Windsor Castle. It was only supposed to be for a week but they would stay for most of the war. The castle had already been prepared for bombings, its pictures and precious artefacts removed, the crystal chandeliers taken down and black-out curtains put in place. Although the girls were used to the castle, everything was gloomy and the staff were understandably tense. The Princesses stayed in their usual rooms in the Lancaster Tower, built in the Tudor period. Elizabeth had her own bathroom and bedroom, which she now shared with Bobo. Next door to them were Margaret and Alah. Nearby was the nursery, overlooking Windsor Great Park. Crawfie was on her own in the Victoria Tower, some distance away, with her own large suite but a bathroom on the roof. There was no central heating, and the electric stoves in the bedrooms were subject to wartime fuel cuts. The only reliable heating was log fires in the sitting rooms.

At first it was rather depressing. The Princesses missed their possessions which were still at Royal Lodge, and Alah was cross, as she always was when worried. High-powered bulbs had been replaced by low-powered ones; Crawfie said, 'We seemed to live in a sort of underworld.' A few nights later they experienced their first bombing. As the alarm went off, everyone went to the shelter in the dungeons, including Lord Wigram, Governor of the Castle, but there was no sign of the Princesses or Alah. Wigram and Crawfie found them putting their clothes on, Alah dressing carefully as usual with her cap and white uniform; Elizabeth told Crawfie, 'We must dress.' They were told just to throw a coat over their nightclothes and get moving. By the time they got to the shelter, the Master of the Household, Sir Hill Child, 'was a nervous wreck' and had to speak to Alah sternly about taking the children to safety immediately the alarm went. While they waited on uncomfortable temporary beds, Margaret fell asleep on Crawfie's lap and Elizabeth read a book. Sir Hill Child made tea, until finally at 2:00 a.m. the all-clear sounded. Eventually comfortable beds were installed, a bathroom provided and a bedroom for the King and Queen, and the Princesses were allowed to keep their treasured items down there; when the raids increased, the family would sleep there all the time.

The same week, following Hitler's threat to capture European monarchs, the King received a call at 5:00 a.m. from Queen Wilhelmina of the Netherlands begging for help. After a dramatic exit from Holland, the King met her and took her to the Palace; then the Dutch army surrendered. She was joined shortly at the Palace by the King's widowed uncle, King Haakon of Norway, and his son.

There was brightness too. 'Monty' came to help with lessons and sang with the children, which they loved. A company of Grenadier Guards soon arrived, which would prove to be a lot of fun for the Princesses. At the weekends the King and Queen stayed whenever they could, and while they observed food rationing, they could supplement the household's meals with game birds and venison from their estates. The Queen's brother Michael became a father again when Betty gave birth to a son at Woolmers.

Henry Marten now came to the castle for Elizabeth's lessons. Beyond its protective walls, the situation in Europe worsened. After the successful Dunkirk operation in late May, the Germans entered Paris on 14 June; on 22 June the French government surrendered. Having lost her ally, Britain was on her own. Churchill warned Roosevelt of the consequences if Britain were defeated: 'You may have a United States of Europe under Nazi command far more numerous, far stronger, far better armed than the New World.'[9] Eleanor Roosevelt wrote a sympathetic letter to the Queen, whose brother had now begun to play a part in bringing America into the war.

David Bowes Lyon was appointed Press Officer to the Ministry of Economic Warfare. The Ministry wanted neutral countries to stop trading with any country that was fighting Britain and thus undermine the ability of the Axis powers to acquire vital war supplies. Britain considered the United States to be the most important neutral because of its economic capabilities and its natural geographic boundaries. However, the barrier that Britain hoped to create around Germany needed to be applied with diplomacy and without antagonising American merchants.[10] From May 1940 there was a new willingness to accommodate the US government in any way that it could, to encourage American aid and involvement in the European conflict.

While David Bowes Lyon was playing his part, the Princesses' other uncle David was again causing concern. With the agreement of the British Military Mission in Paris to which he was attached, the Windsors left as the Germans advanced and went to the south of France. However, on 20 June they had to flee into Spain, where General Franco's fascist government was aligned with Berlin. Ribbentrop, the former Ambassador, knew the Duke had been sympathetic to Germany and wanted to retain him in Spain. A letter dated 7 July 1940, containing news from a British agent, informed the Foreign Office that 'Germans expect assistance from Duke and Duchess of Windsor, latter desiring at any price to become Queen. Germans have been negotiating with her since June 27th.' It said the Germans proposed to form an Opposition Government under the Duke and that 'the Germans think King George will abdicate during attack on London'.[11]

Churchill told the Windsors to move to neutral Lisbon in Portugal, from where a flying boat would take them to England, but the Duke refused unless he received guarantees that they would be royally treated and invited to Buckingham Palace. No such assurances were given. They did go to Lisbon but stayed in a house borrowed from Senhor Esperito Santo, the head of a bank considered to be corrupt. On 15 July, Santo had had a three-hour interview with the German Minister.[12] Churchill learned that Santo said the Duke 'manifested extreme defeatist and pacifist sympathies'.[13] The Windsors were approached by Ribbentrop's men, who were told to give them praise and promises and, if necessary, to force the Duke back to Spain.

To get the Windsors out of German reach, Churchill suggested to the King that the Duke be offered the post of Governor of the Bahamas. The idea was not well received by the royal family but no one wanted them in England. The Duke reluctantly accepted the appointment, and they left Lisbon on 1 August. Later, an agent reported that the Germans had assisted the Windsors in ensuring that all their effects from Paris would be safely transported to Portugal and then to the Bahamas, and concluded, 'The desire of the Germans to please the Duke and Duchess of Windsor was absolutely marked and evident.'[14]

Meanwhile, Britain stood alone, but it was not a situation that unduly worried the King: 'Personally I feel happier now that we have no allies to be polite to & to pamper,' the King wrote to Queen Mary.[15] The feeling of elation and pride after the evacuation of Dunkirk made many British people feel the same way. However, in July, Hitler announced his intention to march into London on 15 September. Now the south-east of England prepared for invasion. The Home Guard was formed, and the security of Their Majesties was increased. The Coates Mission was formed, a handpicked body of officers and men from the Brigade of Guards and the

Household Cavalry, who were equipped with armoured cars and stood ready to take them to a place of safety or defend them against surprise attack by parachute troops. The King and Queen took shooting lessons, as did the equerries, and the King took to carrying a rifle and a revolver in his car. Later, he told a visitor that it was his intention, if Britain was invaded and a resistance movement established, to offer his services at once, in whatever capacity, to its leader.[16] The Queen's nephew, John Elphinstone, was taken prisoner and incarcerated at Colditz with a group called the *Prominente* from well-known families, who were favoured by Hitler as a bargaining tool.

In August, the Luftwaffe increased its bombing raids, and London experienced the Blitz. Surprisingly at that stage there was very little protection at Buckingham Palace. The only shelter was a small room in the basement, a housemaids' sitting room, which was reinforced and divided into small cubicles. On 8 September, the Palace took its first hit. It was a delayed time bomb, but no one was hurt, and the damage was slight. Following the attack, the King and Queen made their first forays into the devastated East End, picking their way through the rubble. On 13 September, the Palace was bombed again in a deliberate hit. A German bomber emerged from low cloud, flew straight up the Mall, and dropped several bombs on the Palace. There was no time to reach the shelter, and the King and Queen were almost killed; however, they told no one, not even the Prime Minister, until after the war. The damage was considerable, and the Chapel was destroyed. However, there was never any question of them leaving London. The Queen wrote, 'I'm glad we've been bombed. It makes me feel I can look the East End in the face.'[17]

They took to sleeping at Windsor, returning to Buckingham Palace during the day. In October Windsor town itself was bombed on two consecutive nights. The Queen told her sister May that 'it was the first time that the children had actually heard the whistle and scream of bombs. They were wonderful.'[18] In London, 145 Piccadilly was almost destroyed, Kensington Palace was bombed, and a land mine exploded in St James's Park, which blew out most of Buckingham Palace's windows. There was no question of the Princesses being sent abroad, as many of their parents' friends were doing. As the Queen reputedly said, 'The children could not go without me, I could not possibly leave the King, and the King would never go.' There was also the question of public morale to keep up. To send the girls away would have conveyed the wrong message. Among those who were evacuated were Davina and Simon Bowes Lyon, aged ten and eight. In July they had arrived in New York with their maternal grandmother and three cousins from their mother's side, and two governesses. Family friend J. P. Morgan sponsored their trip. They stayed in Virginia at the family house of Ronald Tree, an American-born British Conservative MP and journalist.

Now Elizabeth was becoming a symbol of the future, illustrated by what was seen as her first act of leadership. On 13 October that year, 1940, she delivered her first broadcast in the popular programme *Children's Hour*, heard all over the Empire and in the United States. Naturally the speech was written for her, but that did not detract from the fact that here was the young Heiress Presumptive speaking to them. After lots of practice, and in a voice which many thought resembled her mother's, Elizabeth empathised with those away from home: 'My sister Margaret Rose and I ... know from experience what it is like to be away from those we love more than all.' She reassured her listeners that 'we children at home are full of cheerfulness and courage. We are trying to do all we can to help our gallant sailors, soldiers and airmen. . . . And when peace comes, remember it will be for us, the children of today, to make the world of tomorrow a better and happier place.'[19] Elizabeth invited Margaret to say 'Good night', before wishing everyone good luck. The effect was far-reaching and emotional. In South Africa, a novelist wrote, 'It was perfectly done. If there are still queens in the world a generation hence, this child will be a good queen.'[20]

The strain was telling. Crawfie said the Queen was becoming pale and drawn, and the King, who had been visiting Britain's worst hit areas, was looking increasingly like his father. Meanwhile, his brother in the Bahamas had become very friendly with a Swedish millionaire, Axel Wenner-Gren. In December, he lent the Duke his yacht to take the Duchess to Miami for dental treatment and went with them. Wenner-Gren was known by the Foreign Office to be friendly with the Nazis, and it was decided to tell the Duke, particularly when Wenner-Gren came under attack from the American press for his sentiments. However, the Duke expressed surprise at such allegations, saying Wenner-Gren was a friend of Roosevelt's, with whom the Duke had an interview while he was in Miami; he told the Foreign Office it was 'most satisfactory'.[21]

To keep up the Princesses' spirits, as Christmas approached, the Queen arranged for them to join pupils of the Royal School Windsor, with evacuees from London, to give a little concert. Directed by the head-master, Hubert Tannar, the Princesses played piano solos and duets and acted in a scene called *An Apple for the Teacher*. Elizabeth, in cap and gown, played the teacher, while Margaret and other children tap-danced into school. In another scene in a country inn, devised as a setting for drinking songs, the Princesses were waitresses and served the drinks. The Queen was impressed and invited them to perform in the castle. Tannar then devised a nativity play, *The Three Roses,* performed in St George's Hall. Elizabeth played one of the three kings in a golden crown and velvet tunic and led a procession through the audience to the stage. Margaret was the Little Child, whose gift to the baby Jesus was herself. Dressed in a white dress and a string of beads, she sang 'Gentle Jesus Meek and Mild' while kneeling at the crib. The King was overcome: 'I wept through most of it. It is such a wonderful story.'[22] The performance set the precedent for the Princesses' pantomimes of the future.

The royal family's Christmas card that year showed Their Majesties standing in the bomb-damaged Palace. After Christmas at Windsor, on 27 December the family went to Sandringham. Instead of staying in the Big House, they stayed in Appleton, the late Queen Maude's house, which was less of a target. Lascelles thought it a rather miserable little place, but the staff had installed carpets and furniture and made it com-fortable; there was also an air raid shelter in the grounds and protection by armoured cars and guns. Elizabeth thanked Helen Hardinge for her present of an engagement book and said, ever-thoughtful, 'At last we are able to go away for a bit. I hope Mummy and Papa will be able to get a rest too, because I think they deserve it.'[23] Margaret thanked Helen for her 'sweet little picture' and apologised for not writing sooner, 'but I have had lots of letters to write. I hope I don't sound rude because I could easily have written to you before.'[24]

An article described the fourteen-year-old Elizabeth in late 1940: 'Physically the Princess is graceful and straight-limbed. . . . She has about her a sweet reasonableness and this, with her open-hearted generous sympathy, makes her accessible to all; but she has also, very markedly, an innate dignity, which seems, touchingly, to set her in a little space by herself apart. . . . One thinks of Princess Elizabeth now as "standing with uncertain feet to where the brook and river meet."'[25] Despite its sentimentality, the piece captured something of the adolescent Princess, and the poignant sense of her standing slightly apart would be lasting.

CHAPTER 14

Allies at Last (1941)

As 1941 dawned, the royal family started to feel better for their break in Norfolk. The Queen told Queen Mary, 'The children are looking quite different already – I am afraid that Windsor is not really a good place for them, the noise of guns is heavy . . . and so many bombs dropped all around'.[1] The King went shooting most days and was looking refreshed. While they relaxed, Prince Philip was about to see action. Three months earlier, Italy had invaded Greece, which was now on the Allied side. On New Year's Day 1941 at Alexandria, Philip joined the battleship, HMS *Valiant*, part of the Mediterranean Fleet, and headed towards Greece, witnessing attacks on ships on the way. In mid-January, he enjoyed some shore leave at Athens, staying with his mother Alice, who was doing charity work with the families of Greek soldiers.

He also stayed with George II of Greece, where he met the American-born MP and author Henry 'Chips' Channon. After talking to Philip's aunt, Princess Nicholas of Greece, Chips later said, 'He is to be our Prince Consort, and that is why he is serving in our Navy.'[2] However, Philip's sister Theodora said that initially he had wanted to join the Greek Navy and that while Mountbatten had not stopped him, she had, and persuaded him to enter the Royal Navy.[3] Also, while Alice liked to think about 'potential dynastic alliances' for her children,[4] as Philip's biographer has said, 'Even on Princess Nicholas's part, this prophecy seems to have been speculative, to say the least.'

In March, the royal family were dismayed by the actions of their good friend, Prince Paul, Regent of Yugoslavia. The husband of Princess Marina's sister, Olga, Paul was faced with a demand by Hitler to allow German troops to march through Yugoslavia to subjugate Greece. Despite appeals from George VI he felt he had no choice, and then signed a pact with the Axis powers, Germany, Italy and Japan. Now Philip on *Valiant* was engaged in convoying British troops to Crete and Piraeus to bolster Greek defences ahead of the expected German landings.

At the same time the Foreign Secretary Anthony Eden[5] received advice from Ronald Tree in the Ministry of Information. Tree said that 'the question of getting America into the war is now a vital issue. Without her assistance I cannot see how the war can be won or indeed how we can cope adequately with the battle for the Atlantic.'[6] America thought it was doing all it needed to do, he said, by entering into the Lend Lease agreement with Britain (to assist with its defences), and did not feel ready 'to enter the fray'. What was needed was to get the United States 'into that frame of mind that will enable them to support the President in any move he may wish to make'. There needed to be better communications within Britain's organisations in America. Ideally, a head of all publicity in the United States would work closely with the media. Tree considered David Bowes Lyon 'to be admirably suited for that job' because he had gained a very good reputation as Press Officer, had excellent contacts in the United States, and was 'a strong enough personality to be able to put over the policy of Her Majesty's Government'. As a result, Bowes Lyon was appointed the head of the Political Warfare Executive (PWE) Mission in Washington, a position he began in 1942.

He was not universally liked by his colleagues: some thought him 'pleasant but highly unintelligent', others considered him to be an intriguer,[7] and he was sometimes criticised for relying too much on his relationship with the royal family. However, there was no doubt he had Britain's interests at heart. But while the Queen's brother worked towards bringing the United States into the war, the King's brother was doing the opposite.

The Duke of Windsor gave an interview in March 1941 to the American magazine, *Liberty*, which infuriated heads of news services in the United States. The interview contained 'useful ammunition' for the appeasement group. In a report of it in the US Press, which was sent to the King, the Duke said, 'We have got to look at facts not wishes, and since you cannot kill 80 million Germans, and since they want Hitler, how can you force them into a revolution they don't want?' When the war is over, 'there will be a new order in Europe, whether it is imposed by Germany or Great Britain.'[8] There would also be a new World League of Nations, he said, and 'you Americans will have to come in next time'.

The King demanded a copy of the authorised interview. Then, in April, reports were received of a conversation the Duke had allegedly had with an American friend of the Duchess, in which the Duke said, 'It would be an absolute tragedy if your country came into this war. The only thing to do is to bring it to an end as soon as ever possible.'[9] At a dinner at Government House, several people heard him say that it would be 'very ill-advised' of America to enter the war, as Europe was finished anyway; and the Duchess said that if the United States entered the war, 'this country would go down to history as the worst sucker of all times'.[10] Fortunately that year, a new American Ambassador replaced Joe Kennedy. John G. Winant believed that 'no power on earth will beat Britain down . . . you are fighting for those things that mean as much to the US as they do to England.' Winant would be lauded for his work with Churchill on the Anglo-American alliance.

Elizabeth may have known little of the problems her uncle was causing, but it all contributed to the strain upon her father. It was bad enough to learn that their cousin John Bowes Lyon, eldest son of Patrick, had gone missing in action. To brighten the gloom, the Princesses were allowed to give lunch parties for the officers stationed in the castle, which helped Elizabeth with her social skills. Crawfie said she 'played the part of the hostess perfectly. She never left anybody hanging around.' After watching her father host parties, she had a good example to follow. Margaret meanwhile 'began to develop into a real little personality then with the male element about' and made everyone laugh. Sometimes they were invited to tea by the officers and played charades.

During 1941, cousin Margaret joined the Princesses. She was attending a secretarial college which had been evacuated from London to Surrey, so she stayed at Windsor and caught the bus every day. She said the Queen 'managed even during the war when things were black to have fun' and gave the Princesses 'a sense of stability in family life'.[11] When they were on route to the shelter during a warning, the Queen 'absolutely refused to be hurried, despite the efforts of courtiers to persuade her to move faster. . . . The Fuhrer was not going to force her pace.' The Princesses kept up their Girl Guiding activities, camping in the grounds during the day and working for their cooking badges, testing their efforts on the Air Raid Precautions men on look-out duty on the castle walls. In the gardens they tended their vegetables and cousin Margaret said, 'The pudding every day was stewed bottled plums, picked from the garden.'[12]

May 1941 was a particularly grim time. There was a massive attack on London, with nearly 1,500 killed and 2,000 injured, and 11,000 houses destroyed. Around two thousand fires were started, one of which destroyed the Bath Club. Both Houses of Parliament were hit and Westminster Abbey damaged. By June, over two million British homes had been destroyed, over half in London. The Princess Elizabeth of York Hospital for children had already been bombed; the Princess was pleased to receive two cheques from children in Canada towards maintaining the premises in the countryside to where the young patients had been evacuated.

But it was not all gloom. Unlike many people, the royal family still had the facilities for entertainment, and in July, Elizabeth attended her first royal ball. The King was a good dancer and a keen one, and he was not going to let the war interfere with that pastime. A West End band was engaged at the castle to play a variety of music, and guests included Guards officers, with whom Elizabeth danced enthusiastically. Myra Butter was one of those 'lucky enough to get asked'. She says that 'the only party one went to was probably the one they gave'. The occasions were 'absolutely wonderful', and many of the officers 'remained friends for all one's life, until they died. Princess Elizabeth kept all her friends.'[13]

That month Elizabeth helped her parents welcome two hundred guests at an important reception for the heads of Allied States and members of their governments. Among them was King Peter II of Yugoslavia, aged seventeen, a godson of George V. His mother, Maria, was a great-granddaughter of Queen Victoria. Peter had become King at just eleven when his father, King Alexander I, was assassinated in France. As he was too young to rule, his father's cousin, Prince Paul, acted as Regent of Yugoslavia. After Paul signed the Axis agreement, there was a British-supported military coup in which he was deposed and fled the country, and Peter was declared of age. He took over the administration of his country and gained the allegiance of his armed forces. However, a month later Yugoslavia was invaded. Peter had a dramatic escape to the Middle East, where he was helped by the British Embassy in Cairo.

In June Peter came to Britain and joined his mother, and spoke bravely of his intentions for his occupied country. Later he recalled,[14] 'This was my first visit to London since 1934. I was shocked and saddened by the destruction wrought on the city by the blitz, but at the same time heartened by the wonderful morale of the people.' When Peter went to the Palace to see his 'Uncle Bertie and Aunt Elizabeth', they were very kind; the King was 'deeply worried' by the events in Yugoslavia. When the Queen gave him a cup of tea, he noticed, 'we were all allowed only one lump of rationed sugar.' It was decided that, for the time being, Peter should go to Cambridge University to study international law and economics.

Peter spent a weekend in early August with the royal family at Windsor. 'The weather was very fine', he recalled,

and afterwards I walked in the park, talking with Uncle Bertie, and later played bowls with two of the King's ADCs and one of my own. That night I had dinner with the family, and we retired early to bed. My room was very comfortable, though with out-of-date plumbing. Next morning, after breakfast, Princess Elizabeth took me on a tour of the castle with its huge ramparts and interminable corridors. Then I strolled around the grounds with Elizabeth and Margaret and their two corgis. I had never met the two princesses before, and found them charming young girls.

He thought it a lovely weekend and they were 'very sensitive' to the needs of a king in exile. In September the King and Queen would attend a special service in St Paul's Cathedral to celebrate his coming of age.

David Bowes Lyon asked his sister if she would write an article for an American magazine. She refused but agreed to do a radio broadcast on 10 August to the women of America, talking of the heavy burden the British people faced and thanking the Americans for the support they had given so far. Two days later, Churchill and Roosevelt signed the Atlantic Charter, which set out the common principles of their national policies. It was a good start, for the world situation would change very soon.

That summer the family managed to escape briefly to Balmoral, where they entertained the Canadian Prime Minister for two nights in a little cottage. There were virtually no staff, and the Princesses decorated his table for lunch with lettuce leaves from the garden, planted instead of flowers. He found Elizabeth 'very sweet' in her conversation[15] and Margaret entertaining, recording how she would cross her eyes to amuse everyone. The Queen and the Princesses visited the Earl at Glamis, where Margaret celebrated her eleventh birthday, something they had not managed to do the previous year.

For Elizabeth, a highlight came in October when Prince Philip had a rare leave and spent a weekend at Windsor; he had also kept in touch with Osla Benning and seen her during the summer. Philip regaled the King with stories of his adventures in the Mediterranean, and afterwards he wrote to Philip's grandmother: 'What a charming boy he is, & I am glad he is remaining on in my Navy.'[16] His Navy was about to be taxed further. On 7 December, Japan bombed Pearl Harbour. Now the United States entered the fray, declaring war on Japan, as did Britain; then Hitler declared war on the United States. The King sent a message of sympathy to Roosevelt, now the leader of Britain's most important ally. Very soon American troops began to arrive.

The loss of Britain's two main battleships sunk by the Japanese came as a great blow to the King, who was pleased to lose himself in the Princesses' first pantomime, *Cinderella*. He had become very involved near the end of rehearsals, complaining about Lilibet's tunic being too short and behaving 'as if he were arranging a battle campaign', said Crawfie, but he was helpful in organising the guardsmen on the stage. Margaret was determined to play Cinderella, wearing a white wig and crinoline dress and being carried in Queen Anne's sedan chair, while Elizabeth played Prince Charming. All the ticket sales went to the Wool Fund, a charity favoured by the Queen. A fellow member of the group said that although they found it exciting coming to the castle and meeting real princesses, it was all rather uncomfortable, because Mr Tannar made them curtsey and call the Princesses 'ma'am'. No one thought it unfair that the Princesses had the main parts: it was just assumed they would. There were few children of Elizabeth's age, and she seemed unable to relax with those who were: she was more comfortable being protective of her sister or the younger members. Margaret was thought to be the best actress in the little company; Elizabeth was rather stiff. She was never bossy with the other children but was quick to correct her sister if she was messing about.[17]

As the family prepared for Christmas, the happy news came that the Duchess of Gloucester had given birth to their first child, a son, fourth in line to the Throne. In the midst of chaos and destruction, life was going on.

CHAPTER 15

Growing Up (1942)

After Christmas at Appleton, during which the Queen was amused to receive a food parcel from J. P. Morgan in America, the Princesses returned to Windsor Castle in early 1942. Elizabeth was approaching her sixteenth birthday. The concept of the 'teenager', with its connotations of rebellion, was yet to be invented, and in the 1940s, children often went straight from school into war work or the armed forces. Elizabeth's adolescence, affected as it was both by war and by her unique position as Heir Presumptive, left little room for wildness, and her very nature did not incline her to be. She had a reserve which hid a strong will and an impressive intelligence which was noted by many who met her. Her situation might have been hard to cope with but, as one biographer said, 'She seems to have dealt with the peculiarity of her position by becoming as unremarkable as possible in everything she could not change, while accepting absolutely what was expected of her.'[1] It is that stoicism of which her cousin Margaret has spoken and which endures.

One rite of passage that year was her confirmation in March. In the Private Chapel of Windsor Castle the Archbishop of Canterbury, Cosmo Lang, assisted by the Dean of Windsor, performed his last ceremony before his retirement. On Easter Day, she took her first communion at the Royal Chapel and afterwards they enjoyed breakfast and Easter eggs at Royal Lodge. There were many 'firsts' for Elizabeth that year. She received her first public appointment when the King made her honorary Colonel of the Grenadier Guards, the regiment protecting the family at Windsor. On 20 April, she had her first official audience when she received Colonel Prescott, who presented her with a diamond Regimental brooch as a birthday gift. The next day she carried out her first official engagement when she inspected her regiment at Windsor Castle, walking confidently along the long line of troops and taking the march past on the dais. Afterwards, she hosted a party for six hundred officers and men, with a variety performance headed by popular comedian Tommy Handley. At a party in the sergeant's mess, she watched her parents dancing the foxtrot until one of the Guards' drummers, twenty-two-year-old Jack Bensted from Liverpool, rescued her from being a wallflower, and she danced the rest of the number and three encores with him.[2]

Elizabeth was agitating to get involved with war work, especially as two cousins were engaged in VAD duties, but her parents considered her too young. Conscription for women under thirty had been introduced in late 1941, so the law required that she register for work like all girls of her age. Wearing her Girl Guide uniform, she signed on at the Windsor Labour Exchange. As she did so, Osla Benning was working at top secret Bletchley Park, as a multilinguist in the naval section. Like Philip, Osla enjoyed practical jokes; by contrast, Elizabeth 'was always too serious minded ... and never failed to consider what the feelings of other people would be', said Crawfie. Meanwhile, Philip passed his sub-lieutenant's exams, and in June he was posted as a sub-lieutenant to the destroyer HMS *Wallace*, based on the Firth of Forth in Scotland. Its task was to escort merchant vessels on a treacherous passage to Sheerness in Kent, during which they were vulnerable to attack.

Elizabeth was cocooned in many ways, but her father had been involving her in his work for some time. Photographer Lisa Sheridan noticed that when the daily dispatch boxes arrived, the King would draw Elizabeth to him and explain matters 'very earnestly'; there was 'a particular bond of understanding' between them.[3] Now she was taught separately from Margaret and given her own room at Windsor; once a sitting room and decorated in pink tapestry, Elizabeth was delighted to use it as her private apartment, where she could receive official guests and entertain her friends.

On 4 July, the family were delighted when the Duchess of Kent gave birth to their third child, Prince Michael. Early on in the war the Duke of Kent had asked, for the second time in his life, to leave the Royal Navy, and had requested a transfer to the Royal Air Force. The Service was of great interest to his nieces: 'The RAF took their fancy, and the men who went up in aircraft alone were their heroes.'[4] Working in an inspector's role, he flew thousands of miles in Britain and overseas, to RAF stations and aircraft factories, shipyards and blitzed areas. When under fire or shell, witnesses said he was fearless.[5] Princess Marina became Commandant of the Women's Royal Naval Service, known as the Wrens, and also worked as a VAD.

As Michael was born on America's Independence Day, and as his father had visited the Roosevelts the year before, the Kents asked the President if he would be a godfather. He accepted with delight; the King would stand proxy for him at the christening on 4 August, at which one of the baby's given names was Franklin. In joyous mood, the Duke wrote to their friend Lady Desborough on 13 July[6]: 'We are all so pleased and happy with our new son & it is a great relief that all is safely over. His arrival has been the one bright spot in these gloomy times. My wife is going on very well & the baby is sweet & I believe looks like me!' He was pleased that Lady Desborough had seen his 'mama' at Badminton, and said it was 'wonderful' that she had made a new life for herself there. 'It is, I suppose, no good inviting you to Coppins with the petrol difficulties,' he said, regretting that, as he was seldom in London, 'I never see any of my friends.'

He never would again. Six weeks later, on 25 August, he was killed when the military aircraft he was travelling in crashed into a Scottish hillside and exploded, killing all but one of the fifteen passengers. He was thirty-nine. The royal family were at Balmoral, taking a short break. Cousin Margaret recalled how the shocking news came in the middle of dinner. The King was heartbroken: 'I have lost him & all those qualities that were apparent in everything he did,' he told Helen Hardinge. 'He was such a friend & a great help to me in my work. I shall miss him terribly I know in so many ways.'[7] A Court of Inquiry attributed the accident to pilot error, a decision which was subsequently doubted. It was a great loss to the Princesses. They were very fond of their uncle, who used to chase them around the garden at Coppins and knew how to talk to children.

Princess Marina, left with three young children, was inconsolable. Despite the Duke's colourful past and continuing proclivities, theirs was a happy marriage. Putting aside her own grief, Queen Mary went to Coppins immediately, although soon warned Marina that she had a duty to all war widows and should not become self-indulgent in her grief. However, the King realised that the only way to help her was to bring her sister, Olga, from Kenya, where she was living in exile with Prince Paul. It was a sensitive issue, consent for which had to be given by Churchill. Not long after the tragedy, the Queen was grieved to hear that her nephew John Bowes Lyon, missing in action, was confirmed dead.

The visit of Eleanor Roosevelt to Britain in October was timely, for she could also pay her respects in person to Marina. David Bowes Lyon had visited the President in March and given him a letter from the King. It served as his introduction to Roosevelt and thanked him for his plans to help Britain, proclaiming confidence that Britain would win the war. Mrs Roosevelt's visit was designed to maintain relations and to show her how women could help in the war effort. She was taken on a country-wide tour of American camps and airfields and was concerned to discover Britain's proximity to the enemy. She was shown around bomb-blasted London: deeply shocked, she said she 'was in no way prepared for the great area of destruction'.[8]

Even Buckingham Palace was an eye-opener. As much of it was unusable, Mrs Roosevelt was given the Queen's own bedroom, together with the use of the King's sitting room: the Queen's had been dismantled and had no windows. She was impressed by the bedroom's size but could not ignore the cold. The King had recently intensified the fuel measures at the Palace and Windsor. The Palace had been one of the first buildings in Britain to introduce fuel economy; now he ordered that there be no central heating, and fires could only be lit in bedrooms on doctors' orders. Only small electric fires were allowed. In bedrooms in both residences, only one lightbulb was permitted, regardless of the room size. Black lines were painted around baths, restricting the water level to five inches, and boiler use limited.

On Mrs Roosevelt's first night in the Palace, a dinner was given in her honour. The menu was nowhere near the Palace's usual standards due to rationing, although she noticed it was served on gold and silver plates. She spent some time talking with Elizabeth, whom she found 'very attractive, quite serious, with a good deal of character. She asked a good deal about life' in the United States.[9] The night was memorable because that day, 23 October, General Montgomery was to launch at El Alamein the offensive that would eventually destroy German power in North Africa. Churchill, a dinner guest, was jittery for news and even the film shown after dinner could not settle him. It was Noel Coward's film, '*In Which We Serve*', inspired by Mountbatten's experience as Commander of the sunk destroyer, HMS *Kelly*. While they watched, Churchill received the good news he was hoping for.

Elizabeth was all too familiar with the film, because Coward had invited the royal family on set. Mountbatten's daughter, Pamela, was there too, and travelled in the car with the Princesses. As they drove through a small crowd that had gathered near the studio, 'Princess Elizabeth kept reminding her sister that she "really must wave" at the people.' Coward let the girls stand on the 'deck' as the storm scene was being prepared. Pamela said it was constructed 'so that it could pitch and roll in the "swell", and after a few minutes the Princesses and I felt so sick we asked whether we could climb down'.[10] No doubt Philip's response to Elizabeth's feeble sea legs would have been robust. October had brought him further promotion when he was made the first lieutenant of HMS *Wallace*, second-in-command of the ship at just twenty-one, and one of the youngest to hold that position.

President Roosevelt asked that the thousands of American troops now in Britain be allowed to honour Thanksgiving. Services were held countrywide, the largest in Westminster Abbey, after which the King and Queen held their very first Thanksgiving party at Buckingham Palace. Assisted by the Princesses, they greeted over two hundred officers and nurses. Crawfie said the Princesses were fascinated by the American soldiers they saw at Windsor, even though the men told them so often about the girls of their age back home, that Margaret decided there must be 'billions' of them in America.

As the Christmas season approached, Philip received bad news. His best friend, Alex, Myra's brother, had died of injuries in Tunisia while serving with the 17/21st Lancers. He was twenty-four. Myra says, 'Philip was very, very fond of my brother. He wrote a fantastic letter when he died, he's very deep. He thought Alex was a wonderful person. The three boys [with David Milford Haven] were very close, a band of brothers.'[11] In his letter to their mother, Zia, Philip said that Alex 'filled the place of a brother and for that alone I am eternally grateful to him. As the older boy he was the guide and the pillow and in a great many ways I tried to model myself on him.'[12]

Amid all the misery, their pantomime, *The Sleeping Beauty*, was a welcome diversion. Elizabeth played Prince Salvador, and Margaret was Fairy Thistledown. Accompanied by a large orchestra, they performed to hundreds of troops. Lascelles thought it 'an admirable show, largely through the genius of Mr Tannar . . . and the whole thing went with a slickness and confidence that amazed me.'[13] As usual, Margaret eclipsed her sister. The *Sunday Post* reported,[14] 'Princess Margaret in the chief role was outstanding and she sang and danced extremely well. Princess Elizabeth as the prince was in a number of pleasing items with her younger sister.' Margaret's talent flourished as she grew: 'She missed her vocation,' said cousin Margaret. 'She should have been in cabaret.' The Heiress Presumptive would not have begrudged her little sister's talent. After all, she had to have something of her own.

CHAPTER 16

All the Young Men (1943)

In early 1943 the bombing continued, and in Lewisham, south-east London, a bomb fell on a large school, killing many children. The Queen visited the young survivors, taking with her bananas – a rare treat in wartime – brought back by Mountbatten from Casablanca. He had been in conference with Churchill, Roosevelt and President de Gaulle, where they reached the momentous decision for American and British forces to launch from Britain an invasion of Nazi-dominated Europe. The date would be as soon as practicable, they told Stalin in Russia; it would eventually begin in June 1944 with the D-Day Landings.

Elizabeth took a step further towards wartime work, when in February she was enrolled as a Sea Ranger, and she soon achieved the rank of bosun. Her parents encouraged her to accept more public roles and agreed to her becoming President of the National Society for the Prevention of Cruelty to Children (NSPCC). There was time for a little socialising too. A series of parties at Windsor called 'clump parties' helped the girls get to know the officers and made life lighter for everyone. 'The Queen was marvellous at getting the Grenadier Guards to send officers up and they had little dance parties and things,' recalled cousin Margaret.[1] There was an equal number of young men and women, and they played games like sardines (the proximity with another person helping nicely to break the ice) and enjoyed treasure hunts. The Duchess of Kent sometimes came over too. 'She was so glamorous,' Margaret said, 'and always that faintly foreign tinge to her words which made it seem very attractive.' She and her daughter Princess Alexandra were given a ground floor suite of rooms, but it was said that 'they'd more often be seen knitting in the sitting room rather than joining in'.[2]

Elizabeth's seventeenth birthday was celebrated in late March with a dance at Windsor. Most of the guests were British and American officers, many from the Grenadier Guards. A well-known band played and dancing went on until 4:00 a.m. when Elizabeth was seen dancing the last waltz. It was a lovely and lively occasion, one that was especially exciting because of the war, an evening when relationships were formed and friendships furthered. Of Elizabeth's male friends, one party-goer whom Myra Butter remembers fondly was Rupert Nevill, son of the Marquess of Abergavenny and an officer in the Life Guards. There was Patrick Plunket in the Irish Guards, who succeeded to the family title as 7th Baron Plunket at the age of fifteen when his parents were killed in an air crash. Three years older than Elizabeth, he had an irreverent sense of humour and was often said to be the brother she never had. In 1948, he would become equerry to the King and, after Elizabeth's coronation, Deputy Master of her Household. Mabell Airlie's grandson, David Ogilvy, was another old friend; his younger brother, Angus, would marry Princess Alexandra.

Then there were those who were regarded as potential suitors, at least by Elizabeth's parents. Hugh Fitzroy (Lord Euston) was said to be the Queen's favourite and headed a list of so-called 'flirts'. Seven years older, he was heir to the dukedom of Grafton. The family seat was Euston Hall in Norfolk, which gave its name to London's Euston Road and Euston Station, built on land acquired by an ancestor. Tall and good-looking, Hugh was one of the Grenadier Guards at Windsor and one of those who lunched with the Princesses. Later in 1943 he was appointed ADC to the Viceroy of India, but it did not stop speculation. In December, reports appeared in Britain from the United States that an announcement of Elizabeth's engagement would be made the following year. The lucky man was said to be either Hugh or Charles Manners, 10th Duke of Rutland. Charles was another Grenadier, whose mother was the Queen's close friend Kathleen, 'Kakoo', Dowager Duchess of Rutland. Their family seat was Belvoir Castle in Leicestershire.

When the King's Assistant Private Secretary, Sir Eric Mieville, heard the reports, he formally announced that he was not prepared to comment. Years later, as Duke of Grafton, Hugh was asked if he had

'Lilibet' in 1943

ever considered marrying Elizabeth: 'Good Lord, no!' He said a newspaper had telephoned his father at the time to ask if the reports were true; his father had said, 'Go to hell!' and slammed the phone down.[3] After all, flirting with the Heiress Presumptive was one thing; marrying into the royal family was quite another. In 1946 Hugh married into the Smith banking dynasty. As for Charles Manners, Martin Charteris, later Elizabeth's Assistant Private Secretary, said he 'was certainly very fond of her'. However, 'evidently he made a pass at her, which greatly offended her. I once asked her whether he had done so and there was no answer, which tells its own story.'4

Another close friend was Henry Porchester, known as 'Porchey', later the 7th Earl of Carnarvon. When they met, he was twenty and already a horse owner and breeder, and Elizabeth seventeen. His father, then the Earl, knew the King: 'I think the King thought I might be the right kind of chap to accompany the Princess to the races,' said Porchey. 'I'm glad he did. We hit it off at once.'5 They remained close through their love of racing, and later he became her racing manager. He was another of the 'flirts'. Patrick Plunkett was also on the list, but although he was a stalwart dancing partner, he was what was termed 'a lifelong bachelor': a fellow Guards officer said he was 'just neutral'.6 One lady-in-waiting said that when Elizabeth liked someone, they would get 'come-hither looks, a fluttering of the eyelashes. You can't have much going on between you in a Viennese waltz, but there's the look, the pressure of the hand and, in those days, it wasn't so commonplace to want the next thing.'7

Suitors aside, Elizabeth's duties increased. In the week before her seventeenth birthday, she undertook her first public engagement entirely alone when she spent the day with the tank battalion of her Grenadier Guards in Southern Command at Andover. Dressed in a turquoise blue skirt and jacket, on which sparkled her diamond regimental brooch, and wearing a broad-brimmed hat, photographs showed her looking relaxed and happy as she walked along the lines and chatted to the men. Later she inspected a tank, climbing up to examine the turret, and asked to see it in motion.

Elizabeth's cultural education was about to expand, too, instigated by the Queen. The day after Elizabeth's inspection, she took both Princesses to an evening of poetry in aid of charity, organised by her friend Osbert Sitwell and his sister Edith, at which well-known English poets read their work. In spite of the illustrious gathering of poets such as the Poet Laureate John Masefield, T. S. Eliot and Vita Sackville-West, the event was not as successful as the Sitwells would have liked. The lectern was too big and obscured the view of the poets and impaired their voices. Walter de la Mare was too short for the lectern, another poet went on too long and had to be silenced, and when T. S. Eliot read 'London Bridge is Falling Down' from *The Waste Land* the Princesses started to giggle. Another poet, Dorothy Wellesley, was supposed to read, but she got drunk, caused a disturbance and had to be forcibly removed.[8]

A less unpredictable activity was the additional music lessons that the Princesses began to receive from Sir William Henry Harris, the organist and choirmaster of St George's Chapel. Every Tuesday evening they visited 'Doc H', as he was affectionately known, at his house in the Castle Cloisters. He talked to them about the great composers and sent them up into the organ loft while he played for them below. They learned to read musical scores and to conduct, and he introduced them to English madrigal music. Knowing how much her daughters enjoyed singing, the Queen suggested to Dr Harris that they do more of it. The result was a series of musical parties, in which the Princesses' friends joined them to sing madrigals and part-songs. Dr Harris brought in singers to reinforce his little group: four of the senior choristers from St George's, with the lower voices augmented by Etonians, Grenadier Guards and members of local choral societies. When the group reached twenty-five, they had to move out of his house into the Red Drawing Room in the castle; after the war they continued in the Bow Room at Buckingham Palace. Relaxed and informal, the choir sang only for themselves, visited occasionally by the Queen.

It was entirely fitting that in May, Elizabeth should accept the position of President of the Royal College of Music in place of the Duke of Kent. In doing so, the College, which was founded by her great-grandfather, the Prince of Wales (later Edward VII), returned to its tradition of having the heir to the Throne as its President. Elizabeth's appointment was likely to please her grandfather, who was a keen music lover, like his late wife. As a boy at Glamis, Claude and his ten younger siblings used to sing part-songs and operatic selections after dinner. When Prime Minister William Gladstone visited Glamis in 1884, he was so impressed that he asked if the youngsters might let an old man join in the singing, declaring that he had not enjoyed an evening so much for many a month.[9]

Meanwhile, the Foreign Office received from David Bowes Lyon in Washington a request that Elizabeth be allowed to make a four-minute broadcast for *Victory Hour*, the official war programme of American schools. The theme would be 'Youth under Fire', in which she would tell American students what British students were doing in the war.[10] No such broadcast took place: perhaps it was deemed too didactic or too political. However, the Queen agreed to broadcast to the women of the Empire, which would be heard in America too. She spoke of the valuable war work that women were doing, but also of the importance of looking after the family home, now and later: 'These men . . . are counting on us at all times to be steadfast and faithful. . . . We women as homemakers have a great part to play in re-building family life as soon as the war ends.'

The family had a tense time in June when the King flew to Algiers to visit his troops, a trip made possible by the defeat of the Germans and Italians in North Africa. A risky undertaking, it was kept secret; he travelled incognito as 'General Lyon'. His heavy programme included visiting the brave and battered island of Malta, to whose residents and garrison he had earlier awarded the George Cross. He fell sick with the rest of his party with 'desert tummy', and lost nearly a stone in weight. However, it was hugely successful, his troops enthusiastically expressing their pleasure at his visit.

In the King's absence the Queen acted as Counsellor of State. They missed him terribly. Lilibet had been in bed with a cold, she told him in a letter, Margaret had helped the Sea Rangers cook their lunch, and she had taken them to see a new ballet called *The Quest* at Sadlers Wells, which they loved. She also took Elizabeth to her first 'Prom' concert at the Royal Albert Hall, 'a good Bach/ Handel programme', wrote Lascelles, who accompanied them. 'Princess Elizabeth obviously enjoyed the concert and I think may be really fond of music.'[11]

After the King's return, changes took place in the Royal Household that would have a very positive effect. Hardinge, who had gone with him, resigned as his Principal Private Secretary. Relations had been deteriorating since Hardinge's opposition to Chamberlain's appeasement policy. Lascelles had come to realise that Hardinge and the King were 'temperamentally incompatible' and 'rapidly driving each other crazy'. Lascelles confronted Hardinge over an issue and resignation followed: the official reason given was his ill-health. Lascelles accepted the King's invitation to replace him. Helen accused the Queen of having something to do with it, but she rebuked her for thinking she wished Alec ill. 'I am truly devoted to you & Alec and eternally grateful for all your marvellous loyalty,' she wrote.[12] Queen Mary was pleased and thought the atmosphere at Windsor had 'changed completely'.[13] Elizabeth remained friends with their daughter Winifred and her sister, as did the Queen with Helen, although later they would cross swords over a book Helen wanted to write.

Elizabeth's cultural programme continued, and she carried out more wartime duties. At Buckingham Palace the Princesses helped the Queen greet three hundred members of the Women's Land Army, an important civilian organisation of women who worked the land in wartime in the absence of the men. Specially chosen members from different parts of Britain were invited to a tea party to celebrate the WLA's fourth birthday. A Wiltshire land girl, Gwen Robinson, wrote of the thrilling experience for an ordinary person of going to the Palace[14]:

> *I must confess I was getting 'quivvery' with anticipation. When we arrived at Buckingham Palace we were shown through the main door, where ushers and attendants were on either side . . . Just inside a regimental band was playing in full swing.*
>
> *I was eagerly scanning the hall and room into which we were passing. It was gorgeous – great, marble pillars and ceilings, all inlaid with pure gold, great hanging oil paintings of deceased Royalty. . . . And there were great, thick carpets which were absolutely like velvet to walk on. . . . Passing through two great doors we found . . . first the usher, who took our cards and read our individual names out, and then Her Majesty Queen Elizabeth, and, to our great delight, Princesses Elizabeth and Margaret Rose.*
>
> *We then had to drop a small 'bob' curtsey to them and shake hands. As soon as we saw them we forgot they were the highest ladies of the land – they are so perfectly natural and have such a wonderful way of putting anyone at ease.*

Back in the hall, food was laid out 'on tremendously long tables' and waiters poured tea into royal-crested china.

The Queen and the Princesses were among the girls laughing and chatting and you can guess how thrilled we girls of Wiltshire were when we were introduced for the second time, and the Queen asked us about our work, telling us how happy we looked and how proud we could be of our great part in the national war effort. I have never regretted joining the Land Army, but it wasn't until that moment that I realised just how glad I was that I joined it.

That kind of royal recognition and personal touch meant a great deal to people.

By now the tide seemed to be turning on the war front, with an increasing number of Allied victories. However, as the Queen told her brother, 'what a beastly time it is for people growing up. Lilibet meets young guards at Windsor & then they get killed & it is horrid for someone so young.'[15] Elizabeth always wrote to the mothers of dead officers, telling them how much the family had enjoyed his being at Windsor and what they used to talk about. At least one person in her life was managing to cheat death. In July, Philip was heading towards Sicily on *Wallace* when it took a hit from an enemy plane, and it was clear they were to be that night's target. Philip had the idea of fashioning a fake raft to make it look like the flaming debris of *Wallace* floating in the water, then they moved the ship away quickly and cut the engine. When the aircraft returned, it began bombing the raft. Later a shipmate, Harry Hargreaves, said, 'Prince Philip saved our lives that night. It had been marvellously quick thinking.'[16] At Malta shortly afterwards he saw his uncle Dickie, whose destroyer was in port with some captured Italian generals on board. He was about to be made Commander-in-Chief of the new South-East Asia Command, a stellar appointment proposed by Churchill and approved by the King.

His nephew was due to have leave that Christmas, and having 'nowhere particular to go',[17] he was invited to stay at Windsor with his cousin David. He was also going to watch the girls' pantomime, *Aladdin*.

Elizabeth was thrilled, saying excitedly, 'Who *do* you think is coming to see us act, Crawfie?' Philip managed to get to the third performance of five, after being confined to bed in Claridges hotel with flu, and sat in the front row with the King and Queen and his cousin Marina, whose two eldest children were in the cast of forty. Crawfie found Philip 'greatly changed. It was a grave and charming young man who sat there, with nothing of the rather bumptious boy I had first known about him now.'[18]

Philip laughed at all the bad jokes: as the Queen said during rehearsals, 'all the oldest jokes are being resurrected & used boldly once more'. Although the story was Chinese, 'some dreadfully Japanese touches are creeping in, including such atrocities as Nip off to Nippon!'[19] Elizabeth played Aladdin and made her entrance by popping out of a laundry basket. She wore long white silk trousers with a Chinese kimono shirt, and later changed into a suit of red and gold jacket and satin shorts, with silk stockings and buckled shoes. Margaret, playing Aladdin's girlfriend, Princess Roxana, wore the more feminine costume, but she looked small and plump next to her sister. Although Elizabeth was again in a male role, Philip could not have failed to notice her now voluptuous figure, or her features which had so impressed Cecil Beaton when he photographed her just weeks earlier: 'the dazzlingly fresh complexion, the clear regard from the glass-blue eyes, and the gentle, all-pervading sweetness of her smile'.[20] When she tap danced and sang, 'In My Arms', there was big round of applause, and she was said to have 'acted well and sang with plenty of confidence'.[21] But it was Philip's presence that gave her the greatest pleasure. Crawfie 'had never known Lilibet more animated. There was a sparkle about her none of us had ever seen before.'[22]

On Christmas Day, the King made his broadcast, proud of the victories that had been achieved that year but aware that much still lay ahead. At lunch, Philip joined an intimate group of the King, Queen and Princesses and four Grenadier Guards who could not return home for the holiday. Elizabeth told Crawfie, 'We had a very gay time, with a film, dinner parties and dancing to the gramophone'. On Boxing Day evening, they were joined by David Milford Haven and members of the Royal Household, including Lascelles: 'After dinner and some charades, they rolled back the carpet in the crimson drawing room, turned on the gramophone and frisked and capered away till near 1am.'[23] The King too always enjoyed himself on such family occasions and wore 'his tuxedo made of Inverness tartan, which is a source of much pleasure to him'.[24] To his diary he confided, 'Let us hope that next Christmas will see the end of the War.'[25]

After his stay, Philip wrote to the Queen to thank her, and in a characteristic show of self-awareness he said he hoped his behaviour 'did not get out of hand'. A young man of strong opinions, he knew the Queen was another strong character; they seem to have talked about what he should do next if he had the choice, and he told her that she was right, that he would stay in Britain rather than go to America. He asked her whether he might add Windsor to the places he could stay, along with Broadlands (the Mountbattens' home), and Coppins: 'that may give you some small idea of how much I appreciated the few days you were kind enough to let me spend with you'.[26] Elizabeth looked forward to many more.

CHAPTER 17

Rumours (1944)

Philip's stay at Windsor proved to be a turning point, but it did not mean his girlfriends had suddenly disappeared from the scene. He had given Osla Benning a Christmas present, a book by the nineteenth-century caricaturist, George Cruickshank. However, although he had seen her during the last year – she was flat-sharing with Sylvia Heywood, and he would go to their parties and crash on the sofa – they had started to drift apart. Another girlfriend was Gina Wernher, Myra's older sister, dark and beautiful. Gina said she loved being with Philip, a close friend of the family, for he was 'marvellously clever and amusing', but, 'We were best friends and we went out together . . . but nothing really serious happened.'[1]

In early 1944, Queen Mary heard a rumour that the King of Greece was planning to suggest his cousin Philip as a possible suitor. Queen Mary considered Philip very suitable in some ways. She had already told Mabell Airlie that she thought him 'very handsome . . . and seems intelligent too. I should say he has plenty of common sense.' Philip was also on her wartime list for woollen scarves and pullovers: 'I believe she knitted him several,' said Lady Airlie. 'She certainly followed his career in the Navy with interest, for she talked of it when I was at Badminton.'[2] Queen Mary was also pleased that he was the grandson of Britain's First Sea Lord whom George V had held in such high regard.

The King confirmed the rumour and said he considered Philip intelligent, with 'a good sense of humour and thinks about things in the right way'.[3] However, according to Queen Mary, he wondered if 'an Englishman through and through, might not be more popular with the people of Britain'. Also, he and the Queen considered Elizabeth 'too young for that now, as she has never met any young men of her own age'.[4] Nevertheless, they did nothing to discourage the friendship.

Another issue arose early that year. Elizabeth would be eighteen soon, and the question had been asked during 1943 as to whether she would receive the title of Princess of Wales. The idea had been gathering momentum in Wales, where a Town Council petitioned Churchill on the subject, saying it would do much to help Anglo-Welsh relations. The Welsh Parliamentary Party joined the campaign. Now Lascelles wanted a decision made 'before an undignified controversy erupts in Parliament and Press'[5]; not for nothing was he sounding out views for having a 'professional, whole-time 'public relations officer' at Buckingham Palace'.[6] The King consulted Churchill.

Several points had to be considered. The title of Prince of Wales had only ever been held by an Heir Apparent, and Elizabeth could only ever be Heiress *Presumptive*. However, that did not dispose of the question of whether it was possible to call her Heir, even if only Presumptive, and to give her the title the Welsh wanted. Experts found a record suggesting that Henry VIII had considered that whichever of his daughters was heir to the Throne would be called Princess of Wales. The King did not like the idea, saying it was a family matter, but he said the Dominion MPs could suggest a Dominion title if they wanted.

The Cabinet eventually agreed with the King, and on 12 February 1944, the official announcement said that he would not be changing the Princess's title. As he said to Queen Mary, 'How could I create Lilibet the Princess of Wales when it is the recognised title of the name of the Prince of Wales? Her own name is so nice and what name would she be called by when she marries, I want to know.'[7]

The war blasted on. A week later there was an air raid on London in the middle of the night, heavier than any since the Blitz. The reverberations reached Windsor and woke everyone in the castle, during what turned out to be a heavy week for enemy raids. A bomb was dropped in Pall Mall, blasting a corner of St James's Palace and injuring several people, including the Hardinges' recently married daughter, Winifred; they were all taken over to Buckingham Palace, where beds were found for them.[8] Marlborough House also lost many windows.

The year was another of 'firsts' for Elizabeth. In March she went on her first official tour with her parents, spending two days on a military inspection tour in Yorkshire. It was followed by her first civic tour when, as a gesture to the Welsh people following the King's decision, he and the Queen took her with them on their two-day tour of the mining and industrial areas of South Wales. Elizabeth received a warm welcome everywhere and was given the unofficial title 'Ein Tywysoges', meaning 'our own Princess', while the Press enthused about the tour strengthening the link between Wales and the royal family.

Elizabeth was set to become one of the King's Counsellors of State on her eighteenth birthday, enabling her to carry out state business when the need arose. Originally the law prevented her from becoming a Counsellor until she was twenty-one, but her father wanted her to have 'every opportunity of gaining experience in the duties which would fall upon her' when she became queen.[9] He had asked Parliament to amend the Regency Act 1937, and the resulting bill became law in November 1943.

She may have had adult responsibilities, but Elizabeth still enjoyed messing about. At Easter, the family stayed at Appleton, from where the Queen told Queen Mary that 'Luckily Bertie is well & he and the children are out all day on their bicycles & seem most happy. They are rat hunting this afternoon – what a sport!'[10] She also told her about the 'very nice temporary equerry from the RAF called Townsend' they had with them. A brave Battle of Britain fighter pilot, Group Captain Peter Townsend was handsome, charming and, at that time, married. They could not know that he would later divorce and find fame of a very different kind when he and Margaret fell in love. Townsend later wrote that when he met the sisters, he found Elizabeth shy, sometimes to the point of gaucheness, and Margaret as unremarkable as one might expect a fourteen-year-old girl to be, except for her dark blue eyes and her love of attention when she made a wisecrack.

Back in London as a pre-birthday treat, the King and Queen took the Princesses to the Palace Theatre, to see *Something in the Air*, a musical starring Cicely Courtneidge who had been entertaining the armed forces abroad. Among the inevitable birthday eulogies, one newspaper told of how, when Elizabeth was young, her future was never discussed with her. However, one day Queen Mary took her to the theatre to see *Peter Pan*, and afterwards, as the little Princess walked behind her to the waiting car, she was heard to say, 'When I am Queen, I shall always get in first.'[11]

The Times coincidentally continued the theatrical theme in its tribute: 'Without any "building up" of an entrance, a new character has slipped demurely upon the stage of public life. She has few lines to speak at present, but in a later act she will have many.' The piece praised her academic abilities and her riding and swimming skills, although her status did not save her from the sexism of the day: 'Like some others of her sex, she is no mathematician.' At the same time it acknowledged the 'exceptional power' she would have to influence the tradition into which she was born.

It also highlighted the unique and unnatural position in which the Princess was placed compared with others of her age: 'She appreciates and shows that it is a privilege, which few girls of 18 enjoy, to listen to those who bear the burden and possess the experience of great affairs.' But she had not found it easy. Lack of contact with people her own age did not help: 'War has a little narrowed her social contacts.' Elizabeth's contacts with older people were being watched with special interest. Her parents' guests were 'the active leaders of nation and empire', but mixing with them was 'something of a test . . . [she has] a native shyness, which has cost some effort to overcome.' Most importantly, however, in the midst of world turmoil, 'Princess Elizabeth stands for the generation that will inherit the coming victory; she will live in a new world, and will be the representative of those who have to mould it.'[12]

One newspaper recognised that while her birthday was a time for congratulations, it was 'also for sympathetic understanding. The Princess's life has been a happy one. But no one will be so foolish as to think that it has been, or can be, an easy one.'[13] And for the benefit of the millions of children who were fascinated by the sisters, at least one author used her birthday to remind them that 'Princess Elizabeth and Princess Margaret have had to work jolly hard at their lessons, the same as you have had to do.'[14]

On the day itself, celebrations were low-key. The King wrote in his diary, 'Lilibet's 18th Birthday. The Changing of the Guard took place in the quadrangle and we made it an occasion for her birthday. Col. J. Prescott, handed her the Colonel's Standard, which will be used on her future inspections. . . . We gave a family lunch to which Mama came.

It was a lovely hot day. L. can now act as a Counsellor of State.'[15] The lunch was an intimate affair with Queen Mary, the Gloucesters, the Princess Royal and her husband Lord Harewood, and Princess Marina. The Queen gave Elizabeth one of her own small diamond tiaras as a present, and the King gave her a bracelet. Thanking Lady Desborough for 'the beautiful autograph book' which she was 'looking forward to seeing . . . full of interesting people's names', Elizabeth told her, 'My eighteenth birthday was a very busy one, and I spent it amongst the family, and a great many Grenadiers and old friends.'[16]

To Philip it must have seemed as though everyone was 'getting hitched' that year. In March, his cousin Princess Alexandra of Greece and Denmark married the exiled King Peter of Yugoslavia in London, where they had met; she and her mother were both in exile. Philip was close to Alexandra, and after he left Gordonstoun, he had stayed with her and his widowed aunt in Venice, where he had met Cobina Wright. Alexandra had noticed how 'blondes, brunettes and redhead charmers' all came Philip's way and he had 'gallantly, and I think quite impartially squired them all'.[17] Philip could not attend the wedding, but Marina was there.

Then in the spring, Osla Benning got engaged to a young diplomat, although it did not last, and in 1946 she would marry another. Philip became godfather to their first son in 1947, and he and Osla would remain friends until her early death in 1974. Her engagement was followed in August by Gina Wernher's. Her fiancé was Lieutenant Colonel Harold 'Bunny' Philips of the Coldstream Guards. The announcement came as a great shock to the Mountbatten family. For years Bunny had been Edwina's lover, a relationship which Lord Mountbatten tolerated: as Pamela said, 'Quite simply, he made my mother easier to be around'.[18] He was tall and 'thrillingly handsome. . . . Bunny brought great joy to our lives and I loved him deeply.' There were times 'when my father and my sister feared [Edwina] might drown herself'. She did not, and channelled her energy in very positive ways during the rest of the war and in India. Gina and Bunny married in October that year.

Shortly before Elizabeth's birthday Philip was posted to a shipyard in Newcastle-upon-Tyne, to help oversee the completion of the building of HMS *Whelp*, a new destroyer on which he was going to serve. While he waited, he gave his first interview in Britain to a local reporter, Olga Franklin; her editor was adamant she should talk to the young Prince, although the feature had nothing to do with him and Elizabeth. The piece began, 'Very few of the workers in a North-East shipyard are aware that the ash-blond first lieutenant RN, who travels by bus to work among them each day, is a Royal Prince.... Prince Philip, who has the looks of a typical Prince of a Hans Anderson fairy tale, will certainly have been noticed by many a girl worker at the shipyard.' He explained his background and said he had last seen his home in Athens in 1941. 'The Prince was amused at my suggestion that he might find the northern accent difficult to understand,' she wrote. He told her, 'I understand the local people perfectly and I am enjoying my stay.' Clearly Philip spared her the sometimes tactless remarks for which he became known. Indeed, she 'thanked him for the good humoured and kindly way he had accepted "exposure"'.[19]

The effect Philip had on women was lustily captured by Franklin in a letter to her sister. 'I get dizzy looking at him. His beauty is so dazzling. People don't look like this, surely, in real life? . . . This Prince Philip is stunning, with hair like gold coin only paler, a sort of ash-gold; eyes of deep blue, almost violet in the electric light; tall, fine-featured, really a shockingly beautiful figure in naval uniform.'[20] Meanwhile, his grandmother Victoria, at Kensington Palace, had heard marriage rumours about him and Elizabeth but although she had 'touched on it' with Philip recently, as she told Mountbatten, she had found him 'not inclined to confide in me', so she did not press it.[21]

Elizabeth meanwhile was mixing once more with those 'active leaders of nations'. On 1 May, she attended her first official dinner, held for the Dominions Prime Ministers who were in London at the time. Elizabeth was seated between General Smuts of the Union of South Africa and Mr Mackenzie King of the Dominion of Canada. It was shortly followed by her first independent public appearance in the City of London, when she attended the Diamond Jubilee meeting of the NSPCC to give a short speech as President. On the lighter side, she and Margaret entered their first trap-driving competition at Windsor Horse Show and Gymkhana and were delighted when they each won a prize in separate categories – they had had plenty of practice driving around Sandringham. Elizabeth's social life started to get underway, although at that stage, it was largely limited to friends' cocktail parties.

As the preparations for the D-Day landings on 6 June were completed, the tension was immense. Churchill wanted to see the initial attack from one of the bombarding ships and suggested to the King that he go with him. However, when Lascelles heard their plans, he was appalled. He asked the King whether he was prepared to advise Princess Elizabeth on the choice of her first Prime Minister should he and Churchill be killed simultaneously. Lascelles also pointed out the predicament the commander of the ship would face in battle when he knew he had such important passengers. The King took his point and tried to persuade Churchill to abandon his plan. It led to a bitter argument between them, although eventually, and very reluctantly, Churchill agreed not to go.

On the night of 6 June, the King made a moving broadcast, in which he said that 'a supreme test has to be faced. This time the challenge is not to fight to survive but to fight to win the final victory for the good cause.'[22] He called the people to 'prayer and dedication' while soldiers, sailors and airmen were fighting to liberate Europe. When the invasion proved to be progressing positively, the Cabinet agreed that the King should visit the Normandy beaches on 16 June, where he met with General Montgomery.

After the D-Day landings, Hitler's revenge was swift. Elizabeth's cousin, George Lascelles, was taken prisoner as another of the *Prominente*, and on the King's return on 18 June, a tragedy happened close to home. Hitler unleashed two new weapons on Britain, first the pilotless V-1 flying bomb, the doodlebug, then the V-2 rocket. As morning service was being held in the Guards' Chapel, a doodlebug fell on it, killing sixty-three servicemen and women and fifty-eight civilians; a hundred more were wounded. Among the dead were the sister of the Queen's friend, Arthur Penn, who discovered her body when he went to help clear up; and Captain Ivan Cobbold, whom the King knew from shooting parties and whom Lascelles had seen just the day before. Ivan and his wife Lady Blanche, a daughter of the 9th Duke of Devonshire, had just celebrated their Silver Wedding anniversary. Little wonder that the Queen felt moved to write to 'Darling Lilibet', telling her of 'one or two things in case I get 'done in' by the Germans!' She was sure she had left all her own things to be divided between her and Margaret, 'but I am sure you will give her anything suitable later on – such as Mrs Greville's pearls, as you will have the Crown ones.' In any case, she knew Lilibet would 'always do the right thing, & remember to keep your temper & your word & be loving'.[23]

The Princesses had their own sighting of a V-1 when they were with Crawfie in Windsor Great Park with the Guides. Crawfie and the Guide Captain spotted it coming and made everyone lie down. Crawfie threw herself over Margaret, who was next to her, and they watched it pass over them. It eventually dropped on the Windsor Race Course a few miles away. They were shaken by the explosion and Crawfie said that around that time, the Princesses 'showed signs of strain. Conversation would break off and I would know they were listening.' The doodlebugs were 'so utterly inhuman, like being chased by a robot'.[24]

Now Elizabeth needed her own household. It began in July with the appointment of her first lady-in-waiting, Lady Mary Palmer. Until then Elizabeth had been accompanied on formal engagements and assisted in correspondence by her mother's ladies, but they were all much older. Young women nearer her own age, who could be friends too, were sought. It was a requirement that they be married, and although Mary was not, she was engaged to be married in November.[25] Aged twenty-three, she was already known to the family, as was always the case in such appointments: she had 'come from good stock which has served its country well'.[26] Her father, Lord Selbourne, worked with David Bowes Lyon in the PWE, and her mother was the daughter of the 1st Viscount Ridley, a former Home Secretary. Mary had attended the prestigious St Paul's Girls' School and had been working in a day nursery in London among refugees from Gibraltar; that work was coming to an end. Both the King and Queen liked her.

Soon Elizabeth had her chance to act as a Counsellor of State, when the King left on a ten-day visit to his troops in Italy. 'Lilibet and I have signed a few papers dismissing people from the Services for various 'orrible offences!'[27] the Queen told the King. They also signed the Royal Assent to several new Acts of Parliament and, significantly for Elizabeth, on 1 August she received with the Queen an Address from the House of Commons and replied on behalf of the King.

Rumours about Elizabeth and Philip continued. Philip sometimes stayed with Princess Marina at Coppins when he had leave. Even his mother Alice, living in Nazi-occupied Greece, heard that, at Easter, he had paid 'an interesting visit' while at Coppins and had lunched 'with a certain young lady & her parents'. In July, Lady Desborough's cousin, Sir Michael Duff, was staying with the Elphinstones at Beaconsfield. At the same time Philip and Elizabeth were staying with Marina. Elizabeth later said, 'I spent a weekend at Coppins while he was there, but that was the only time I saw him except at Windsor.'[28] The Elphinstones invited them all to dinner. Duff thought Prince Philip

CHARMING and I consider [him] just right to perform the role of Consort for Princess Elizabeth. He has everything in his favour, he is good looking, intelligent, a good sailor, and he speaks ONLY English, the latter quality most admirable and necessary when one considers the point of view of the man in the street, who has an innate prejudice against any language but his own . . . I gather he goes to Windsor a lot. He is 24 and ripe for the job. But whether he likes P.E. or she him, I can't say.[29]

In Europe, light started to appear at last at the end of the long dark tunnel, and in August the liberation of Paris began. London was still suffering, however. The family escaped to Balmoral. During a week of fine weather and quiet, the Princesses soon had 'very bright eyes and pink cheeks again – the life at Windsor is rather trying right now, but they are really rather good about it all.'[30] Certainly Scotland felt a million miles from the war. Earlier the King had 'angelically' lent Birkhall to the Hardinges' son George for his honeymoon, where 'that part of Scotland is untouched by war and there's a great deal to eat!'[31]

Scotland also had the honour of Elizabeth's first official visit. In Edinburgh, attended by her aunt May Elphinstone, she accepted purses of money for the YMCA and made a speech. With the Queen she inspected a training centre of the Auxiliary Territorial Service (ATS), the women's branch of the British Army formed during the war. Not an obviously thrilling engagement, but Elizabeth was very interested, because she had wanted to join the ATS since she was sixteen. After much cajoling of her father, he had finally relented, and she would join early the following year.

Some visits still had to be kept secret, including Elizabeth's first launching of a ship. It was a significant event for her when, on 30 November, she went to Clydebank where the most powerful battleship in the world, HMS *Vanguard*, lay ready to be launched in the shipyard of John Brown and Company. For the first time the Princess's personal standard was flown from the flagstaff. She played her part well, smashing the traditional bottle against the prow and praying for good luck to the ship and all those who sailed in her. The coming of victory meant that the ship would not be needed for battle after all, and her first important service would be to take the royal family to South Africa in 1947.

While news in Europe continued positively, at home more sadness lay in store. The Queen and Princesses spent two days at Glamis visiting the Earl, who had been suffering from flu and was very weak. He was eighty-nine and had 'always been so active & virile that one could not wish him to live as an invalid', the Queen told Queen Mary.[32] She was intending to return to Glamis the following evening but early the next day, 7 November, he died. Crawfie said it was the only time Lilibet ever sought comfort from her. His son David could not justify a journey from the United States in wartime, but Rachel attended the funeral. The ceremony was as simple as the Earl would have wished. His coffin was carried by foresters and gamekeepers to a farm lorry drawn by two horses, and the procession to the burial ground was accompanied by the plaintive sound of four pipers from the Black Watch. The Princesses sent a wreath of white and pink carnations and a card that read, 'In loving memory of darling Grandfather, Lilibet and Margaret.'

Patrick Bowes Lyon was now 15th Earl of Strathmore and Kinghorne, but Glamis Castle stood empty, at least temporarily. Telling David about the funeral, the Queen said 'Pat' was determined to live at Glamis, for he seemed to love it. However, his wife Dorothy, with whom he lived in Surrey, was either reluctant or unable to move and had not attended the funeral due to illness. Patrick had not been in good health, either, resigning his commission with the Black Watch earlier that year, and he and Dorothy had suffered much sadness when their son John was killed.

Rather wistfully, the Queen said, 'Perhaps he will become more ordinary and easy when he is "himself" at Glamis.'[33]

Philip also suffered a loss when on 3 December his father, Prince Andrea, died in Monte Carlo, aged sixty-two. Philip's parents had not seen each other since 1939, although Alice received sporadic news of him. She knew he had been living for some years with a beautiful French Countess, but did not hide the fact that she would have liked to make a fresh start with him. Philip was on HMS *Whelp* in the Indian Ocean when he received the news via a naval message, which Alice managed to get Dickie to send. Even though Philip had become estranged from his father, his friend Mike Parker said he really loved him and the news was a great shock. There was no way that Philip could leave the ship for the funeral in Nice. When his ship stopped at Colombo, he was able to join the Mountbattens, who were lodging up in the hills.

That year Elizabeth had no handsome prince to perform for in their Christmas pantomime, which was 'Old Mother Red Riding Boots.' For once she played a woman, Lady Christina Sherwood, and emerged from a bathing machine on 'Brighton beach' wearing a bathing costume of the 1890s. Margaret, playing the Hon. Lucinda Fairfax, sang a solo and as usual received particular praise, but both girls were said to dance well in the ballet scene, choreographed by Miss Vacani. Philip may not have missed much. Lascelles, who usually thought the pantomimes very well done, found this one 'too long and the funny parts were not funny'. However, he thought it was 'redeemed' by the seaside scene and its ballet.[34]

As the King delivered his Christmas message, his wife and daughters sat in the room with him for the first time: he wanted to emphasise the idea that Christmas is a family festival. In a message that now could convey real hope, he said, 'The darkness daily grows less and less. The lamps that the Germans put out all over Europe, first in 1914 and then in 1939, are being slowly rekindled.'[35] It was the last Christmas of the war.

CHAPTER 18

Freedom (1945)

In January 1945, as Philip operated a rescue mission by HMS *Whelp* for the Allied victims of a Japanese bomber, Elizabeth made her second broadcast, this time in French, to thank the children of Belgium for toys they sent after their liberation. Margaret was supposed to do it, but she was ill with mumps, the first one in the Royal Household to catch it. The speech emphasised the familiar notion of self-sacrifice for the greater good: 'It is so very hard to part with one's toys – I know that from experience,' Elizabeth said, 'but you will believe me when I say that, for that very reason, your presents are all the more valuable to us.' She hoped that the personal bond between their countries, 'created by our common hardships, will . . . help us to build a better world'.[1]

At last she joined the Auxiliary Territorial Service (ATS). The Queen told Queen Mary, 'I think it will be a good thing for her to have a little experience from the inside into how a women's service is run. She will learn something about the inside of a car as well, which is always useful. The course takes about six weeks, I believe, & she can do it by day.'[2] In March, Elizabeth began at No. 1 MT Training Centre at Camberley, where she was gazetted to an honorary commission as Second Subaltern. Although the Palace announced her commission, her whereabouts had to be kept secret. She had never driven a car so she began her course – the theory and practice of mechanics – with a stationary car on blocks. As her first lesson began, she did not even know where the clutch was, yet in a short time she learned to drive a heavy Bedford lorry, then a Wolseley staff car, and became very efficient at stripping and reassembling an engine. When Margaret saw her sister driving a large field ambulance, Crawfie said her resentment at being confined to the schoolroom 'burst out once again', and she complained that she was 'born too late'.

Elizabeth was thrilled to wear her uniform, feeling that she was properly a part of the war effort, and pleased that in most respects she was treated exactly the same as the other girls, expected to salute her senior officers and subject to the same discipline. It was unfortunate that she went down badly with mumps after Margaret, which left her run down, and with the course itself being demanding, she got overtired and had to take time off. That was where the difference lay between the Princess and the other girls: there cannot have been many trainees whose Commander made enquiries of their well-being every day via their governess, and who were allowed to sleep in their own homes rather than in the barracks.

Crawfie took Margaret to tea in Elizabeth's mess, an experience which Margaret enjoyed, seeing all the 'hearty lady officers' drinking sherry and smoking cigarettes. Crawfie was determined to distance her beloved charge from such conduct: 'Lilibet has never smoked and does not do so now. Nor has she ever adopted the fashion of blood-red nails but paints hers only a very pale pink.'[3] Her presence there was only revealed when the King and Queen visited, and their daughter, dressed in overalls, proudly showed them how to put a disabled lorry into working order. After driving Commander Wellesley around London to the Palace, wearing her 'L' plate, the officer pronounced the Princess 'a very good and extremely considerate driver'.[4] However, as Dermot Morrah drily remarked, 'whether the fact that she found it necessary to drive twice round Piccadilly Circus on the way was due to high spirits or to a less than absolute mastery of the roundabout system has not been determined by an absolute authority'.[5] Elizabeth was soon wearing the three stars of a Junior Commander. She told Winifred Hardinge, 'My short time with the ATS was a great experience and I had a wonderful insight into the working of the transport side of the service.'[6]

Back at the Palace, arrangements were made for her to have her own suite of rooms, together with a footman and a housemaid. Her household expanded with her second lady-in-waiting. Mrs Vicary Gibbs, born Jean Frances Hambro,[7] was three years older than Elizabeth and already a widow. In September 1944 her husband, a Captain in the Grenadier Guards, was killed in action. He was twenty-three and Jean twenty-one. She was left with their four-month-old daughter; their first child had died at two months. Happily the following year Jean would marry the Princesses' cousin, Andrew Elphinstone: she met him at the Palace, where he was now lodging with his sister Margaret, as it was convenient for their work. Andrew and Margaret were given a self-contained apartment on the second floor, which was 'lovely, very ritzy'.[8] The Queen may have been their aunt, but it did not save Margaret from censure from the Master of the Household, Sir Piers Leigh, who told her off for putting their milk bottles on the window ledge to cool, in the absence of a fridge. He said it defaced 'the architectural purity of the Palace facade', but as the Palace had been bombed nine times, Margaret thought he might have had more to worry about.[9]

On 13 April came the shocking news of the sudden death of President Roosevelt. The King ordered a week's Court mourning and sent a message of condolence to his widow, saying, 'In him, humanity has lost a great figure and we have lost a true and honoured friend.' A Memorial Service was held in St Paul's Cathedral, attended by all the royal family. Ambassador John Winant elegantly read the lesson, but Churchill broke into tears during prayers. Roosevelt was automatically succeeded by the little-known Harry Truman. If he had lived a little longer he would have learned of the final events that led to victory. On 28 April Mussolini was executed, and on the thirtieth Hitler committed suicide.

On 7 May, the *Prominente*, who included Winant's son, were picked up safely by the United States 7th Army: 'After tea saw John and George, who flew back today,' wrote Elizabeth in her diary about her cousins. 'John just the same.'[10] And then came the glorious confirmation of the unconditional surrender of the German armies to the Western Allies and to Russia. An official announcement told everyone to expect broadcasts the following day from the Prime Minister and the King, and said the next two days were to be public holidays.

Tuesday 8 May, VE Day, was fine and warm after a night of thunderstorms. At 3:00 p.m. Churchill broadcast the official pronouncement of the end of the war. As he made his way on foot with his Cabinet to a thanksgiving service, the thousands of people outside Buckingham Palace began to start cheering and shouting 'We want the King!' Immediately the royal family made the first of a series of balcony appearances. The King wore naval uniform, Elizabeth ATS, and they all looked radiantly happy. In the crowd, Noel Coward said the King and Queen were 'looking enchanting. We all roared ourselves hoarse . . . I suppose this is the greatest day in our history.'[11] When they came back out later with Churchill, the crowds grew even noisier. Celebrations started all over the country.

Even the Princesses were allowed to let their hair down. Just after Roosevelt's death, the King had shown sympathy with Elizabeth's lack of a social life when he let her attend a party held by the Countess of Selbourne, 'sensibly ruling that it would be an unnecessary deprivation for [Elizabeth] to stay at home on account of Court mourning', said Lascelles. 'I am very sure that *his* father and grandfather would unhesitatingly have decided in the opposite sense!'[12] On VE Day, Elizabeth benefitted again from her father's fond indulgence: 'Poor darlings, they have never had any fun yet', he wrote in his diary.[13] After making his moving Victory broadcast, he entrusted his daughters to the care of some officers they all knew and let them join the crowds. 'This sort of freedom was unheard of as far as my cousins were concerned,' said cousin Margaret, who was with them.[14] There were about sixteen of them, accompanied by the King's Equerry, 'a very correct Royal Navy captain in a pinstripe suit, bowler hat and umbrella. No-one appeared less celebratory, perhaps because he took his guardian responsibilities too seriously.'[15] Elizabeth pulled her peaked cap over her face to disguise herself, but one of the officers insisted she dress properly. Elizabeth reluctantly put her cap on correctly and hoped she would not be recognised.

One officer unlikely to have joined them was Elizabeth's friend and rumoured beau Charles Manners, the Duke of Rutland, who had arrived home in April from the 1st Grenadiers after shooting himself in the foot. However, Porchey was there. He was dining in the Palace when the suggestion was made. 'We were mixed up in the crowd,' he recalled. 'No one recognised Princess Elizabeth or Princess Margaret, and we went round up Whitehall, up Piccadilly, into the Ritz Hotel – I used to have a little room there – and back through Hyde Park Corner, down the Mall. Everyone was very jolly, linking arms in the streets and singing Run Rabbit Run, Hang out the Washing on the Siegfried Line.'[16] They danced the Conga, newly arrived from Latin America, and the Hokey Cokey, then went back to the Palace, where the Princesses stood outside the gates and joined in the shouting for their parents to appear again. Their Majesties made eight appearances that evening, the windows remaining open until after midnight.

Although the blackout had ended in April, lighting was not yet fully restored. Plenty of raucous and bawdy behaviour was going while the Princesses were out there, and the sheer density of people was potentially dangerous. An aristocratic army wife told her husband, still in Germany, what it was like. Having downed whisky and rum, her group joined in the crowds at Whitehall. 'We had quite a good dinner and then stumbled across f.....g couples in the dark to the Palace where the King and Queen had just been out,' she wrote. 'Parliament Square was a seething mass. We actually all got on to a jeep but thank heaven – it got so bad we couldn't move, as otherwise I should have been killed.'[17] Whether or not the Princesses noticed the seedier scenes, they survived their adventure; cousin Margaret said it was 'a Cinderella moment in reverse', in which they 'could pretend that they were ordinary and unknown'. They were allowed out the next night too, Elizabeth recording on 9 May, 'Out in crowd again – Trafalgar Square, Piccadilly, Pall Mall, walked simply miles. Saw parents on balcony at 12.30 am – ate, partied, bed 3am!'[18]

Victory parades began, and on 13 May, there was a major procession to St Paul's Cathedral for a thanksgiving service, in which the family and their personal staff rode in open landaus and Queen Mary accompanied the foreign royals in stately motor cars; in Edinburgh the next day they attended a similar service. In the Palace of Westminster the Queen and Princesses sat with the King as he delivered a response to an address by both Houses of Parliament 'with a dignity and eloquence surpassing anything that I have yet heard from him', wrote Lascelles.[19]

But all was not peace. War with Japan continued. Russia and the United States had been strengthened by the war and their relationships with Britain needed to be evaluated. The King and Queen were exhausted, the King particularly looking shattered. The ever-present problem of the Duke of Windsor did not help. His tenure as Governor of the Bahamas had ended in May. He had been offered the Governorship of Bermuda in 1943 but declined it; the preferred choice was David Bowes Lyon, but Rachel did not want to move there. There was much discussion about what public service the Duke might undertake. He was still pushing to return to England and for his wife to be received.

Lascelles was seriously concerned that most options would have dangerous consequences for the King's health. Churchill advised the Duke to stay in the United States for a while, rather than returning to the South of France where life was still unsettled, so they went to Miami. In October he came to England alone and met with the King. Lascelles pressed home to the Duke that his brother had taken on 'the most difficult job in the world' so that he could marry Mrs Simpson, and Lascelles urged the Duke to stop making his constant demands. Soon afterwards, they settled in France and undertook no public duties on behalf of Britain or any other country.

Meanwhile, Elizabeth's diary became busier and her public face increasingly polished and, where necessary, inscrutable. In June she attended a council meeting of Girl Guides at Cardiff and addressed over three thousand people. The Lord Mayor publicly suggested – rather mischievously, as the King had already settled the matter – that she might be called the Princess of Wales: however, 'she made no movement and gave no indication of her thoughts'.[20] Her position as a leader of her generation was important, and she accepted appropriate appointments. She attended the Empire Youth Service in Westminster Abbey, which reminded the nation that its youth should never have to live again in days of war.

Plans were made for her to go to Brussels in July to take the salute at a Guards' parade. Her friend Winifred, whose husband was still away with the Grenadier Guards, wanted to go with her; Elizabeth told her their plans were already made but that they did not know if the parade would come off at all, owing to the state of affairs in Belgium. Elizabeth said she understood Winifred's 'very natural request. Perhaps before long the wives of people serving over in Germany will be allowed to go out to places in France & Belgium – I only hope that moment would come quicker.'[21] The visit was indeed cancelled, much to the relief of Lascelles, who feared she might be shown the famous statue, the 'Mannequin Pis',[22] which the British public might think would embarrass their Princess and thus cause an international incident.

Individuals who had helped bring the war to an end were rewarded by the King. But for Churchill, who had done so much for Britain in its darkest hour, there was great disappointment when he was defeated in the general election of July. Now the Labour Party was in power under Clement Atlee, who had been his deputy in the coalition government. The King was very disappointed; he had come to value Churchill greatly. Further concern arose in August when President Truman cut the Lend-Lease agreement, which Churchill had negotiated with Roosevelt. Now Britain would have to renegotiate its loans with the United States, and instead of looking forward to rebuilding the damaged country, a new austerity dawned. The new government immediately cut imports of food, tobacco, textiles and fuel. Such measures would demoralise Britain further and eventually lead to Labour's defeat.

Nevertheless, keen to foster the positivity of victory, the King and Queen held a dance at Windsor to celebrate both peace and the Queen's forty-fifth birthday. Earlier in the day they attended Ascot with Elizabeth and were delighted when the King's horse won its first victory. Then came news of Japan's unconditional surrender and on 15 August the Pacific War was finally over. The freedom that Elizabeth had enjoyed for VE Day was repeated, and she wrote, 'VJ Day. Out in crowd, Whitehall, Mall, St J St, Piccadilly, Park Lane, Constitution Hill, ran through Ritz. Walked miles, drank in Dorchester, saw parents twice, miles away, so many people.'[23] The next day she was out again, recording that she sang until 2:00 a.m. and went to bed at 3:00 a.m.

The one person with whom she would have loved to share her freedom was back at sea after being in Australia. After undertaking rescue missions earlier in the year, Philip went to Australia in May, where *Whelp* had a refit. It gave him an enforced three months of shore leave in Sydney and Melbourne. Philip attended parties at the house of society photographer Jo Fallon, where another guest was Robin Dalton, a divorcee and friend of David Milford Haven. Robin said Philip had two girlfriends in Australia at the end of the war, Sue Other Gee and Sandra Jacques.[24] Sue's real name was Priscilla, and in July 1941 her engagement to Lord Adam Granville

Gordon had been announced.[25] However, Gordon married someone else in 1947, so what Sue's romantic status was when she met Philip is unclear. A picture of her in 1937 shows a good-looking, dark-haired woman, who appears older than Philip, which accords with Robin's view. Robin did not know how serious their relationship was. By contrast, she said Philip had 'a very full love affair' with Sandra Jacques[26], a beautiful singer and model, and that he kept in touch with her. How accurate Robin could have been about their relationship is uncertain; even she has said that Philip was 'always cautious, emotionally tight.'[27] His friend and fellow officer, Australian Mike Parker, said he was 'quite reserved. I don't believe [he played the field].... We were young, we had fun, we had a few drinks, we might have gone dancing, but that was it. In Australia, Philip came to meet my family, my sister and their friends. There were girls galore but there was no-one special. Believe me, I guarantee it.'[28]

In late July, Philip left Sydney on *Whelp* to escort the flotilla's flagship, *Duke of York*. They were on their way to assist in the intended invasion of Japan when Hiroshima, and then Nagasaki, were bombed. *Whelp* became one of the first Allied ships to enter Japanese waters, and Philip witnessed the historic signing of the Japanese surrender on board. Philip's crew members already knew that their first lieutenant and Princess Elizabeth were 'courting' because their letters came and went from the ship's mailroom. At Buckingham Palace, Elizabeth displayed a picture of Philip, and Crawfie asked her if it was wise: after all, people would gossip. Elizabeth replaced it with one of Philip sporting a beard but Crawfie said that the 'oddly piercing, intent blue eyes were much too individual'.[29]

Although they did not see each other during that summer of 1945, there was indeed gossip, which seemed to originate abroad. In early September, Buckingham Palace was moved to say that 'nothing was known of rumours in monarchist circles in Athens linking the names of Princess Elizabeth and Prince Philip of Greece'. The rumours may have come from Philip's mother Alice, whom Harold Macmillan had found living in very humble conditions after the German occupation, during which she ran soup kitchens and orphanages. She also saved the lives of a Jewish family by sheltering them in her house and, when interrogated by the Gestapo, feigned simple-mindedness. She must have seemed an eccentric figure, which probably assisted her: she was stone deaf and always wore a grey nun's veil and gown, the dress of the religious order she founded. Her courage would bring her honours.

Philip himself had already been mentioned in the newspapers in another context. In April his sister Sophie gave an interview 'in perfect English' from her husband's family's castle near Frankfurt, which was headlined in the Press, 'HUSBAND fought for Nazis, BROTHER for the Allies.' Sophie's husband Prince Christoph of Hesse, a Luftwaffe major, had been killed in October 1943 in an Italian air crash. Sophie told the paper that her husband and her brother Philip 'had been very close to each other on opposite sides during the invasion of Sicily. She revealed that about two years ago Hitler ordered that all members of royal families serving with the German armed forces be withdrawn from the fronts and thought it might have been because the Nazis feared that some of the princes might try to set up in opposition to Hitler.'[30] The mysterious circumstances surrounding the crash had given rise to speculation that it had been ordered by Hitler; also Christoph had been rethinking his affiliations before his death. Even though such connections were not of Philip's making, they would not make life any easier for him in the next few years.

The royal family's visit to Scotland in September was the first since the end of the war, and their engagements were particularly significant. Elizabeth visited a school for children who were unable to walk, some in iron callipers at a time when polio was still a crippler. She had just recovered from an injury herself, having been thrown from her bolting horse, bruising both legs and badly gashing one. She also scratched her eye and it was fortunate, as the Queen told Queen Mary, that it was not far worse. However, she recovered sufficiently to visit the circus in Ballater, a treat attended by both Princesses and various cousins: Simon and Davina Bowes Lyons, back from their evacuation in the United States, Margaret Elphinstone and the Kent children.

The King was still exhausted, but there was no real break for him; in addition to their engagements, he had to work his way through state papers every day. The Queen worried about him, as did Lascelles: he smoked too much, was over-diligent and short-tempered, and told his brother the Duke of Gloucester that he felt 'burned out' and blamed the war. However, he took up stalking again and introduced Elizabeth to it, which took them out into the fresh air and probably amused him too: there were no clothing coupons to spare for sporting garments, so Elizabeth had to wear the plus-four trousers of one of his suits.

After their return came the happy event of the christening in Westminster Abbey of King Peter and Queen Alexandra's son, Prince Alexander, at which the King and Elizabeth were godparents. The baby was born in July in a room in Claridges hotel, which Churchill had declared to be part of Yugoslavia so that the child was not born in exile. To Peter's sorrow, in November Yugoslavia was declared a Republic by General Tito, and a new chapter of that country's history began. Armistice Day was particularly poignant, and this year Elizabeth played an active part, laying a wreath at the Cenotaph for her own generation. For the first time women were part of the Guard of Honour of the three services, and for the first time the dead of two world wars were remembered.

Happily for Elizabeth, her social life was expanding and included a pre-Christmas night out to see Noel Coward's play 'Sigh No More' at London's Piccadilly Theatre. She was dressed glamorously in a fur coat and a red crepe dress, which Crawfie had encouraged her to buy, as it 'brought out her lovely complexion.' Afterwards she had a new taste of freedom when she had supper for the first time in a West End restaurant, *The Bagatelle*. With a party that included four officers from the Life Guards, she danced a rumba and a tango to Edmondo Ros and his band. But freedom was relative. Detectives were on guard, and word always got around, so that wherever she was, she would come out to find an excited crowd waiting. It was the shape of her life to come.

Chapter 19

Courting at Last (1946)

As if to reinforce Elizabeth's increasing independence, a remaining link with her childhood was broken just two days into 1946 with the sudden death of her nanny, Alah. As usual she was with them for Christmas, which they had celebrated back in the 'Big House' at Sandringham for the first time in several years. Crawfie said that, like her royal master and mistress, Alah would never admit to feeling ill. She was sixty-two and had been with the royal family and, before that, the Elphinstones and Bowes Lyons, for forty-five years. Thanking Lady Desborough for her letter of sympathy, Elizabeth wrote, 'It was a terrible shock for us all when Alah died so suddenly, but I am very thankful that she did not suffer. She will be greatly missed by all who knew her, and for us here, she has left a great gap. She was a wonderful person in every way, and we shall not forget her.'[1] Her funeral took place in her home village of St Paul's Walden Bury, where she was buried in a grave next to the Queen's brother, John.

As the first full year of peace began, so did adjustment to post-war life. It was different for everyone. Mabell Airlie joined a cheerful and sprightly Queen Mary at Sandringham in the New Year and was pleased to learn she had settled back into life in Marlborough House. Lady Airlie had not been to Sandringham for some years and noticed that the atmosphere had changed; it was younger and less formal. Tables were covered with jigsaw puzzles. The younger members of the party, including Elizabeth, were surrounded by 'several young Guardsmen from morning till night. The radio, worked by Princess Elizabeth, blared incessantly.' No medals were worn when they met for dinner. Although she did not like the change at first, she soon changed her view. The atmosphere was 'much more friendly than in the old days . . . One sensed far more the setting of ordinary family life in this generation than the last', from Margaret's sulking 'like any fifteen-year-old girl' when the Queen told her to put on a warmer coat, to Queen Mary referring ironically to the officers as 'The Body Guard'. What she did not like was the appearance of the King: 'His face was tired and strained and he ate practically nothing. . . . He had been working on his Boxes before dinner and he was going to work again afterwards. . . . I felt a cold fear of the probability of another short reign – and a great personal love for him.'[2]

At Windsor Castle, too, the staff had to adjust. They missed not only Alah – 'a very dear friend and pillar of strength in the nursery' – but the Princesses, who had left just before the end of the war. 'Dear Princess Elizabeth . . . what a lovely character she is, so natural and human', wrote Alice Bruce. 'We miss the Princesses very much here. <u>No</u> laughter or music, <u>no</u> dogs barking & everywhere so dull. This is my first experience of the Castle being empty after five years of every tower being occupied', but she knew she had to get used to 'the new life'.[3]

Philip was also finding life dull. He had remained in the Far East with *Whelp*, bringing home prisoners of war, and arrived back in Britain in mid-January. After overseeing the ship's decommissioning, he took up an onshore post as a naval instructor at HMS *Glendower* in North Wales and complained to the Queen that he was 'still not accustomed to the idea of peace, rather fed up with everything and feeling that there was not much to look forward to'.[4] He rather grudgingly accepted the idea of continuing in the navy in peacetime. But as Elizabeth said later, it was 'great luck that he was given a shore job just then',[5] for they would be able to see more of each other.

Life in the royal houses also experienced change. Staffing had become a problem. Of those who went to war, many did not return; those who did often did not want to return to service. Newly made millionaires now paid better wages; no longer did being a member of the royal staff fulfil people's ambitions. Another issue was the continuing austerity that gripped Britain during 1946: the King expected his family and household to endure the rationing and restrictions. At least they could be assured that the Labour Party would not start to rock the monarchical boat. Although the Party had promised changes when it was elected after the war, in 1923 it had voted overwhelmingly not to make republicanism its policy, a decision attributed largely to the involvement of Edward VII and George V in social and charitable causes.

For the Princesses, post-war life revived some of the old customs. In the mornings they spent time with their parents again. The sisters still had nursery breakfast together, which would continue until Elizabeth's wedding. However, Elizabeth no longer had time for lessons. At 10:00 a.m., as Margaret began hers, Elizabeth would ring for her lady-in-waiting and deal with her correspondence. In the afternoons she often had official engagements, although she usually found time to go into the gardens with the dogs. The madrigal group the girls had enjoyed at Windsor started again, with even more members, and afterwards they enjoyed sherry and biscuits in the Bow Room.

Elizabeth was settled in her new suite. Her bedroom was pink and fawn with flowered chintz and plain white furniture. Nothing was particularly grand or ornate, but she took little interest in furnishings and was quite happy to accept a room that had been arranged by someone else, unlike Margaret. There was a lovely view towards Big Ben. 'No wonder you are always so punctual,' Margaret said tartly one day, 'you can't very well help it.'[6] Elizabeth's wardrobe now extended, within the confines of post-war clothing allowances. She enjoyed looking at the sketches her dressmakers showed her, which were then exhibited on Norman Hartnell's models, but she still lacked the passion for clothes that Margaret had shown since she was young, drawing beautiful sketches of svelte women wearing gorgeous garments. However, Elizabeth did take notice when Philip commented. On the weekend she spent at Coppins, she wore a blue dress. Philip said, 'Blue becomes you, Ma'am', so she made sure she wore blue the next time.

Philip now started going to London when he could. 'Philip enjoys driving and does it fast!' Elizabeth wrote. 'He has his own tiny MG which he is very proud of. He has taken me about in it, once up to London, which was great fun, only it is like sitting on the road and has wheels which are almost higher than one's head! On that one and only occasion we were chased by a photographer, which was disappointing.'[7] They both enjoyed the theatre and dancing, but they had to be discreet, dancing with other people so as not to encourage gossip.

Elizabeth's official engagements began to fill her diary and increase her public profile. In March she undertook a major solo engagement when she went on a three-day visit to Northern Ireland, where her aunt Rose's husband, Admiral Earl Granville, was Governor. It was her first visit alone away from Britain's mainland. She was accorded all the naval ceremony proper to an heir to the Throne, travelling in the cruiser, HMS *Superb*, which was the first naval vessel to fly her personal standard. The main purpose of her visit was to launch an aircraft carrier, HMS *Eagle*, then the biggest in the world. Arriving at Belfast's shipyard, Harland and Wolff, with her aunt and uncle, Elizabeth was greeted by thousands of shipyard workers and their families, many packed on top of giant cranes to get a view. At a luncheon attended by six hundred guests, her speech paid tribute to the earlier *Eagle* which had been sunk in 1942. To invoke in those post-war months a sense of Britain's maritime history struck the right cord. Later Rose told the Queen that Elizabeth had her 'wonderful gift of looking as if she was loving it all'.[8]

After visiting more towns and villages, carrying out inspections and giving speeches, her tour was remembered as 'a truly royal acknowledgement of all that Ulster had done to speed the victory of the British Commonwealth in the Second World War.'[9] It was followed in April by a visit to Co. Durham, home of her Bowes Lyon ancestors. In the war-scarred city of Sunderland she launched a tanker, *British Princess*, and opened an eye hospital. The value of the visits of the sweetly smiling and enthusiastic Princess in those grim years of post-war Britain cannot be underestimated, as the thousands of people who waited for her under leaden skies and heavy drizzle demonstrated.

At the end of May, Elizabeth was delighted to be a bridesmaid at the Westminster wedding of her cousin Andrew to her lady-in-waiting, Jean Gibbs. Guests included George II of Greece, Philip's cousin, who had been in exile since the German occupation, and Philip himself. Afterwards he and Elizabeth appeared together in Press photographs but with other people in the frame. Philip had recently returned from another wedding, that of his widowed sister, Sophie, in Germany, who married Prince George of Hanover; Philip 'was devoted to his sisters', says Myra Butter.[10] He turned up unexpectedly; he and Sophie had not seen each other since 1937, and she was shocked to see how like their late father he was, including his sense of humour. Afterwards he went to Monte Carlo with Mike Parker to collect his father's personal effects from his mistress. Although Prince Andrea had left Philip the bulk of his estate, it turned out to have huge debts; Philip's grandmother deduced that the Comtesse must have 'sucked him dry'.[11]

While Jean Elphinstone went on her honeymoon, Elizabeth's third lady-in-waiting began her duties. Scottish-born Lady Margaret Egerton, known always as Meg, was eight years older than the Princess. Sporty and musical, and a member of the ATS from early in the war, she had something of a free spirit about her which was not always appreciated. The Queen noticed she would fly into the Palace forecourt on her bicycle, her hair loosely in a headscarf. 'You must speak to her,' she told her daughter. 'She really can't come here like that! She must wear a hat!' Elizabeth took issue with her mother's attitude: 'Don't be old-fashioned, Mummy. These days girls simply don't *have* a hat.'[12]

The summer was busy. In July Elizabeth received an Honorary Degree of Bachelor of Music from London University, conferred on her by its Chancellor, her great-uncle, the Earl of Athlone, and in a historic and symbolic ceremony in August, she was admitted to the Circle of the Bards of Wales at the Eisteddfod. With Margaret she spent several days on a Sea Cadets training ship in Devon, rising at 6:45 a.m. when Elizabeth's first tasks were to light the galley fire, make breakfast and peel potatoes. At Buckingham Palace she co-hosted with the King and Queen the first garden party since 1939, attended by seven thousand guests and described as 'London's biggest and best post-war fashion parade'. She wore a tailored dress of turquoise blue and matching hat; Margaret was in pale blue. Even though guests included foreign royalties and many dignitaries, it was noted that the tea was on 'austerity lines without the usual raspberries and cream'.

There was still time for courting, though. Philip wrote to the Queen in June apologising for the 'monumental cheek' of having invited himself to the Palace but said that, however 'contrite' he felt, 'there is always a small voice that keeps saying, nothing ventured, nothing gained – well, I did venture and I gained a wonderful time.'[13] He often had dinner with both Princesses in the nursery, which was now Margaret's sitting room, or 'Maggie's Playroom', as Philip changed the sign to read. 'The food was of the simplest,' said Crawfie. 'Fish, some sort of sweet, and orangeade.'[14] The three of them would play games 'and race about like a bunch of high-spirited children', although Crawfie sometimes removed Margaret on some pretext or other because her attention-seeking presence was not helping the romance.[15] Philip stood no nonsense from Margaret, although generally he was very good with her. Myra Butter recalls his kindness to her as the younger sister of Gina: 'He was always sweet and kind and funny to me. He was always gadding about. I used to get all his bus tickets – God knows why I wanted them! He was giving like that.'[16] Crawfie said she now liked Philip 'immensely. It was clear to all of us that he was very much in love . . . he was a forthright and completely natural young man, given to say what he thought. There was nothing of the polished courtier about him.' Indeed there was not, and that would prove to be another stumbling block.

That summer Elizabeth met Prudence Stewart Wilson, who was engaged to Major Eric Penn of the Grenadier Guards; he was a nephew of the Queen's friend, Sir Arthur Penn, and had known the Princesses for years. Pru and Elizabeth were the same age and would become good friends. She recalls having dinner at Buckingham Palace after watching an American musical with the Princesses: 'I sat next to the King. He was absolutely charming, lovely and sweet to me, because I was young and he was very interested in what I'd been doing in the war. He was a very gentle, lovely man.' As for her friend, 'Princess Elizabeth was so beautiful to look at. She really was enchanting. She had a wonderful figure and wonderful skin, and such a vivacious, lovely face when she smiled.'[17]

Philip had the chance to appreciate Elizabeth further at Balmoral, where he stayed for the first time that summer. He was thrown in the deep end with the Queen's family and old friends, but at least Marina and her children were there. He attended Craithie Church and was photographed walking and chatting with Michael Bowes Lyon.[18] At the Balmoral Ball he danced reels and old country favourites with tenants and estate workers, where Elizabeth, wearing a gown of soft cream satin and a tartan sash, hardly left the dance floor. If the pair managed to make physical contact, it was fleeting: country dances were not designed for intimacy, but perhaps that added to the frisson.

Philip joined the King and his party to shoot grouse and go stalking, something for which he had no suitable clothes and no experience, unlike the King and his daughter: Peter Townsend said of Elizabeth, 'She was a tireless walker and an excellent shot.' By contrast, Philip's shooting was erratic compared with other guests, including David Bowes Lyon. Conscious of sneers and being determined and quick to learn, Philip watched and improved. Tension was relieved in the evenings when, after a good dinner, everyone played games or was entertained by Margaret; she played the piano and sang well-known songs in different voices, causing hilarity. Philip nearly blotted his copybook, however, when he made one of his first gaffes. He did not have a kilt, so had to borrow one. Wearing it for the first time, he dropped a deep curtsey to the Queen. The King was not amused.

While Elizabeth and Philip snatched as much time as they could alone, in early September rumours began in some newspapers of their engagement, some saying it was based on 'insider information'. Lascelles found it necessary to issue a denial. Nevertheless, it was at Balmoral that year when they told her parents they wanted to get married; Philip has maintained that it was the first time he had thought about marriage seriously. Although the King loved his daughter dearly, he could not accept that she was ready for marriage. 'Princess Elizabeth was his constant companion in shooting, walking, riding – in fact everything. His affection for her was touching,' said Mabell Airlie. 'I wondered sometimes whether he was secretly dreading the prospect of an early marriage for her.'[19] As Elizabeth was under twenty-five, she had to seek the King's consent. He wanted them to wait before making any announcement, until Lilibet was twenty-one and after their South African tour the following year. The King and Queen had accepted the invitation of General Smuts, and they would all be away for four months from February; he was on his way to Balmoral to discuss details. For Elizabeth the tour must have been a cloud on the horizon: just as their relationship was blossoming, they would have to be apart. The couple agreed to keep their engagement secret.

Afterwards Philip wrote an exuberant letter to the Queen: 'I am sure I do not deserve all the good things which have happened to me. To have been spared in the war and seen victory, to have been given the chance to rest and readjust myself, to have fallen in love completely and unreservedly, makes all one's personal and even the world's troubles seem small and petty.' At last, he said, life had a purpose.[20] After another visit, he told the Queen that he hoped his behaviour had not got out of hand: he had started 'a rather heated discussion', for their political views were quite different. Philip's views were inclined more to the left than the Queen's. Perhaps he took after his uncle: Myra Butter says Dickie Mountbatten 'had very definite opinions', as did Philip. Edwina Mountbatten particularly was left-wing: 'She didn't live left-wing, mind you,' says Myra. 'My mother used to call her "the drawing room pink". I suppose that washed off onto [Dickie]. I can remember my mother saying, "Oh come on, Dickie!"'[21] However, Philip hoped the Queen would not think him 'violently argumentative and an exponent of socialism' and asked her to forgive him if he had said anything he should not have.[22]

Philip left Balmoral on 13 September and began an instructor's post at Corsham in Wiltshire. His Commanding Officer, Sir William O'Brien, recorded that he gave Philip his petrol coupons so he could drive to London to see 'his girl'.[23] He also managed to crash his MG in October when it skidded on a corner, which badly damaged the car but only slightly injured Philip. It was just as well, for he was to be an usher that month at the wedding of his cousin, Patricia Mountbatten, to Lord Brabourne, her father's Aide-de-Camp. Famously their wedding gave rise to the photograph that supposedly told the world there was something going on between Philip and Elizabeth. Heavy rain had been falling on the morning of the wedding, which was taking place at Romsey Abbey in Hampshire, with the reception at Broadlands. In spite of the rain thousands of people lined the streets for the biggest society wedding since the war; also the bride's father had just been created Viscount Mountbatten of Burma for his wartime services as Supreme Allied Commander, South-East Asia Command.

Both Princesses were bridesmaids with Princess Alexandra and the bride's younger sister, Pamela. 'When we reached the door of the abbey,

Princess Elizabeth turned to Philip and he casually reached behind Princess Margaret and took her coat,' Pamela recalled. 'This small act jump-started a media frenzy, as the press realised that it had glimpsed, however fleetingly, an air of ease and understanding between the pair. Newsreels confirmed the rumour and royal gossip went into overdrive.'[24] A picture appeared of the pair looking directly at each other as Elizabeth began to shrug off her fur coat. In fact, newsreels show the exchange was actually brief and part of a longer action, in which Philip waited as Elizabeth began removing her coat, but Margaret was quicker, so he took hers first, then turned back to take Elizabeth's. Nevertheless, the photograph was presented as being meaningful, thus fuelling rumour and selling papers.

Shortly afterwards many friends met again at the marriage of Myra to Major David Butter of the Scots Guards. Queen Mary and the Princesses were there, as were the Mountbattens and Philip's mother Alice, who was now in England and staying with her mother in Kensington Palace. Guests also included staff from the hospital where Myra worked as a nurse during the war. She says, 'Looking back we were all so grown up. I married at 21,[25] Princess Elizabeth married at 21. My husband was 26 but he'd been right through the war, been wounded. Philip was only 26. They all seemed so much older, like men of 35, 36, but they were full of fun.'[26]

According to Gina, one of Philip's detractors was Elizabeth's uncle, David Bowes Lyon. Gina called him a 'vicious little fellow' who 'had it in for Philip right from the start.'[27] In November he was with the Queen and Elizabeth at St Paul's Walden Bury, where his sister unveiled a church window in their father's memory; perhaps the subject of Philip arose then, although it is unlikely the engagement would have been mentioned, for the Queen did not tell her other siblings. There would be time enough for David and others to voice their misgivings. Meanwhile the Press continued to speculate, especially as Philip's application for naturalisation as a British subject was being considered by the Home Office.

Philip's application meant renouncing his membership of the Greek and Danish royal families, and it was commonly supposed that it was in preparation for marrying Elizabeth. However, its original purpose was for his naval career and had been contemplated some time earlier. Even though he had lived in England since he was eight and had served in the Royal Navy throughout the war, his position was covered by temporary Admiralty regulations,[28] which said he could only receive a permanent commission if he became a British subject. The King felt it proper to get the consent of George II of Greece first, which he gave in the autumn of 1944. Philip's application was then put on hold because of the unsettled situation in Greece. On Christmas Day 1944 Churchill and Anthony Eden had made a dramatic visit to Athens, which resulted in a Regent and new Prime Minister being appointed and was followed by a period of armed conflict between different political factions. To proceed at that time to naturalise Philip, a member of the Greek Royal Family, could be open to misinterpretation. George VI was advised that it should wait until after March 1946, when the Greek general election and a plebiscite on the monarchy would take place.

On 28 September 1946, George II was returned to the Throne, but that made the timing for Philip's application sensitive again. There was also the question of what title he would have. The King was willing to grant the right and privilege of the title 'His Royal Highness Prince Philip', which the Prime Minister and Mountbatten (of course) agreed to. However, Philip himself turned down the King's offer, saying he would rather be known simply as Lieutenant Philip – plus a suitable surname – RN. Impressed, the King agreed. As the royal house of Greece and Denmark had no family surname, the Home Secretary suggested Philip take his mother's name, Mountbatten. Finally, in December 1946, the application proceeded.

Inevitably it sparked speculation again about an engagement, which was denied by the Palace, and in the House of Commons the question was asked as to why 'priority' was being given to Philip's application. The Home Secretary, Chuter Ede, replied that Philip had submitted an application in accordance with the arrangements he had announced in February 1946 enabling 'early consideration to be given to applications . . . from foreigners who have served during the war in HM Forces.'[29] The foreign Press got its wires crossed, and said that the announcement of the engagement was being delayed because of the situation in Greece. Meanwhile

Mountbatten used his formidable contacts in government and the Press to start emphasising his nephew's Britishness. He told his friend, Labour MP and journalist Tom Driberg: 'He left Greece at the age of one and has only spent three months of his entire life in Greece and cannot even speak the language.'[30]

As Christmas came and went, the royal family's preparations for their South Africa tour were near completion. Crawfie thought Elizabeth seemed quiet and subdued as she packed. Mabell Airlie said that when she remarked to Elizabeth that it would be sad to be away for her twenty-first birthday, she replied, 'but when I come back we will have a celebration – perhaps *two* celebrations.' To a Princess in love, that moment must have seemed an eternity away.

CHAPTER 20

A Royal Announcement (1947)

Britain in January 1947 was suffering one of the most severe winters in history. For the first time, Big Ben froze and missed the chime of 9:00 p.m. At Windsor, the Thames froze. Coalmines stopped working and ports closed. A fuel crisis made electricity cuts common and took the country back to the darkness of wartime blackouts. Virtually bankrupt after the war, 'Austerity Britain' meant rationing was still in force. It was with reluctance that the King prepared to leave for South Africa at such a time, but he knew General Smuts anticipated their visit eagerly, hoping the tour might help promote unity in his country. The King and Queen had taken lessons in Afrikaans in preparation for a country that had two capitals and two languages, and where the opposition Nationalist Party were agitating for apartheid.

On 29 January, shortly before their departure, the Queen and Elizabeth attended the wedding of Eric Penn and Prudence Stewart-Wilson. Lady Penn says, 'I think people realised that Elizabeth and Philip were seeing each other but not how serious it was.'[1] The Mountbattens held a small farewell dinner for the royal family which Philip attended, and afterwards he wrote to the Queen to thank her for 'the heartening things' she had said to him, which would 'keep my spirits up' while they were away.[2] Philip also wrote to Mountbatten, saying it was clear he liked 'being General Manager of this little show and I am rather afraid that [Elizabeth] might not take to the idea quite as docilely as I do'.[3] He did not want his uncle Dickie to spoil things.

Mountbatten and his family were also preparing to leave Britain. He had been appointed last Viceroy of India, to oversee its independence from Britain, which would not be an easy task. Mountbatten had accepted the post reluctantly. He told Sir Frederick 'Boy' Browning: 'I need hardly tell you how much I tried to avoid this appointment and what a sad disappointment it is to me that I shall not now go to sea in two months time. I am afraid I am in for another difficult job.'[4] He went to see the King: '"Think how badly it will reflect on the family if I fail," said Mountbatten. The King replied, "Think how well it will reflect on the family if you succeed," and told him he must go.'[5]

On 31 January, the day of the royal family's departure, all the staff assembled in the Bow Room in Buckingham Palace, as they always did when the family was going away. The King was wearing his naval uniform and Crawfie thought he looked 'desperately tired'. The Queen looked 'very sweet and pretty'. Margaret, whose lessons were to take a break, seemed 'very grown up' and promised to write. Lilibet, however, 'was sad and we all thought that she did not want very much to go': after all, the tour was about to break in with some force on her romantic life. Ten immediate members of the household were going with them, including Lascelles and an Assistant Private Secretary, Michael Adeane, Equerry Peter Townsend and Elizabeth's most recent lady-in-waiting, Lady Meg Egerton. Elizabeth also took Bobo Macdonald, who now served as her dresser. There was also a doctor, clerical staff, police officers and footmen.

A procession of semi-state landaus was supposed to take them to Waterloo Station but was cancelled due to severe weather to spare the horses. At Portsmouth they boarded HMS *Vanguard*, where they were greeted by 101 officers and 1,715 crew members, including 189 Royal Marines, who would be on duty for the voyage. They set sail on 1 February, in the snow. The weather in the Bay of Biscay was terrible, and the ship was damaged. The King and Princesses kept to their cabins; the Queen was the first to be able to face dinner. When they reached calmer waters, they could start to relax, although the King kept worrying about the dire situation in England. However, he enjoyed the entertainment: the nightly films and concerts and the deck games, where the crew joined in; Elizabeth had fun too, telling Crawfie, 'The officers are charming. . . . There are one or two real smashers'. But other handsome men did not stop her putting Philip's photograph on display in her cabin, and she wrote to him; however, she said later that the story that she wrote to him every day in South Africa was 'quite untrue', because she had little free time.[6] Other friends

Eleanor Roosevelt with the royal family in the Bow Room at Buckingham Palace, 1942
LIBRARY OF CONGRESS

also got letters from her, including Porchey. She and Philip managed to speak on the telephone, and he wrote to her.

For Elizabeth, the journey was particularly significant. Not only would she turn twenty-one but she was also travelling outside the British Isles for the first time, to a Commonwealth country whose sovereign she would one day be. Excitement grew as they crossed the Equator, when she and Margaret had to undergo the fun of nautical rituals, such as having their noses powdered and eating a giant 'pill' in the form of a candied cherry. There was also drama when Meg Egerton went down with a severe chill and had to be taken off the ship. When they reached Cape Town on 17 February, to be met by General Smuts, it was the first time a reigning British monarch had set foot on Union soil. A huge civic Ball was given to welcome them, where five thousand guests danced to a fox-trot specially composed for Elizabeth, called 'Princess'. The first and most important constitutional duty was in Cape Town itself, where the King opened the Union Parliament.

Then the tour began that took them to forty-two locations in nine weeks, with few breaks. There were guard inspections, receptions, parades, garden parties and more balls. The family received a tumultuous reception with none of the republican sentiment they had anticipated. However, Betty Shew Spencer, one of the few journalists officially invited to write about the tour, said: 'Yet it seemed to me that at first they hesitated to admit Princess Elizabeth to their affections with the same completeness of surrender they made to the Queen', something that might be expected to an extent, for it was Their Majesties who were in the foreground. However, she found that journalists did not seem to know what to say and perhaps 'fell into the error of thinking [the Princesses] lacked more positive qualities'.[7]

She noted that those reservations soon disappeared when Elizabeth made her first solo appearance on 3 March, opening a new graving dock at East London, the second most important city of Cape Province. When she gave her speech, not only did she come across as gracefully unaffected, she endeared herself to the crowd by dealing with the problems of a windy day. She had to stop her skirt from billowing up, keep her hat on her head and at the same time turn over the fluttering pages of her manuscript, all of which she achieved 'with an admirable sang-froid' that belied her lack of experience. When she saw it later on film, Margaret remarked, 'Lilibet needs three hands.'[8]

For thirty-five nights the family's home became the White Train. Made up of fourteen carriages and a third of a mile long, it took them nearly 7,000 miles around the country. Other journeys were made in Daimlers and in aircraft. The family were dazzled by the country, its heat, colour, and the difference from austerity Britain. Margaret recalled the vastness and the 'amazing opulence, and a great deal to eat'.[9] Elizabeth told Queen Mary, 'When I caught my first glimpse of Table Mountain I could hardly believe that anything could be so beautiful.'[10]

They met people from widely different communities and, because apartheid was not yet in force, attended a 'Coloured Ball'. The public particularly liked to see or read about the Princesses at play, especially out riding in the early mornings, when 'they would gallop across the vast emptiness of the Veld, dressed alike in jodhpurs and yellow shirts'.[11] Elizabeth endeared herself further when she was inspecting a parade of Guides and Brownies and saw at a distance a busload of Girl Guides brought from a leper colony in Basutoland, who were kept segregated. She made a point of going over to them and walking around the bus, smiling and waving at the girls. Elizabeth remembered her filial duty too. In Rhodesia they were visiting the grave of Cecil Rhodes. Half-way up the granite slopes of the hill, the Queen's shoes became too slippery to walk, so Elizabeth handed over hers and continued in stocking feet; later she made an exasperated comment about mummy never having the right footwear.

In the Kruger National Park, they were thrilled by its wildlife, and at the Kimberley diamond mines, Elizabeth was presented with a superb stone weighing six carats. At the Zulu ceremony at Eshowe, five thousand warriors danced the 'Ngoma Umkosi', the Royal Dance. Elizabeth found it very impressive and wrote that it ended 'with a terrific charge to the edge of the dais where we were. This they were allowed to do only because Mummy begged them to be allowed to come nearer.'[12] At the last minute a line was diplomatically omitted from the warriors' address, which was intended to read: 'We hear, O King, your eldest daughter,

Princess Elizabeth, is about to give her heart in marriage, and we would like to hear from you who is the man, and when will this be.'[13]

Inevitably the tour was not all sweetness and light. In early April they were making a journey of 120 miles to Johannesburg in an open car, in intense heat, and all along the route people were crowding the car and screaming their excitement at seeing the family. The King was fractious: hot, weary, losing weight and worried about affairs back home, he began berating the chauffeur, who started getting anxious. His wife and daughters tried to humour him but to no avail. Eventually his equerry, Townsend, could take it no more and uncharacteristically shouted at him: 'For Heaven's sake shut up or there's going to be an accident.'[14] Worse was to come. They saw an agitated policeman running towards the car and then another man, 'black and wiry, sprinting with terrifying speed and purpose' towards the car. He was clutching something in one hand, and with the other he seized hold of the side of the car. The Queen thought they were being attacked and 'with her parasol, landed several deft blows on the assailant before he was knocked senseless by policemen', said Townsend. 'As they dragged away his limp body, I saw the Queen's parasol, broken in two, disappear over the side of the car. Within a second, Her Majesty was waving and smiling, as captivatingly as ever, to the crowds.'[15] Everyone was shocked, but it was made worse when they discovered that the man was an ex-serviceman who had been loyally calling out, 'My King! My King!' as he held a ten shilling note, a birthday present for Princess Elizabeth. The King wrote to him and apologised profusely.

For many people the most significant event of the tour was Elizabeth's twenty-first birthday which fell when they were back in Cape Town. The day was declared a public holiday, although for Elizabeth it began a little disappointingly. Heavy rain cloud meant that plans to ascend Table Mountain had to be abandoned, so she spent the morning at Government House reading her birthday wishes and opening presents. Diamonds were the order of the day: flower-petal earrings from the Diplomatic Corps, a brooch from the Royal Household and a badge from her Grenadier Guards. From Britain, where the bells of St Paul's were rung in her honour and tributes paid all over the country, came a message from the Prime Minister, acknowledging that she had 'lived through some of the

King George VI and Queen Elizabeth with the Princesses at Johannesburg, South Africa, 1947
UNIVERSITY OF SOUTHAMPTON

hardest yet noblest years of these islands' long history' and speaking of her 'simple dignity and wise understanding'.[16]

The sun came out in time for a massive birthday parade, attended by General Smuts and his Cabinet, at which Elizabeth reviewed more than seven thousand troops, and then went on to a youth rally where ten thousand voices sang 'Happy Birthday to You'. At the City Hall, the Mayor of Cape Town presented her with a golden key; and later, looking radiant in a white tulle evening gown, sparkling with diamante and sequins, she attended a young people's ball at Government House, where Smuts presented her with eighty-seven diamonds in a silver casket.

Her speech that evening was, and continues to be, considered the most moving she has ever made. It was written by Lascelles, and when Elizabeth read a draft she told him it made her cry. As Ben Pimlott has said, it 'was both a culmination of the tour and a prologue for the Princess'.[17] At the threshold of her own destiny, she sat in a small room in

Government House and spoke to the many millions of her future subjects across the world, asking to be heard as the representative of her generation. It was the last part of her speech that was unexpectedly personal and thus all the more moving when she said she would like to make a 'solemn act of dedication with a whole Empire listening':

> *I declare before you that my whole life, whether it be long or short, shall be devoted to your service and the service of our great Imperial family to which we all belong, but I shall not have the strength to carry out this resolution along unless you join in with me, as I now invite you to do. I know that your support will be unfailingly given. God help me to make good my vow and God bless all of you who are willing to share in it.'[18]*

The speech affirmed the British Monarchy as the stable link between the diverse nations of the Commonwealth, while the sincere and earnest nature of the Princess's vow, connecting her directly with the people, had a powerful effect. As one veteran member of the Royal Household wrote to another, 'Who wouldn't kill a dragon for Princess Elizabeth now?'[19] Lascelles had done a good job and as the tour came to an end, he reflected on its success. He was particularly impressed by Elizabeth's blossoming:

> *She has got all P'cess Marg's solid and endearing qualities plus a perfectly natural power of enjoying herself. . . . Not a great sense of humour, but a healthy sense of fun. Moreover, when necessary she can take on the old bores with much of her mother's skill, and never spares herself in that exhausting part of royal duty. For a child of her years, she has got an astonishing solicitude for other people's comfort; such unselfishness is not a normal characteristic of that family.[20]*

Ultimately, the tour did not have the effect Smuts wanted: the next year he lost the election and new racial laws were introduced, weakening links with the Commonwealth Union and leading to South Africa's withdrawal. However, the effect of the tour lingered.

As the royal family were all too aware, Britain had suffered miserably while they sweltered in the heat. When they arrived back in Portsmouth on 11 May, however, they were greeted in bright sunshine amid the greenery of spring by thousands of people who put misery behind them to welcome their royal family back. Certainly they were glad to be home and Elizabeth was seen dancing a little jig on the deck. She would have to wait a little longer, though, to see Philip, for he was not allowed to meet the ship. The Press loyally reported that the King looked tanned and healthy, and the Queen and Princesses had a 'rosy glow'. However, Crawfie was shocked at their appearance. The King and Queen 'looked positively worn out': he had lost 17 lb. She was 'horrified to see how thin Lilibet had gone. She had also lost all her pretty colour and looked pale and drawn', although she seemed to have 'a sort of inner radiance'.[21] Margaret looked the worst, 'ill and tired out', although she was pleased to see she had grown up. They were keen to tell Crawfie all about their experiences.

However, Crawfie had news of her own. She had a fiancé, George, whom she wanted to marry before the war but put it on hold because the royal family needed her at a difficult time. Now they wanted to proceed; after all, Lilibet was grown up and Margaret nearly seventeen. The Queen acknowledged the sacrifice she had made but told her that a change for Margaret at that stage would not be desirable. Crawfie found herself reassuring the Queen that she would continue her work and live at the Palace 'for as long as they wished me to, even after I was married' and settled down to educating Margaret to a final level. The Queen said nothing about Lilibet's plans.

The absence of Philip at Portsmouth gave rise to speculation that the relationship had ended, fuelled by the fact that no announcement had been made. While they were away, however, Mountbatten had continued priming the Press. When a poll in the *Sunday Pictorial* suggested some people did not favour Elizabeth's marriage to a foreign prince, Mountbatten continued his campaign. Aiming particularly at Lord Beaverbrook, who was hostile to Mountbatten, and his *Express* newspaper group, he persuaded the two *Express* editors and their chairman to attend a meeting at his house; Philip was present but did not play any active part. The pressmen were unable to think of any reason why the public should oppose Philip's change of nationality, so when the news broke they were hardly in a position to manufacture any of their own.[22] Philip's name appeared in the London Gazette in March 1947 in a list of 817 naturalisations. He was now a commoner known as Lieutenant Philip Mountbatten RN.

Elizabeth meanwhile had become a significant public figure in her own right. New honours were heaped upon her. In an ancient and symbolic ceremony at the Guildhall on 11 June, she received the Freedom of the City of London, making her only the third woman to be so honoured. On the King's official birthday, he conferred on her the Imperial Order of the Crown of India, intended to mark the royal family's leaving the historic Indian Empire. Later that day, Elizabeth took part for the first time in the Trooping of the Colour, the first such ceremony since the beginning of the war. As Heiress Presumptive, she rode as the principal supporter of the King, with the Duke of Gloucester following, and in doing so she also symbolised the great advance in the position of women who had been admitted to the armed forces during the two world wars. This year, instead of the usual brilliant scarlet and gold costumes, it was a battle-dress parade. Elizabeth wore the dark blue uniform of the Grenadier Guards and looked composed and confident as she rode side-saddle on her chestnut horse with practised elegance.

She also made two new acquisitions: her own personal guard, newly-promoted Inspector Alexander Usher from the Metropolitan Police, whom she already knew and who would accompany her on all official duties; and 'an 18 hp Daimler car which the King gave me for a 21st birthday present. I found it waiting for me when I returned from South Africa. Its registration number is no longer HRH 1! We both drive each other about',[23] for Philip had soon begun to appear at the Palace again. Philip's friend Gina said he used to talk to her about Elizabeth before they got engaged: 'He said "I think we could do a lot together."'[24] Now there was no reason to wait any longer. On 11 June Philip wrote to the Queen and said he was sure that the delay had been right but that he and Elizabeth now wanted to start their new life together. Little wonder, though, if he was a little nervous: getting married is a major event in anyone's life, but marrying the heir to the Throne was a rather different undertaking. One day Philip's Commanding Officer at Corsham found him 'sitting rather solemnly in the library':

> *I said something like, 'What's up?'*
> *He replied: 'I am going to marry Princess Elizabeth.'*
> *'Good Lord! I said (and this is not so stupid as it sounds since, for all the rumours, none of us had any real idea whether the romance was real or not). 'Well, I wish you the very best of luck.'*
> *'Thank you very much,' replied Philip with a wry smile. 'I am going to need it.'*[25]

The Queen was supportive, if anxious, about her daughter's decision: 'You can imagine what emotion this engagement has given me,' she wrote to Lascelles. Elizabeth had 'such a burden to carry, and one can only pray that she has made the right decision, I <u>think</u> she has – but he is untried as yet.'[26] The same day, 7 July, the Queen told her sister May Elphinstone: 'This is one line to tell you <u>very secretly</u> that Lilibet has made up her mind to get engaged to Philip Mountbatten. As you know, she has known him since she was 12, & I think that she is <u>really</u> fond of him & I do pray that she will be very happy. . . . We are keeping it a deadly secret, purely because of the Press.' She said that May's daughter Elizabeth, whom she admired, had had a long talk with Philip and 'liked his interest in many things & ideas'.[27]

Philip was still at Corsham and when in London stayed with his mother in Kensington Palace. One July evening Elizabeth said, 'Crawfie, something is going to happen at last! He's coming tonight.' Unfortunately the Queen was in bed with laryngitis and was not there to see Philip, but apologised in a note. She had hoped to tell him in person 'how happy we feel about the engagement, and to say how glad we are to have you as a son-in-law. It is so <u>lovely</u> to know you so well and I know we can trust our darling Lilibet to your love and care. There is so much that can be done in this muddled & rather worried world by example & leadership & I am sure that Lilibet & you have a great part to play.' She acknowledged that it would not always be an easy part, but she had 'great confidence' in his good judgement and knew he would be 'a great help & comfort to our beloved little daughter.'[28]

That evening, 9 July, Buckingham Palace issued the announcement in the Court Circular:

> *It is with the greatest pleasure that the King and Queen announce the betrothal of their dearly beloved daughter, the Princess Elizabeth, to Lieutenant Philip Mountbatten R.N., son of the late Prince Andrew of Greece and Princess Andrew (Princess Alice of Battenberg), to which union the King has gladly given his consent.*

Shortly afterwards, Elizabeth left to attend a private dinner party at the Dorchester Hotel, and then on to a dance at Apsley House, and was immediately mobbed by crowds who had already heard the news. Looking radiant in a dress of lime green taffeta embroidered with gold sequins, under an ermine cape, she smiled as people cheered and shouted their congratulations. Naturally the next morning, the newspapers were full of the story. 'I have never seen her look lovelier than she did on that day, not even on her wedding morning,' said Crawfie. 'She wore a deep yellow frock, a shade that has always suited her very well.'[29] Her engagement ring was a three-carat diamond solitaire flanked on each side by five smaller diamonds, all set in platinum. The diamonds came from a tiara owned by Philip's mother, and the ring was created by a jeweller in London's New Bond Street. Philip was heavily involved in the design, but it meant Elizabeth had been unable to try it on, and it was a little big. Nevertheless, she wore it for the engagement photos that followed.

Margaret was delighted: 'One day I scarcely thought I knew him; and then suddenly he was engaged to Lilibet.'[30] On 31 July, the King formally gave consent through his Privy Council. Elizabeth wrote, 'One of the Councillors present told me afterwards, it was most unanimous and touching and 'you can now get married with our hearty approval!!'[31]

Philip, though, was still an unknown quantity as far as the public were concerned. In the inevitable coverage of his life, one newspaper said, surprised, 'He is said to speak without any trace of a foreign accent.'[32] Elizabeth took him to see Queen Mary at Marlborough House, and then the pair made their first semi-official public appearance at the last Garden Party of the season at Buckingham Palace; it was attended by six thousand people, keen to catch a glimpse of the man they had just heard was to marry the Princess. Elizabeth wore a coffee-coloured two-piece outfit with lace-trimmed hat, Philip was in naval uniform. Lady Penn was there: 'She introduced me to him and I was absolutely stunned by how wonderfully good-looking he was. And they looked such a wonderful couple together.'[33] Princess Alice was there to see her son with his fiancée, who wore 'her happiness like a garment, plainly for all to see'.[34] At 9:15 p.m. that evening, the couple appeared on the balcony before joining the King and Queen for a family dinner. Elizabeth looked lovely in a long white gown, and the crowds alternated between shouting for her and for Philip.

Not everyone was so impressed. Sir Michael Duff, who had been so positive when he first met Philip, had revised his opinion. He spent the weekend after the announcement with the Duchess of Kent at Coppins, and Elizabeth and Philip came to Sunday lunch:

> *Princess E looked radiant & he not quite so much – I have known him for years & think him charming in a rather dull way. I don't think he has very endearing qualities but they may grow, he's a bit 'naval' if you know what I mean, & none of the gaiety of 'Dickie' Mountbatten . . . and his manners are a trifle rough. She really looked very pretty & they are both going to be called the Duke & Duchess of something or other which I think quite right.*
>
> *Philip of Greece gives the impression of taking all the wrong & trivial things to heart & not the things that really matter – which is just a lack of a sense of proportion. However, time will tell, he scowls a bit as though a fly were a permanent guest on his nose! I think that all Royalty scowl, the male members especially. I suppose it's done in self-defence!*[35]

He also wondered if they would 'be forced to have an austerity honeymoon in keeping with the austerity wedding?' the latter having been raised in the Press because of all the shortages. Duff was clearly feeling generally critical. He had been at the Garden Party and noted, 'The Duke of Gloucester looked quite stuffed . . . as though he had been bedded out for the summer . . . Margaret Rose [looked] as painted as any inmate in a chic brothel!'[36]

Unlike Duff, Lady Airlie was uncritical of Philip when she met him at the Garden Party, noticing he

> *shook hands rather shyly. I noticed that his uniform was shabby – it had the usual after-the-war look – and I liked him for not having got a new one for the occasion as many men would have done, to make an impression. Observing him I thought that he had far more character than most people would imagine. I wondered whether he would be capable of helping Princess Elizabeth some day as the Prince Consort had helped Queen Victoria. I felt that he would, although I should not live to see it.*[37]

No longer could Philip make do with shabby clothes. His engagement to the Heir to the Throne meant he could not shamble about like the commoner he had elected to become. He was given a secretary to organise his social diary, a detective and a valet, John Dean, who used to be the Mountbattens' butler. When Dean had unpacked Philip's bag for weekends with the Mountbattens, he noticed his civilian wardrobe was 'scantier than that of many a bank clerk'[38] and often all he took with him was a razor. He also noticed he carried a photograph of Elizabeth in a battered leather frame. Dean would wash and iron Philip's shirt, not because Philip expected it but because Dean liked him. Now he had a job trying to smarten Philip up: his favourite kit was flannel trousers, 'not always very new or creased',[39] and open-neck tennis shirt with rolled-up sleeves. Dean had to keep reminding him not to put his hands in his pockets, which ruined the shape of his jackets. He also began a battle to get Philip to give up smoking: Elizabeth disliked it and worried about how much her father smoked.

Mountbatten's friend Tom Driberg had continued to ensure Philip's Britishness was emphasised, to the extent that Elizabeth's new Private Secretary, Sir John 'Jock' Colville, noted: 'An effort has obviously been made to build him up as the nephew of Lord Louis Mountbatten rather than a Greek Prince.' However, there was concern from some left-wing quarters as to how much a royal wedding would cost and at the suggestion that Philip might receive an allowance. Mountbatten told Driberg that any rights Philip had to a salary from the Greek Civil List, he had renounced with his rights of succession; that his private means were very small; and that he was almost entirely dependent on his Naval pay of around £300 a year after tax. His MG car had 'made a big hole in his private pension' and, except on naval business, he usually travelled by third-class train. Philip himself had no complaints about this, and he was going to continue in the Navy, but he would still be expected to carry out some public duties himself. Mountbatten pointed out that Philip 'could hardly be expected to uphold the dignity of this nation on £300 a year any more than the Prime Minister was able to uphold the dignity of his office on £10,000 a year! . . . It really amounts to this: you have either got to give up the Monarch or give the wretched people who have to carry out the functions of the Crown enough money to be able to do it with the same dignity at least as the Prime Minister or Lord Mayor of London is afforded.'[40]

Although many photographs appeared after the engagement, clearly not everyone was on the ball. Two days later Elizabeth went to Ascot with the King, Philip and Margaret, and so well did they blend with the crowds that as Elizabeth approached the entrance to the royal enclosure, the gateman challenged her because she was not wearing a badge. Her detective had to identify her before she was admitted, an incident which she no doubt took in good humour.

The King favoured the following spring for the wedding, but Elizabeth was loath to wait any longer. A three-week wait for the Palace to release the date was stressful for staff in the Home Office's Central Office of Information (COI), who were responsible for preparing pre-wedding publicity for Britain and the Commonwealth. Apart from the amount of work to be done, there were severe paper shortages: 'If it is next spring we can do a much better job', read one anxious note, 'but if it is to be October we shall have to move with the utmost speed. Provisional steps have been taken to reserve poster paper'.[41] The official Crown posters in question were to contain up-to-date, full-colour photos of the couple and of the King and Queen, rather than merely tinted photos. Language was a problem, too. If the wedding was in October, they could only produce the posters in English; if it was next spring, 'they would be required in probably sixteen languages'. Orders were already coming in for the posters and for royal supplements, too. An eight-page pre-wedding supplement was to be produced for *Today* magazine, with a run of 70,000 for the Colonies and Indian Dominions, as well as a souvenir brochure about the wedding itself. Countries in the Middle and Far East also ordered brochures, and Brazil and Mexico wanted everything.

While the COI waited for a date, it tried to get the photos taken. The venues were to be the White Drawing Room at Buckingham Palace in the morning and the gardens in the afternoon. 'It seems there is no question of Mountbatten's family being in the group,'[42] noted one memo, a reference to the fact that Philip's sisters were not being invited. Processing the colour photos was quite a palaver. They were to be taken by Fox photos, flown by Pan Am to America, where they would be processed, then flown back to Britain for selection. A two-month embargo on releasing them, which expired on 19 October, gave the only clue as to when the wedding might be. Working with the Palace was not easy. 'I'm afraid the arrangements for the Royal portraits are far below what we all hoped,' said a frustrated lady in the COI, 'but we have had quite a struggle with the Palace even to get as far as we have done.'[43] It was made worse when she found that, although the COI had to tell their preferred photographer that they could not grant exclusivity, the well-known society photographer Dorothy Wilding was designated by the Palace for the afternoon session. Eventually, the date of 20 November was announced, leaving less than four months for preparations.

Meanwhile, Philip went with the royal family to Scotland, finding the usually drab Euston Station specially decorated with a floral tribute from the railway's Chairman: a large heart made of hydrangea petals with the letters 'E-P' worked in small rosebuds and surrounded by blooms. In Edinburgh, Elizabeth received the Freedom of the City, a ceremony at which Philip was formally and warmly welcomed to Scotland, although he was spotted with his arms crossed, looking bored. That evening, at a Ball for the National Association of Girls' Clubs, they danced together in public for the first time, Philip handsome in formal naval dress, Elizabeth lovely in a crinoline-skirted gown of rose pink net. After further engagements, they returned to London and in August went to Balmoral.

Elizabeth knew that some courtiers and others close to the family did not like Philip. There were various reasons. He had not been to Eton. His German connections were considered unfortunate. They saw his youth and breeziness as a potential threat to their traditional ways. Some, including Lascelles, considered him brash and ill-mannered and thought he was unlikely to be faithful. Lord Brabourne, husband of Philip's cousin, Patricia, said: 'We were at Balmoral that year and they were absolutely bloody to him. They didn't like him, they didn't trust him, and it showed.'[44] Whether it upset Elizabeth or whether she shrugged it off was hard to tell, for as Lady Penn says, 'I think whatever she did feel she never would have said anything if she thought he was being unfairly assessed, she would just have risen above it, which is her great strength. She thinks a lot and she just quietly gets on with what she has to do.'[45]

Jock Colville was on his first Balmoral working holiday and noticed the luxury and gaiety, compared to the austerity of London: picnics on the moors, siestas in lovely gardens, singing and games. Colville cautiously liked Philip and noticed 'the very English atmosphere that surrounds the Royal Family',[46] especially when their friends from old families like the Salisburys were present. He thought Philip did not seem very demonstrative towards the Princess, but he was hardly likely to be amid hostile company.

Meanwhile, Crawfie married and returned to the Palace to look after Margaret as agreed; her husband now had a job in a London bank. Crawfie noticed Philip had made significant changes to Lilibet's sitting room, which greatly improved it: he had 'strong ideas about furnishings'. Much later, and on a far bigger scale, he would take on Windsor Castle after the fire of 1992: 'It's entirely thanks to him that it's been so wonderfully restored,' says Lady Penn.[47] Crawfie also found wedding preparations in full swing. At the end of September, Philip was formally received into the Church of England by the Archbishop of Canterbury at Lambeth Palace. Lady-in-waiting Lady Katherine Hamilton said, 'It is lovely seeing Princess Elizabeth so happy & confident & looking so pretty.'[48] Soon the day she had waited for so patiently would arrive at last.

CHAPTER 21

Light and Hope (1947)

The lead up to the wedding was a whirl of arrangements and formalities, headaches and festivities. Inevitably at such a difficult time economically, questions were raised in the House of Commons about the cost, although isolated protests over the alleged 'wasteful use of public money' found little support; in any event, the King himself was anxious to avoid overlavish displays. The Chancellor of the Exchequer, Hugh Dalton, was able to inform MPs that public funds were to be used only to pay for decorations in Whitehall and outside Buckingham Palace, and all other expenses were to be paid by the King's Civil List. More tricky was the question of the cost of the Princess herself. The marriage of an heir to the Throne automatically entailed a review of the Civil List, and the Palace was seeking £50,000 a year for the couple – an increase of £35,000 on what Elizabeth had received. A series of delicate and complex discussions followed and eventually in December, under a new Chancellor, the matter was resolved satisfactorily.

If there was ever a more potent reminder that Elizabeth was primarily a public figure rather than an individual, it was surely in relation to her wedding. Even though it was essentially a personal event, everything was open to scrutiny, to be examined or explained or justified, a situation exacerbated by post-war hardship. While the royal family were great supporters of British industry, the wedding dress, by Norman Hartnell, raised questions. Lascelles responded testily to the Prime Minister's request for information, including the nationality of the silkworms: 'The *wedding dress* contains silk from Chinese silk worms but woven in Scotland and Kent,' he replied. 'The *wedding train* contains silk produced by Kentish silk worms and woven in London. The *going-away dress* contains 4 or 5 yards of Lyons silk which was not specially imported but was part of the stock held by the dress maker (Hartnell) under permit.'[1]

The King was sensitive to the clothing coupon situation: the Home Office noted, 'The Board of Trade have not, by the King's instruction, issued special coupons for the trousseau, although in view of the major national importance of the occasion, some concession has been allowed in respect of the wedding and going-away dresses.'[2] Such was the affection in which the Princess was held that women all over the country sent her their own clothing coupons, which she was prevented by law from accepting, so they were returned with grateful thanks. Rules applied to wedding presents, too. The King made it a policy that when it came to gifts from businesses, they could only be accepted from trade associations, not from individual firms, and be 'of reasonable size and value'.[3]

Naturally, Hartnell wanted details of the dress to be kept secret, which proved to be a nightmare; he was pestered day and night by reporters, causing him to whitewash his workshop windows and hang thick curtains. He begged the King and Queen for help. The Palace Press Secretary, Commander Richard Colville, suggested that a formal statement be made to the Press that it was the Princess's wish that details of her dress be kept secret. He also faced questions from the Women's Press Club of London about what cosmetics she would wear, who would help her get ready on the day, and so on. The dour Commander asked them if journalists really thought such details worthy of publication: 'Yes,' came the reply. He said he 'was not prepared to publicise the private lives of the Royal Family', although he would provide details of their charitable and welfare works: not exactly what they were hoping for, and an example of his misunderstanding of the relationship between the royal family and the Press.

With a swirling skirt and full court train thirteen feet long, Elizabeth's dress was exquisite. James Laver, design expert at the V&A at the time, enthused about Hartnell's creation:

> In a design based on delicate Botticelli curves, he has scattered over the ivory satin garlands of white York roses carried out in raised pearls, entwined with ears of corn minutely embroidered in crystal. By the device of reversed embroidery he has alternated star flowers and orange blossom, now tulle on satin and now satin on tulle, the whole encrusted with pearls and crystals.[4]

Hartnell liked to recount how his manager, returning from America, was asked at the customs if he had anything to declare: 'Yes,' he replied, 'ten thousand pearls for the wedding dress of Princess Elizabeth.'[5]

Hartnell also designed the bridesmaids' dresses. Elizabeth's attendants, in order of precedence, were Princess Margaret, aged seventeen; their cousin Princess Alexandra, eleven, the King's niece; Lady Caroline Montagu-Scott, twenty, daughter of the Duke of Buccleuch; Lady Mary Cambridge, twenty-three, great-niece of Queen Mary; Lady Elizabeth Lambart, twenty-three, daughter of the late Field Marshal the Earl of Cavan; the Hon. Pamela Mountbatten, eighteen, Philip's cousin; and cousins the Hon. Margaret Elphinstone, twenty-two, and the Hon. Diana Bowes Lyon, twenty-three, nieces of the Queen. Elizabeth also had two pages, her cousins Prince William of Gloucester, nearly six, eldest son of the Gloucesters, and Prince Michael of Kent, five, youngest child of the Duchess of Kent. Philip's best man was to be his cousin David, Marquess of Milford Haven.

Cousin Margaret remembered being fitted for her dress: 'Before the wedding I'd never been old enough to even think of walking across the doorstep of Norman Hartnell, and to do so to try on a bridesmaid's dress was very exciting!'[6] Pamela Mountbatten and her parents came back from India shortly before the wedding, where on 15 August independence had been declared. Pamela only had time for two fittings, but the expertise of Hartnell's team meant her dress fitted perfectly. 'Our white dresses had an ethereal beauty,' she said, 'tight-waisted, with full skirts over many layers of tulle, over white satin petticoats.'[7] As the dresses were sleeveless, the bridesmaids wore a tulle fichu draped over their shoulders, fastened by a satin bow and edged with star-shaped lily heads made from seed pearls and crystal beads. Their skirts were sprinkled with the same design, echoing that on the bride's dress. Delicate tiaras of silver orange blossom and ears of corn, and long white gloves with little pearl buttons, completed their outfit.

From the New York Institute of Dress Designers, Elizabeth received a gift of twenty-five dresses; she gave nineteen away to young women also called Elizabeth and aged twenty-one, who married on 20 November. For the wedding guests, the dress code was simpler than usual. On 15

September the Lord Chamberlain announced that for men, morning dress, lounge suits or service dress was to be worn, and for women morning dress with hats: 'This will be the first time that lounge suits have been permitted at a royal wedding. It is an austerity departure from the tradition of court dress or full dress uniform.'[8]

Schoolchildren were to have the day off at the King's request. The Ministry of Education urged schools to spend as little as possible in their efforts to mark the occasion, yet ingenious headmistresses still managed to give their children ices and even cakes saying 'Happiness to the Princess' in pink icing, despite the sugar shortage, for overall the public mood was expansive and carefree. One newspaper reader spoke for many when she wrote: 'Away with austerity. Let us make it a day she – and all of us – will remember.'

Family tree showing connection to European royalty (photo by Marcus Adams)
CAMERA PRESS

The wedding would see the largest meeting of foreign royals since before the war: 'a gathering of the remnants of European royalty – a vast, rivalrous, beleaguered, mutually suspicious and mutually loyal, and frequently impoverished, extended family.'[9] They included 'the flotsam of two world wars and many revolutions', in short, the world from which the bridegroom had come. It was thus an occasion to remind the world of the enduring survival of the British monarchy. 'When I am back behind the Iron Curtain,' said Queen Helen of Romania to Chips Channon, 'I shall wonder whether all this was a dream.'[10] Organising the reception of that 'extended family' was a major exercise in itself, undertaken by the Lord Chamberlain's office. Individual slips contained meticulous details of who was arriving when and where; who would meet and transport them; who would officially receive them and where they would be staying. Monarchs themselves received top-level attention, for example,[11]

Arrival of the King and Queen of Denmark
Date – Sunday 16 November
Port – Harwich
Hour – 1.30pm.
To be met by – Viscount Allendale
Proceeding to London by – LNER Train
Station – Liverpool Street
Hour – 4.45pm.
To be received by – The King
Cars required – 2 cars for Their Majesties and Suite (Red Crowns)
Baggage – 1 vehicle
Residence – Buckingham Palace
Police Escort through City.

Lesser royalty received the next level of attention. Prince Jean and Princess Elizabeth of Luxembourg were to be met by Brigadier Streatfield and received by a Gentleman Usher-in-Waiting. No police escort was deemed necessary, and they would be staying at the ordinary-sounding 1, Arkwright Road London; however, as it was in the wealthy area of Hampstead, it was unlikely to be a hardship. Those not invited included the Windsors, and Mary, the Princess Royal, boycotted the wedding apparently in protest at the way her brother had been treated since the Abdication. Philip's sisters were hurt at not being invited, and Sophie told Mountbatten that the Press kept insisting that they must be estranged, which made it worse. Afterwards their mother sent them a detailed description of the wedding, and they were pleased to learn that their brother had signed the register with the gold pen they gave him.

As the big day approached, Mabell Airlie said, 'It was a week of gaiety such as the Court had not seen for years.'[12] On 17 November the King and Queen gave a dinner party to welcome their royal guests and the Commonwealth Prime Ministers, followed by dancing, in which the King led a conga line. That evening, Elizabeth wore for the first time the kingfisher-blue ribbon of the Order of the Garter, which the King had recently bestowed on her. The next evening, the State Apartments in Buckingham Palace, closed for eight years, were opened to receive 1,200 guests at a pre-wedding ball. Noël Coward called it a 'sensational evening. Everyone looked shiny and happy.' Elizabeth and Philip were 'radiant. The whole thing was pictorially, dramatically and spiritually enchanting.'[13]

The week was marred, however, by the shocking news of the suicide in America of ex-Ambassador John G. Winant, which greatly saddened the royal family and Churchill. The King was represented at a memorial service held just the day before the wedding. Later it emerged that the married father of two had had a love affair with Churchill's daughter, Sarah, who had refused to marry him.

Some of the thousands of wedding presents were on public display at St James's Palace, and came from all over the world, from the very rich and the very poor. For once, the convention of returning presents from people Elizabeth did not know was overturned. The variety was extraordinary, from the large – the cinema from the Mountbattens – to the bizarre, such as the piece of cloth woven specially by their friend Gandhi, which Queen Mary thought was his famous loincloth and pronounced 'disgusting'. It nearly provoked an argument with Philip, who felt bound to defend Gandhi's reputation and called him 'a great man'. A string bag and tea cosies made by elderly ladies were appreciated as much as the pigeon-blood rubies from the Burmese Government. The Aga Khan's gift of a chestnut filly (stabled elsewhere) cannot have exceeded the affection with which a plastic brooch and earring set was made by a thirteen-year-old schoolgirl. Glassware came from the new US Ambassador, Lewis W. Douglas, and President Truman. The New York Veterans of Foreign Wars sent a cigar humidor with rare cigars to Philip, who was a favourite with the American GIs. Marie Stopes, the pioneer of birth control, gave the couple a copy of her controversial book *Married Love*, which may have got thumbed more often than Winston Churchill's gift of his tome, *The World Crisis*.

From her parents, Elizabeth received a necklace of diamonds and rubies and two strings of pearls. Margaret gave her sister the very practical and modern gift of a cream plastic picnic set for four and table glassware. Queen Mary surely surpassed herself in her presents, which included a diamond tiara, earrings and brooch, as well as fine pieces of antique furniture and linens. Crawfie thought Elizabeth was unnerved by the sudden lavishness of the presents: it had never been the King and Queen's policy to endow great luxury on their daughters, and she had always been happy with quite simple gifts. At Elizabeth's request, some wedding presents took the form of charitable bequests. Wedding cakes were displayed, too. Of twelve presented to her, the gorgeous four-tier creation by McVities and Price Ltd was the one she chose to be cut at the reception. Measuring 9 feet high and weighing 500 lb. it took three craftsmen five weeks to prepare and needed ten hours to bake.

Just before dusk, on the cold evening of Wednesday 19 November 1947, an excited crowd began to gather around the Victoria Memorial at the end of the Mall. Clutching thermos flasks, blankets and pillows, nibbling hot roast chestnuts, they positioned themselves at a place where many intended to spend the night and most of the following day. How delighted they were to be rewarded with the sight of the royal party leaving Buckingham Palace for Westminster Abbey for a rehearsal. Those who had gathered even earlier may have glimpsed the arrival of the wedding dress, delivered in a discreet grey van bearing a cardboard box, whose ordinariness disguised the fabulousness of the creation inside.

Princess Elizabeth and the Duke of Edinburgh on their wedding day,
20 November 1947
ROYAL COLLECTION TRUST/© HER MAJESTY QUEEN ELIZABETH II 2017

As darkness fell, faces were lit not only by the anticipation of seeing
the royal family on the balcony but also by the spectacle of the floodlit
Palace, enhanced by the individual lighting of a semi-circle of yellow and
white banners bearing the initials E and P. Along the processional route in
Whitehall, those already waiting had seen the drab window boxes outside

government offices replaced with brilliant blooms, while those encamped outside the Abbey admired the canvas canopies freshly coloured with red and gold decoration. The Household Cavalry shook out the mothballs from their ceremonial scarlet and blue tunics not used since 1939, and in the West End coloured bunting last seen on VE day was refreshed, adorning shop windows festooned with bright flags. Everywhere was an explosion of light and colour.

Like a beacon out of the darkness came the brilliant occasion which so many had looked forward to since July. On Thursday, 20 November, even the usual fog and rain kept away. That morning it was announced that the King had bestowed on Philip the Order of the Garter (after Elizabeth's, so that she would be senior) and had created him a Royal Highness. His titles would be Baron Greenwich, Earl of Merioneth and Duke of Edinburgh; however, as the wedding service sheet had to be printed well in advance, he still appeared on it as plain Lieutenant Philip Mountbatten RN. The King told his mother: 'It is a great deal to give a man all at once but I know Philip understands his new responsibilities on his marriage to Lilibet.'[14] Philip had celebrated his last night of freedom at the Dorchester Hotel with his uncle Dickie and old naval comrades, and when his valet John Dean woke him that morning, he seemed cheerful and confident. Later, however, having breakfast with his cousin Patricia Brabourne at Kensington Palace, he said, 'I'm either being very brave or very stupid.' She told him he was being brave; it was a lot to take on but she thought 'the characters of Philip and Princess Elizabeth matched extremely well'.[15]

With Elizabeth's breakfast tray came a large bouquet of white carnations from Philip. Afterwards she went to see her parents as usual, the last time for that childhood custom. Crawfie thought how grown up she looked and how Alah would have loved to have seen her darling Princess. Pamela Mountbatten said the wedding day 'was like being part of a fairy-tale'. As they all got ready, 'the atmosphere was a mixture of frenzy and calm as the professional dressers helped us prepare'.[16] Elizabeth's doughty dresser, Bobo, buoyed her up during a series of mishaps. The bouquet got lost: a footman remembered it arriving but no one knew where it went. Eventually he remembered he had put it in a cupboard to keep cool. Then

Elizabeth wanted to wear the pearls her parents gave her, which were on view at St James's Palace. Jock Colville went to get them, but the policemen there did not know him: he ended up being escorted back to the Palace with the necklace in case he absconded. Finally, as her tiara was being fitted over her veil, it broke, so an aide was bundled into a taxi and sent across London to the jewellers.

The bridesmaids left the Palace first; cousin Margaret said, 'I remember driving in the car up the Mall on the way to Westminster Abbey and waving one's white-gloved hand at the crowds in a rather lordly way.'[17] Thousands of people cheered all along the route as they caught a glimpse of the Princess, her sunray-shaped diamond tiara glittering in the late morning light, sitting in the Irish state coach with her father. Escorted by a procession of plumed and proud Life Guards with scarlet tunics and gleaming breastplates, they arrived at Westminster Abbey just before 11:30 a.m. Elsewhere in Britain and throughout the Commonwealth, millions of people listened to the ceremony on their wireless, and a few very lucky ones watched on television. One guest, the bride's friend Elizabeth Longford, said: 'People had not much believed in fairies during the war – more in demons – and here was a royal princess suddenly reappearing in the fullest outpouring of magic.'[18]

In the Abbey, two thousand people watched Princess Elizabeth walk slowly down the long aisle on her father's arm. She carried her bouquet of white orchids as her little pages, dressed in kilts of Royal Stuart tartan and white frilled shirts, lifted her train and her eight bridesmaids walked elegantly behind. When Princesses Margaret and Alexandra lifted the veil from her face, 'everyone could see the beauty of her peaches and cream complexion', said Pamela. The music, chosen by Elizabeth, began with 'Praise my Soul the King of Heaven'. Her lady-in-waiting, Lady Meg Egerton, had come to the rescue when the Princess announced shortly before the wedding that she wanted the Crimond setting of 'The Lord's my Shepherd'. Since no written score was available in London, Lady Meg, who had sung it in Scotland with the Princesses, repeated it in her fine soprano voice for the organist of Westminster Abbey, who took down the notes and then taught the Abbey choir.

In the congregation, Princess Alice watched with pride the son from whom she had been unwillingly parted. Her choice of dress was eccentric, resembling her usual nun's habit. Peculiar or not, Philip was glad of her attendance, for she was his closest relative present. Now he looked ahead to a new and very different life. The Archbishop of Canterbury conducted the wedding ceremony, each of them clearly saying their vows. Then the Archbishop of York spoke to the couple, reminding them that notwith-standing the splendour and significance of the service in the Abbey, it was essentially the same for 'any pair of lovers who might that day be married in some quiet church in a remote village somewhere in the Dales'.[19] They signed the register in the Chapel of St Edward the Confessor before twenty witnesses; the section for Philip's 'Rank or Profession' said 'HRH the Duke of Edinburgh'; his wife's 'Princess of the United Kingdom of Great Britain & Ireland'.

After a service of exquisite music, quiet devotion and splendid pag-eantry, one of the most moving moments was said to be at the end, when the bride and bridegroom, holding hands, paused to curtsey and bow to Queen Mary. *The Times* wrote: 'Here were the leaders to whom the coming generation will look for inspiration doing reverence to the representative of the leadership of yesterday.' Outside the Abbey, the crowds roared and cheered even louder as their beautiful Princess and her handsome hus-band smiled and waved to them from the fairytale glass coach as they returned to the Palace. The crowd sang 'All the nice girls love a sailor' as they waited outside the gates.

After photographs, the couple and the royal party went on to the balcony where Pamela said they 'were met by an incredible sight: the police had been holding everyone back around the Victoria Memorial, but when we came out, they let them go and we could see – and hear – a sea of people surging forward. Every time the newly-weds waved, the volume of cheering increased.'[20] At the wedding breakfast 150 guests enjoyed fish and partridge, ice cream and cake, at tables decorated with smilax and white carnations, and each place had a little bunch of white heather, sent from Balmoral. The King made no speech, just raised his glass to 'the bride'. Philip, too, kept it short and then distributed gifts to the bridesmaids: silver powder compacts in the Art Deco style with a gold crown above the bride's and groom's entwined initials and a row of six dark blue sapphires running down the centre. Princes William and Michael, the pages, were 'thoroughly overtired, grew peevish, and almost came to blows';[21] wrapped in large shawls, they were promptly removed by nannies.

Elizabeth changed into her going-away outfit, a powder-blue frock and matching coat, and a beret of the same colour with a feather cockade. They were going to Waterloo Station to begin their honeymoon, and as they made their way across the Palace forecourt towards their carriage, they were chased by the bridesmaids who pelted them with paper rose petals: guests were surprised to see the King grab the Queen's hand and join in running excitedly after the couple. As they got into their open landau, Elizabeth was delighted to find that Susan, her favourite corgi, had been hidden under a rug, and shared with her the hot water bottle that had thoughtfully been placed there to keep the bride warm on a cold, damp night.

As Michael Duff had speculated, it was an austerity honeymoon too, although luxurious by most people's standards. The Mountbattens had to return to India and lent them Broadlands for the first week. Although the house was sumptuous, they were bothered by photographers and members of the public who peered into the gardens and spoiled their visit to church. Yet, despite the irritations, Elizabeth was blissfully happy, telling her mother, 'We behave as though we had belonged to each other for years! Philip is an angel – he is so kind and thoughtful and living with him and having him around all the time is just perfect.'[22]

With Elizabeth's marriage, as with any other, adjustments had to be made by everyone. Her mother told her she had thought of her every minute since she left, but they wanted nothing except her happiness. No parents, she said, 'ever had a better daughter, you are always such an unselfish & thoughtful angel to Papa & me. . . . It is lovely to think that your happiness has made millions happy too in these hard times & it is a wonderful strength to the country that we can feel like one big family on such occasions.'[23] The King wrote touchingly:

when I handed your hand to the Archbishop I felt that I had lost something very precious. You were so calm & composed during the

Service & said your words with such conviction, that I knew every-
thing was all right. I am so glad you wrote & told Mummy that you
think the long wait before your engagement & the long time before the
wedding was for the best. I was rather afraid that you thought I was
being hard hearted about it. . . . Our family, us four, the 'Royal Family'
must remain together, with additions of course at suitable moments!!
. . . I can, I know, always count on you, & now Philip, to help us in
our work. . . . Your ever loving & devoted Papa.[24]

During the second week of their honeymoon, they went to familiar Birkhall, which was far more relaxing, if cold: they enjoyed walking and then lying in front of roaring fires. Now Elizabeth considered the adjustments that her husband was facing: 'Philip is terribly independent and I quite understand the poor darling wanting to start off properly, without everything being done for us,' she told her mother.[25] He wanted to be 'boss in his own home'. Writing affectionately to him, the Queen told Philip, 'I _do_ hope you won't find public life too trying, for the people _are_ demanding when they like you . . . I remember at Balmoral last year, you told me that you had always played a lone hand, and had to fight your own battles, & you will now have a great chance for individual leadership, as well as "married couple" leadership, which is so important as well.'[26]

Philip's reply must have comforted her: 'Lilibet is the only thing in this world which is absolutely real to me,' he wrote, 'and my ambition is to weld the two of us into a new combined existence that will not only be able to withstand the shocks directed at us but will also have a positive existence for the good. . . . I thank God for Lilibet and for us.'[27]

CHAPTER 22

Getting Settled (1948)

Elizabeth had been exposed to the notion of public duty since childhood. She had also been a dutiful daughter. Now at just twenty-one she was married, but unlike other young wives of the time, her position meant her duties extended beyond the needs of her husband. Life was not plain sailing after the honeymoon. Jock Colville noted that when they got back in mid-December, she was looking very happy and 'suddenly a woman instead of a girl'. Philip 'also seemed happy but a shade querulous, which is, I think, in his character'.[1] No doubt he was wondering where they were going to live. They were supposed to move into Sunninghill Park, an eighteenth-century Crown property near Ascot, but it had been gutted by fire in August 1947, shortly after it was announced they would live there. Elizabeth wondered if it was done deliberately but arson was ruled out after an investigation. Instead they obtained a lease on a house called Windlesham Moor in Surrey. However, it was not immediately available and was for weekends only. Their London home was to be Clarence House, home to the Duke of Connaught until his death in 1942. However, not only did it need updating, it had been badly bombed during the war, so it required a lot of work before it was fit for occupation; they would eventually move there in July 1949.

Fortunately, early in 1948 Elizabeth's great aunt and uncle, the Earl and Countess of Athlone, went to South Africa and in their absence the newly weds were able to borrow their rooms in Kensington Palace, moving in on 27 January. At that time, Philip had a desk job working for the Director of Operations in the Admiralty, whose office was in the Mall. Philip would drive them both from Kensington to Buckingham Palace, attend to his paperwork and then walk down the Mall to work, leaving Elizabeth to attend to hers.

The fact that he was now married to Elizabeth did not make life any easier for Philip as far as some courtiers were concerned. Cousin Margaret said, 'In the early days of marriage he suffered dreadfully from thinking he was a new broom and therefore he wanted to change everything, so one instinctively thought, "Oh, he's a bit of a bore."'[2] Philip certainly had little patience with things he regarded as waste of time. 'He says things that people don't like,' says Myra Butter. 'You always get an answer; you may not like it but he always considers it. He's so interesting as a person but you've got to know your stuff because he doesn't suffer fools gladly!'[3] The courtiers tended to overlook him, taking the view that only the Princess needed to be consulted on matters which concerned them both. In February, Colville suggested they should visit Paris, to bolster relations with Britain's wartime ally. Philip complained that Colville should have checked with him first before discussing it with the King and the Foreign Secretary. Nevertheless, he agreed to go and the date was fixed for May, *The Times* noting, 'The visit has been so timed at the holiday season that it does not interfere with the Duke's self-imposed resolution to spare himself no part of the routine of naval service while playing his ceremonial part as a member of the Royal Family.'[4] The Duke was committed to attend a staff course at the Royal Naval College, Greenwich, designed for senior officers like himself, which would begin on 30 March and last until mid-September. After all, part of 'being his own man', the phrase used by Elizabeth, was his desire to remain in the Royal Navy.

Colville still needed time to get used to Philip, finding he became impatient if his interest was not immediately aroused. By contrast, he had become accustomed to the Princess, having been her Private Secretary since mid-1947, aged thirty-two. He quickly found that 'she had not only a highly attractive personality but also a natural shrewdness of judgement and the most estimable honesty'. That honesty was of a 'rarer kind' than most people's: 'a refusal to pretend anything she did not believe and an ability to tell what she believed to be the plain, unvarnished truth to anybody, whoever they might be, without being the least aggressive, arrogant or impolite in the process'.[5] Honesty was something Elizabeth liked in others too, as did Philip: 'You have to be honest with him and not go toadying around the place, he doesn't like it,' says Myra Butter.[6]

Colville also discovered that the Princess lacked experience of the workings of politics and social affairs. With the King's permission, Colville arranged for her to be included in the distribution of Foreign Office telegrams and took her to a Foreign Affairs debate in the House of Commons. Other outings followed, for example, to a juvenile court. Colville also arranged a dinner party for the younger members of the government and their wives, such as (future Prime Minister) Harold Wilson, then President of the Board of Trade, and Hugh Gaitskell, the Minister of Fuel and Power. After dinner Colville arranged for each of them to spend fifteen minutes in conversation with the Princess on the sofa, an experience which might have been good for her education but which was unlikely to make her shout for joy. Although Gaitskell thought she had a 'very pretty voice and quite an easy manner' he thought her 'not very interested in politics or affairs generally'.[7] Clearly, Colville had more work to do.

Philip had support of his own in the form of his friend Mike Parker, who was now his equerry. Philip and Elizabeth then appointed a Comptroller and Treasurer of their joint household, Lt General Sir Frederick 'Boy' Browning. Philip said later, 'His seniority in the Army, his connection with the Grenadier Guards and his wide circle of friends in positions of responsibility were immensely valuable to the Queen and myself in the early years after our marriage.'[8] Before the Athlones returned from South Africa, the couple had to move out of Kensington Palace, and the only place to go was to 'Hotel Buckingham', as the Queen called the Palace.[9] Living there was not ideal for the newly weds; Crawfie said Lilibet continued to seek her mother's approval on things. However, she said Philip was 'a great help' in helping Lilibet become self-reliant and brought her more in touch with the outside world.[10]

While Philip was at Greenwich he stayed in the officers' mess, so for a few months, they saw each other only at weekends, except when he had leave. However, now they had Windlesham Moor as their weekend retreat and enjoyed making it homely, something Philip particularly liked. Within easy reach of Windsor, it was a partly furnished modern house, standing on fifty acres of grounds, which included a nine-hole golf course, and had five main bedrooms and six staff rooms. Myra and

David Butter lived at nearby Sunningdale and sometimes socialised with Elizabeth and Philip and other friends: 'It was great fun because we were all young couples, we all married around the same time, the Brabournes, the Penns . . . and we've remained friends all our lives.'[11] The couple also kept an eye on the refurbishments to Clarence House, doing the odd job themselves. Philip's valet John Dean said he 'enjoyed taking off his coat for such tasks as hanging pictures and moving chairs to wherever the Princess thought they would look best'.[12] Like his uncle Georgie, Philip loved gadgets and enjoyed visiting design shows: Dean recalled him buying a washing machine, on another occasion tins of soup.

Elizabeth remained devoted to her dogs and every afternoon at 4:30 p.m. 'a special tray was laid with a cloth, silver spoons and forks, a plate of biscuits, a plate of chopped meat, a plate of vegetables and a jug of rich gravy, so that she could feed them herself', said Dean.[13] Soon she would have a different mouth to feed, for in April 1948 she found she was pregnant, the baby expected in November. The timing of her discovery, five months into her marriage, chimed nicely with her parents' Silver Wedding anniversary. Although it was essentially a private event, it was marked on 26 April by a Thanksgiving Service in St Paul's Cathedral. In words that could also apply to their daughter and son-in-law years later, the Archbishop of Canterbury said of the King and Queen, 'The evidence and example of their steadfastness, rooted in the serenity of a happy home life and expressed in selfless service to their people, have steadied and encouraged the whole nation and stood as a living symbol in our midst of those simple sanctities wherein man's true life consists.'

Two other important occasions took place that month. On 12 April, the third anniversary of President Roosevelt's death, the royal family met with his widow to unveil a statue of him in London's Grosvenor Square, along with Churchill and Ambassador Lewis Douglas. Afterwards Eleanor Roosevelt stayed at Windsor and was impressed that Elizabeth asked her a question about homes for young women offenders: clearly, Colville's work was making a difference. Then, on St George's Day, Elizabeth attended a service in St George's Chapel to mark the six hundredth anniversary of the institution of the Order of the Garter, at which she, Philip and the new Knights Companion of the Order were formally installed. In a simple but profoundly symbolic service, before a congregation of one thousand, they were admitted by the King into the ancient brotherhood, all wearing the magnificent plumed hat and blue velvet mantel. Observed on the way into the Chapel in 'merry conversation' with Philip, the Princess showed 'with what unexpected harmony the beauty of modern girlhood can be framed in the "old look" of 1348'.[14]

Elizabeth needed no reminder that 'girlhood' was behind her when, three months pregnant, she faced a heat wave in Paris when they made their four-day visit in May, the hottest Whitsun weekend ever recorded there. Much had happened to France since her parents' visit, when Hitler was preparing his onslaught on Czechoslovakia. Ostensibly the purpose of the visit was to open the Exhibition of British Life, in the presence of President Auriol, but really it was a chance to restore friendship after difficult years. As *The Times* opined, 'It is right that the first visit of the Heiress Presumptive to any country outside her father's dominions should be paid to France. She now takes up her part in one of the most important functions of royalty . . . representing the peoples of the Commonwealth among their friends in other lands.'[15]

Elizabeth opened the Exhibition with a speech in excellent French. From the President she received the Grand Cross of the Legion of Honour and Philip the Croix de Guerre with palms, and at the Arc de Triomphe they laid a wreath on the grave of the Unknown Soldier. The public seemed to love them, and the government feted them extravagantly. At a lavish lunch at Versailles, the tablecloths and napkins had been embroidered with 'E's and 'P's in their honour; they were taken in a triumphal progress down the Seine, followed by a dinner and reception at the British Embassy. The French appreciated the Princess's beauty in a white décolleté evening gown with turquoise beading, split at the front to reveal a turquoise underskirt, all of which set off the scarlet ribbon of the Legion of Honour. A diamond necklace and diadem headdress completed the magnificence.

Their hosts took them to the races, and later they danced at a fashionable nightclub. The climax was a gala performance at the Opéra, where the crowd outside clamoured all evening for the Princess to appear on the balcony. She was willing to do so, but the security chiefs refused to let her, for fear there might be an 'incident', not caused by their own countrymen but by 'foreigners'.[16] There were a couple of low points. Elizabeth became tired and listless, Philip got a stomach upset and, while they were in a restaurant, spotted a camera lens, so 'was naturally in a frightful rage', said Colville.[17] However, overall the visit was a huge success. In spite of the heat and her pregnancy, Colville said Elizabeth 'carried out a gruelling programme of engagements so faultlessly that not even the most perfectionist of diplomats could find anything to criticise'.[18]

Not everyone was happy. The Scottish Lord's Day Observance Society heard about Their Royal Highnesses gallivanting on a Sunday to the races, nightclub and theatre, and told the General Assembly of the Free Church of Scotland, which formally voiced a complaint. The Church was disappointed that the royal couple should have behaved so while on an official visit, for it set 'a most regrettable example' to the youth of the nation.[19]

On 20 May, shortly after they arrived home, the Palace announced that Margaret had measles; she had been taken ill during the weekend Elizabeth was away, and it emphasised that 'during the period of infection Princess Margaret has had no contact at any time with Princess Elizabeth'.[20] In the 1940s a link between measles and complications in pregnancy was gaining recognition, but even if the Palace had considered that possibility, it was unlikely to mention Elizabeth for that reason when her condition had not yet been announced. More likely it was so that no one who had been near Elizabeth recently would be worried.

Soon the world did find out, when on 4 June the Palace announced that the Princess would undertake no public engagements from the end of June. When she and Philip arrived at the Epsom Derby the next day, a million spectators made it clear that they had heard the news, as they did that evening at the National Festival of Youth and Sport, where police had to hold back the crowds as the couple got out of their car. Their household was now increased by the appointment of an Extra Equerry, a part-time, unpaid post, to assist Mike Parker when necessary at public functions.

Elizabeth's pregnancy raised a question that had been vexing Lascelles: whether it was truly necessary for the Home Secretary to be present at a royal birth. It had been happening for centuries and caused much inconvenience when Margaret did not arrive when expected. Lascelles asked the Home Office to look into it, and in June, Chuter Ede told him it was a custom only, had 'no statutory authority behind it and there is no legal requirement for its continuance'.[21] Lascelles suggested to the King that the custom be abolished. However, the Queen thought it might damage the dignity of the Throne, and the King was indecisive. A visit to the Palace by the Canadian High Commissioner helped settle the matter. The Princess's pregnancy came up in conversation, and the envoy said he presumed that, when the moment arrived, he and the representatives of the other Dominions would be invited to attend, along with the Home Secretary. It was a revelation to Lascelles, for when Elizabeth was born it had never occurred to him or anyone else that the Dominions should be invited, but certainly it was constitutionally correct. When Lascelles told the King that there would be seven ministers sitting in the passage, he was horrified at the prospect, and the custom was abolished forever.[22]

Very soon Elizabeth was inundated with good wishes and presents from all over the world. As with the wedding presents, Elizabeth was allowed to keep the baby gifts, but of course, there was far more than she could ever need; the vast surplus of shawls, bootees and matinee coats were made into layettes for other mothers whose babies arrived at the same time. Particularly touching were letters Elizabeth received from German mothers, who told her they shared her happiness and admired the King and Queen and their children, and liked to have news of them.[23] Those letters were passed on to the Foreign Office. Others saw the Princess almost as a deity, who could solve their problems. One mother said her son was in prison, and as the Princess herself was to become a mother, she could have him released. Such letters could not be answered personally by the royal family but had to be dealt with by the Home Office.

That Elizabeth and Philip were starting to be viewed as a joint entity was reflected in one 'London Letter' column:

When Princess Elizabeth and the Duke of Edinburgh appear in public, they get a reception which can only be compared to what we read of Queen Victoria in her young days. . . . There is sympathy in them, as well as affection; and every word that either says. . . helps to

*strengthen the bond. In some ways, of course, they are amongst the for-
tunate of the earth. In others they have not only a high but an arduous
duty to perform. They show that they know it and they have dedicated
themselves to it – both of them in their different but conjoint spheres –
quite wholeheartedly.*[24]

Elizabeth was still seen in public after the end of June but not in an
official capacity. In July she watched with Edwina Mountbatten as their
husbands took their seats in the House of Lords.[25] Philip began to receive
praise for his speeches, the *Evening Standard* saying that royalty 'have
not produced a speaker of such charm and friendliness since the days
of the Prince of Wales'.[26] However, his refusal to let anyone else write
them caused concern, as there was no chance to have them checked for
anything inappropriate. Harold Macmillan said, 'I fear this young man is
going to be as big a bore as Prince Albert and as great a trouble. Let us
hope the king may live to be a great age'.[27]

There was also concern about some of Philip's friends. A photographer, Baron Nahum, whom Philip already knew via Mountbatten, invited
him to join his club, the Thursday Club, which met in Wheeler's fish restaurant in Old Compton Street. Other members included David Milford
Haven and Mike Parker. Editors of popular newspapers belonged, as did
a group of well-known actors, including Peter Ustinov and David Niven.
The club was known for riotous stag parties, which were said to be not
always all-male.

Baron also knew some less desirable people, and invited them to
parties at his studio in Mayfair, according to Robin Dalton. In October,
Baron introduced Philip and an equerry to a showgirl called Pat Kirkwood,
a beautiful dark-haired musical comedy star. They all went out to dinner,
and she and Philip danced. Inevitably, it was alleged Philip had an affair
with her. Years later when he met Kirkwood again, he openly acknowledged he had enjoyed himself that night, putting paid to the rumour that
anything more had happened. Kirkwood herself said they had not danced
closely, and they had all gone back to Baron's flat afterwards for scram-
bled eggs, before Philip left.[28] Because of his good looks, his energy and
his status, he would always be dogged by rumour. As he would say wryly,

with a private detective always with him, there was little chance of getting up to anything.

Elizabeth would have been more anxious if she had been aware of her father's illness, but the King insisted she be told nothing until after the birth. He had been troubled by cramps in his feet and legs, which became worse and kept him awake with numbness, then pain. On 12 November, his doctors confirmed that he was suffering from arteriosclerosis and feared his leg might have to be amputated. They were in no doubt that the King's heavy smoking was at the root of it, causing obstruction to his circulation. The habit against which James I had railed so vehemently was loved by the later royal family and contributed to the deaths of George V and Edward VII. Even Queen Mary smoked and had given Bertie a cigarette case for his eighteenth birthday. But as Hardinge told his son, the King smoked because of the stress he was under: 'He literally died for England.'[29] The King reluctantly postponed a tour of Australia and New Zealand that was planned for him and the Queen, with Margaret.

Meanwhile, preparations for the birth were completed. Mr William Gilliatt was appointed as gynaecologist; President of the Royal College of Obstetricians and Gynaecologists, he had attended at the births of the Kent children. The old pram in which Alah had pushed both Princesses was brought out and done up. As the couple were still not settled in a house, and Windlesham Moor was not appropriate, the birth would take place in Buckingham Palace, just below Elizabeth's second-floor bedroom. The baby's cot and basket were done up in buttercup yellow silk, with lace trim: the royal family did not go in for traditional pinks and blues. From all over the world predictions as to the sex were proclaimed, each method crankier than the next, and old wives everywhere passed on to the young Princess ancient words of wisdom about childbirth. The King declared by proclamation that the children of the Princess and the Duke of Edinburgh would have the title of His or Her Royal Highness, which was not usually the case for children born to the Sovereign's daughter.

Elizabeth was still up and about on 12 November, when she and Philip had dinner with the Brabournes at the Mountbattens' house in Chester Street. It was cutting it fine, for the next day she went into labour. However, by the evening of the fourteenth nothing had happened, so

Philip went to play squash with Mike Parker on the Palace's court, then had a swim in the pool. At 9:14 p.m. the baby was delivered, and Lascelles rushed in to tell the Duke he had a son. Philip immediately went to his wife, who was still under anaesthetic, so was taken to see his son in the nursery. The King, who fortunately was able to walk, arrived with the Queen, and Philip took them to see their grandson. Queen Mary was there too, thrilled with her first great-grandchild. Philip opened champagne to toast the medical and household staff, and when Elizabeth was awake, he was at her bedside with a bouquet.

The Prince had fair hair and blue eyes and weighed 7 lb. 6 oz. He was heir apparent to the Dukedom of Edinburgh and his father's other peerages, and he was his mother's heir. However, as she was only Heiress Presumptive, the Prince would always be second heir presumptive until she became Queen. According to Crawfie, Elizabeth breastfed him for the first few months, and after a month, when the nursery nurse was no longer needed, he was put in the care of Miss Helen Lightbody. The daughter of an Edinburgh textile worker, she had looked after the Gloucesters' sons and would become known as 'No-Nonsense Lightbody'. She was joined by an assistant, twenty-two-year-old Mabel Anderson, another Scot, whose policeman father had been killed in the Blitz.

Margaret was not around when her nephew was born, for she was at the home of the Earl and Countess of Scarborough in Yorkshire, but she called the Palace frequently for news. Her position in the line of succession went down a step, but she was gradually finding her own role and was in Yorkshire to carry out public engagements. She was a godparent at the Prince's christening, which was performed on 15 December by the Archbishop of Canterbury, in the Bow Room at Buckingham Palace; the chapel had not yet recovered from the effects of wartime bombing. Fortunately the King was able to attend, because after two weeks of treatment, the danger of amputation had passed and his doctors even thought he should be able to do the Australian tour after all; however, for practical reasons, it was replanned for 1952.

The Prince's full name was Charles Philip Arthur George. Elizabeth and Philip had chosen names that mostly had historical significance, but the first name was simply one they liked. Coincidentally at the time of his birth, the film *Bonnie Prince Charlie* was having its first showing in London's West End, with David Niven playing in the title role; the actor had joined Philip at a celebratory all-male party he held a few days after the birth. His godparents were the King, Queen Mary, Princess Margaret, King Haakon of Norway, David Bowes Lyon, and Philip's relations, his grandmother Victoria, his uncle Prince George of Greece and his cousin Patricia Brabourne.

The official christening cake was formed from the top tier of his parents' wedding cake and redecorated with colonnades and a silver crib. Other splendid cakes were also welcomed by the Palace, one decorated by ex-Service silversmiths, another made by young cookery students with marzipan from New Zealand and ingredients from all over the Empire. It was the sort of innovation that the infant, who one day would create the Prince's Trust to help young people in work, would come to appreciate. What no one could have imagined at the time was that Prince Charles would also become the oldest and longest-waiting Heir to the Throne in history.

CHAPTER 23

Princess, Wife, Mother (1949–1950)

1949 is said by Elizabeth's friends to have been the start of the happiest period in her life, although no one knew at the time how short it would be. However, it started badly when she caught measles. They were at Sandringham in the New Year, where Elizabeth was confined to bed. The illness made her eyes hurt, so the Queen had to read everything to her. Eventually, Elizabeth could tell Lady Desborough, 'I am now able to write again, and it is wonderful to be allowed out and about, and also to be able to read once more! Measles is a horrid illness, and I am really rather thankful to be over it. Luckily the baby is in wonderful health, and has put on 3 pounds since he has been here! He is a great joy to us and of course, his grandparents and his <u>great</u>-grandmother find him a very lovable creature!'[1]

The King's health, too, still caused concern. Initially he seemed to be improving, telling Lady Desborough, 'I am much better now & the required treatment to my legs has made a big improvement in my health. It is very nice to be here at Sandringham once again when I can get out of doors for a few hours a day.'[2] The Queen told a friend that 'the one good thing is that he is having the first rest since 1936'.[3] However, in early March he was disappointed when his doctors decided his improved state of health could only be maintained if he lived the life of an invalid, which his temperament alone would make impossible. Upon their advice, on 12 March he reluctantly had an operation on both legs. To his relief, and that of the public, it was successful, and by May he was able to undertake some duties.

Declining an invitation in May to join the Hardinges at Avon Tyrell in Hampshire, Elizabeth said, 'Unfortunately we have a very busy summer ahead of us, and life is very hectic, with every day mapped out to the second. It was so wonderful to spend ten very peaceful days at Birkhall without having to worry about anything!'[4] Earlier that month she and Philip had enjoyed their Scottish break, without the baby, then undertook a four-day tour of Northern Ireland, in which they received the Freedom of the City of Belfast.

In between engagements they enjoyed a lively social life. On Elizabeth's twenty-third birthday in April, for instance, they watched *The School for Scandal* and afterwards dined at London's fashionable Cafe de Paris, where they were joined by the stars of the play, Lawrence Olivier and Vivien Leigh. They all danced, then went on to a nightclub to continue the fun. Royalty and show business would always fascinate each other. At Windlesham Moor, Philip's valet saw Danny Kaye, the American comedian, 'capering around Princess Elizabeth' on the lawn.[5] Chips Channon noticed that at a ball at Windsor, the couple was surrounded by the smart, artistic members of the emerging 'Princess Margaret set'.[6]

The King was able to attend the Trooping of the Colour in June, but rode in an open carriage instead of on horseback to carry out the inspection. This time he wore the splendid scarlet uniform of the pre-war ceremony and was able to stand for a while on a dais to take the salute. As he got back into his carriage, he noticed Elizabeth, riding behind with the Duke of Gloucester, having trouble with her horse, Winston, who kept prancing and backing away. Eventually, she managed to calm him and drew a compliment from the King, who walked across to talk to her. The crowd could not help but notice the increasingly frail and prematurely old man and his young and blooming daughter. It must have been increasingly clear that in Elizabeth, the future was not far away.

At last, on 4 July, they moved into Clarence House. At 2:00 p.m. the Princess's personal standard was flown or 'broken out' from the flagstaff, and a sentry of the Welsh Guards, in scarlet and bearskin, was posted outside. Built in 1825 for the Duke of Clarence, later William IV, the four-storey house enjoyed magnificent views across St James's Park and shared a garden with St James's Palace. For Philip, it was his first permanent home since childhood and one where he could establish a proper base for their family. When his mother, back in Greece, heard about the birth of her grandson, she told her brother Dickie that Philip 'adores children &

also small babies. He carries it about himself quite professionally to the nurse's amusement.'[7]

The couple's bedrooms were adjacent with a linking door, as was common among the upper classes. Philip never wore pyjamas, as Boy Browning discovered when Philip stayed in Cornwall with him and his wife, the novelist Daphne du Maurier, and John Dean said that while he was attending the Duke, and Bobo was helping the Princess, the couple 'would joke happily across the half-open door'. Philip and Elizabeth had consulted their staff about their workplaces, with the result that 'the staff quarters were as near ideal as could possibly be imagined', said Dean.[8] The royal couple were considered highly considerate employers who liked to live simply when they could, with a lack of pomp and ceremony. Dean said Philip took more interest than Elizabeth in the way the house was run.[9]

For a little while longer their social life continued to buzz. Shortly after moving in to Clarence House, they were invited to a fancy dress party held by vivacious blonde socialite Sharman 'Sass' Douglas, daughter of American Ambassador, Lewis W. Douglas; he would always remember his time in Britain because he nearly lost an eye in April when a hook got caught in it while he fished in Hampshire, and he had to wear an eye patch from then on. Sass was already a good friend of Margaret, and they had all partied together in 1948 when Sass was a bridesmaid to a family friend. For her party, Philip and Elizabeth turned the tables: he went as a butler, Elizabeth as a maid, in a black dress, white apron and black and white cap. By contrast, Margaret went all out in a 'low-cut red and black fancy costume with huge red bow at the front, black stockings and very high heeled shoes. Her small black hat was surmounted by high red feathers',[10] and she sported sparkly butterflies in her hair and on her dress. Clearly, she had put behind her the 'horrible & vulgar article'[11] that the *Sunday Express* had published about her in February which speculated on her love life. Elizabeth and Philip enjoyed a weekend in August with the Duke and Duchess of Buccleuch and met Sass again; her friendship with Margaret would continue all their lives. In November, Margaret was spotted smoking at a charity ball and spending most of the time walking around with Sass rather than dancing. While her elder sister was the dutiful Princess with her handsome husband and adorable heir, Margaret was the beautiful, amusing, unattached attention-seeker with admirers everywhere.

Their father, meanwhile, seemed to be bearing up, and at Balmoral in October the Queen told Helen Hardinge he was slightly better, 'which is a great relief, so now we are behaving like people going back to a horrid school & counting & hoarding each last hour & day before getting into the train at Ballater & going back to gloomy, horrible but dear London'.[12] Philip had been agitating to get back to active service and was delighted that month when the King approved his taking an appointment as second-in-command of HMS *Chequers*, leader of the first destroyer flotilla based in Malta. The Mountbattens were there too. His uncle Dickie had taken command of the First Cruiser *Squadron*: rather a comedown

Lady Edwina Mountbatten with Prince Charles and Princess Anne in Malta
UNIVERSITY OF SOUTHAMPTON

from his previous wartime role, and his position as Viceroy of India, but he wanted to be back at sea.

Shortly after Philip arrived, Mountbatten was in the news for other reasons. A Bill he had proposed was passed in the House of Commons, after modification, which allowed married women to anticipate the income from fortunes left to them in a trust fund. In the Mountbattens' case, it would allow Edwina to draw from the £1,400,000 left to her in a trust by her grandfather, Sir Ernest Cassel. The Bill had faced much opposition by Conservative MPs, which Lord Mountbatten's Labour supporters said was because of their animosity towards him: that as Viceroy of India, he had carried through a policy in which the Opposition did not believe. Whether or not that was their reason, there was certainly opposition to his Bill, on the grounds that lifting the existing restriction would see wives going on an orgy of spending: it was '"the lucky ladies" Bill', sneered one Conservative MP. While 'Mountbatten's Bill', as it was originally called, was intended to benefit Edwina, it ended up helping all married women, however small their trust fund: 'We are seeking to alleviate the position of these ordinary little people', said the Attorney General, Sir Hartley Shawcross, 'and enable them to realise their money and spend it as they will'.[13] While the result was positive, it reflected something of society's attitude to women, and from which even Elizabeth's position did not always protect her.

As Philip's ship was undergoing a refit, he stayed with the Mountbattens at the Villa Guardamangia in Valetta. Just after celebrating Charles's first birthday, Elizabeth left him with her parents and flew out to Malta in time for their second wedding anniversary, intending to return for Christmas. Cousin Margaret said that being in Malta 'was the nearest she's ever come to leading a totally normal life. She was just being the wife of a naval officer',[14] albeit one who had staff and could leave her child behind when she needed to. Edwina Mountbatten flew out with Elizabeth and her entourage: lady-in-waiting Meg Egerton and Equerry Mike Parker, Bobo Macdonald, a footman and detective, and Philip's valet. Philip met her at the airport, along with the Governor of Malta and other dignitaries, then drove them both off in the only Rolls Royce on the island, lent to them by the Commander-in-Chief. Edwina

Princess Elizabeth with Lord Mountbatten on a ship
UNIVERSITY OF SOUTHAMPTON

gave up her own quarters in the Villa and moved into Dickie's bedroom, obliging him to move to another.

After their initial welcome, the people of Malta tended to leave the couple alone. Nevertheless, Elizabeth's visit had to be formally acknowledged, so on her first day came a 21-gun royal salute and a welcome in the Legislative Assembly, and all ships in the Mediterranean Fleet were 'dressed overall'. While Philip was at work, she did some window shopping, drove around Valetta and visited his ship. She enjoyed watching a polo match, a game that sportsman Dickie wanted his nephew to try. However, Philip said he was not going to 'ponce around on a horse' and called it a 'snob sport',[15] preferring to play hockey on his ship. Eventually, he did try polo, proved to be a natural and came to love it.

Elizabeth's few engagements were important but not too demanding. She could drive around in her own Daimler car, either with a companion or by herself, and she and Philip spent time alone when he was free (always followed at a discreet distance by a plainclothes police officer). At other times they joined the Mountbattens for picnics and boat trips 'in the admiral's barge', as Pamela Mountbatten remembered. Entertainment was plentiful: the Governor's dinner at San Anton Palace; a dance on *Chequers*; the Saddle Club Ball and the State Ball. They did some entertaining of their own, hosting a Flotilla Cocktail Party and a dinner at the Villa. Mike Parker said Elizabeth 'generally mucked in with the other wives. . . . She spent only ten per cent of the time being a Princess', and that was because of Mountbatten, who 'tried to get her into the admirals' strata'.[16] Never before had she experienced such 'normality'.

Meanwhile, Prince Charles had developed tonsillitis, which child experts said was unusual in a young child. On 13 December, Clarence House announced that the Princess would stay on in Malta for Christmas, with no return date yet announced. It also said that Prince Charles was recovering and making 'excellent progress'. Clearly, Elizabeth talked about him while she was away. Pamela recalled that 'one evening the Princess proudly showed us the films she had taken herself of her son Charles, who was now walking and was very sweet.'[17]

The Queen told Elizabeth that she and the King would miss her very much, for it was 'the first Xmas without our very darling daughter', but they were glad she would be spending it with Philip. The Queen had seen Charles the previous day and 'he seemed in very good form', although his teeth were troubling him and after his 'rather violent attack', it may take him a while to get back to normal. The King 'seems well, but gets a bit tired with all the worries – Uncle David came & had one of his violent yelling conversations, stamping up & down the room, & very unfairly saying that because Papa wouldn't (and couldn't) do a certain thing, that Papa must hate him.' It was so unfair, she said, because the King had been so 'scrupulously fair & thoughtful & honest about all that has happened'.[18]

The Duke of Windsor had been on a three-day visit, staying with Queen Mary, and had a private meeting with the King, in which he again demanded that Wallis be made HRH. Queen Mary told Bertie beforehand, 'Giving *her* this title would be fatal, and after all these years I fear lest people think that we condoned this dreadful marriage . . . I hope that you will be very firm and refuse to do anything about it, and that the Government will back you up.'[19] After their difficult meeting, the King reminded his brother that he had chosen to renounce the Throne for himself and his descendants and to do his bidding would reverse that decision. He also reminded him that he had made Wallis a Duchess, 'despite what happened in December 1936. You should be grateful to me for this. But you are not.'[20]

The King did not know that in 1946 the Duke had started discussions with a minor aristocrat and confidant, Kenneth de Courcy, about how the future for him and his Duchess might look. When the King's health started to fail, de Courcy saw a time when he may not be able to appear in public but would need a Regent. The obvious person would be Princess Elizabeth, but de Courcy played on fears that the Mountbattens might seize the opportunity. De Courcy wrote to the Duchess on 13 May 1949: 'I may tell you confidentially that a Regency has already been discussed and it seems likely enough that presently [a Regent] will be appointed.' He said that if the Regency was 'primarily influenced by the Mountbattens, the consequences for the [Windsor] dynasty might be fatal. [They] . . . will do everything in their power to increase their influence.'

In the letter, he presented a bleak picture of the King's health and suggested to the Duchess that the Duke could make it 'impossible for the Mountbattens to become the decisive political and social influence upon the Regency and the future Monarch'. He suggested the Windsors buy an agricultural property near London and for the Duke to practice modern experimental farming, which 'would make a great appeal to the country'. If a constitutional crisis erupted, the Duke would be on hand to 'help', and it would give him an opportunity to reassert his place in history. If David ever did consider acting upon de Courcy's suggestion, he left it too late, because the King seemed to be recovering.[21]

Elizabeth eventually left Malta on 28 December. 'My mother remarked that it was like putting a little bird back in its gilded cage,' said Pamela.[22] She went first to Clarence House, seemingly not in any great hurry to see her son, who was still at Sandringham. After four days of catching up on correspondence and other matters, she went to the races and saw her horse Monaveen, which she owned jointly with the Queen, win at 10–1. Then she went to see Charles.

Elizabeth was probably a more demonstrative wife than a mother. Like the Queen, she was necessarily a working mother in the days when it was still unusual: she was not a wage-earner, of course, but she was sustained partly by the public purse and expected to play her part. The Queen nevertheless frequently spoke of the importance of women being at home and looking after the family. In October, Elizabeth had spoken at a rally of Mother's Union wives, in terms similar to those her mother had used, denouncing the effects of marriage breakup on children. It was not easy writing speeches: Jock Colville said 'they had to be presented in such a way as not to be socially or politically provocative. On the other hand it was important that [Elizabeth's] speeches should not be flat, conventional and uninspiring.'[23] Elizabeth told the 3,600 wives that their first duty was to 'uphold the sanctity of marriage'. She spoke of the 'havoc' that breakups can have on children, saying, 'we can have no doubt that divorce and separation are responsible for some of the darkest evils in our society today'.[24] But the war had wrought changes in society, practical and moral, and her speech caused protests from those who wanted the divorce laws changed. The chairman of the Marriage Law Reform Committee protested that the harm done to children where the parents were always arguing could be far worse. Given that the views were essentially hers, she could not escape responsibility for the sentiments. Colville admitted later that the speech was 'on a rather high moral plane'. Her own wider family had recently experienced a breakup. The previous year her cousin Anne divorced Viscount Anson: she had been unfaithful to him, but he agreed she could bring the petition on the ground of his desertion. They had two children, who would gain a stepfather when Anne married Prince Georg of Denmark in 1950.

On her own family front, in early 1950 Elizabeth discovered she was pregnant again, the baby due in August. It was wonderful news, although at the same time the royal family were preoccupied with the 'disloyalty' of Crawfie. She had retired in January 1949, aged forty, and was given a grace and favour apartment in Kensington Palace and a pension. She was asked to write some articles for an American magazine *Ladies Home Journal*. Crawfie told the Queen, who initially did not reply, but in April she reminded Crawfie of the need to be 'utterly oyster' about the family. After dialogues and entreaties on all sides, Crawfie signed a contract to write a book. The Queen was sent a copy of the manuscript to approve before publication but was given only three weeks to respond. Publication date was to be January 1950: in fact, extracts were already appearing in the British Press in December 1949. From being a much-loved member of the household, Crawfie became *persona non grata*. She was allowed to keep her apartment but later moved back to Scotland. The Queen later told Helen Hardinge of their disappointment:

> *Poor Miss Crawford's effort is lamentable in every way – it is vulgar and inaccurate and altogether a very depressing affair. I think that something awful happened to her after she married, for she was always the soul of discretion; and that someone so utterly trusted as she was should write in this way about our most intimate & private affairs is absolutely inexplicable. Anyway, it's one of the saddest things that has ever happened to us, & it was such a shock to the children who were so fond of her.*[25]

Queen Mary's view was similar on matters of confidentiality: 'Crawfie's articles appalled Queen Mary, as you know, and all that sort of publicity is, to HM, <u>most</u> distasteful!'[26]

The Queen was not opposed to articles about the royal family as long as she approved of them. Her letter was prompted by a feature Helen had written about the monarchy and sent to her for approval[27]:

> *I do think that it is <u>charming</u> – in fact, the description of Lilibet's wedding was so touchingly and delightfully written, that the slow tears of old age stung their way into my eyes. . . . It cannot do anything but good to have the monarchy written about in such sympathetic and understanding terms, and so important that it should be done on a serious note. As you say most of the stuff is tittle tattle. I am sure that the monarchy needs an occasional sensible & realistic article, just to balance the many stupid and often mischievous & ignorant ones.*

On 18 April 1950, the Press announced the Princess's news. Leaving Charles with his grandparents again, she flew to Malta to join Philip for her twenty-fourth birthday. They also helped Pamela Mountbatten to celebrate her twenty-first, 'at the Phoenicia, complete with Scottish reels and country dances. The Dashing White Sergeant traditionally broke the ice at the beginning of the evening and the reels allowed the other officers to pluck up the courage to ask the heir to the Throne to dance. She danced extremely well and loved it.'[28] Freddie Mizzi was a clarinet player with the Jimmy Dowling Band who played at the Phoenica when Elizabeth and Philip were there: 'She and the Duke used to dance a lot. She was always so beautiful and always so nice and kind. We used to play their favourite song, *People Will Say We're in Love* from *Oklahoma!*'[29] While she was away the Queen sent her news of Charles: 'It has been snowing <u>hard</u> . . . Charles was fascinated by the snowflakes. He pressed his little face against the window, & watched them falling for ages.'[30] Elizabeth arrived back in Britain on 10 May, after a four-week holiday.

In July came the good news that Philip had been promoted and appointed to his first command, on the frigate HMS *Magpie*. The Queen sent congratulations and told him about Charles, of whom he had seen little: 'such a strong manly little boy, & extremely brave too! . . . how he will love having you home.'[31] Philip was given leave for the birth; Princess Anne was born on 15 August 1950 in Clarence House. Elizabeth took longer to recover than before, and rather than resuming her engagements in October, she was ordered by the doctors to postpone or cancel them for another month. In September, Philip returned to Malta to take up his new command. Elizabeth told Helen Hardinge:

> *We are very delighted and proud to have a little girl as well as a boy – and it will be such fun when they are older. The baby is quite unlike Charles, who appears fascinated by her and treats her with great care and affection – so far! I am hoping very much to get up to Balmoral as soon as I can for a welcome change, as London is no place to be at this time of year, and now that my husband has gone back to join his ship, it will be even worse.*[32]

She was able to get to Malta in November and found that *Magpie* was to escort the Commander-in Chief's vessel to Philip's cousin, King Paul of Greece, in Athens. Elizabeth went with him, the first time she had been to Philip's homeland. They stayed with the British Ambassador and his wife, who formed the impression that the Princess was 'very shy and rather withdrawn, a bit of a shrinking violet, in fact, and Philip was young and vigorous and jollied her along.'[33] In December, Elizabeth was delighted when Margaret joined them in Malta; she enjoyed herself thoroughly and told the Queen that they were angelic to her. She went home in time for Christmas with the family, which included her nephew and niece: Elizabeth was remaining in Malta again. Their freedom, however, was drawing to a close.

CHAPTER 24

Rehearsing the Future (1951–1952)

Elizabeth now had a new Private Secretary, Martin Charteris, whose appointment was one 'of pure nepotism', he said later. 'I knew Jock Colville . . . who wanted to return to the Foreign Office, and my wife was friends with Alan Lascelles. . . . There was no vetting, no security clearance, no board interviews, nothing like that. In fact, years afterwards when it was too late it was realised that I had never signed an Official Secrets document.'[1] He would remain in her household until his retirement in 1977.

1951 was set to be a busy year for the royal family, not least because the Festival of Britain was taking place, a vast enterprise for which preparations had been ongoing for four years. The Festival would mark the one hundredth anniversary of Prince Albert's Exhibition of 1851, when the Crystal Palace was built in Hyde Park, and would show the world how much Britain had achieved since the war. However, the King's health was giving more cause for concern. Early in the year he went down with influenza and his programme of public engagements was curtailed. His appearance began to give rise to public comment.

The continuing stress on the King caused by the Duke of Windsor was never far from the Queen's mind. Now he was writing his memoirs, which worried her, as did a book that Helen Hardinge was intending to write. The Queen agreed to look at her draft:

The only thing that worries me very much is the fact that you are writing something about the abdication. I do hope that you won't do this dearest Helen, for several reasons and the most important one being, that the information you have, & the light you shed on that agonising bit of history, must be as the wife of the King's private secretary.

Any information Helen had acquired through her husband 'should be treated as sacred', and could put Alec 'in a horribly difficult position':

> *I do understand very well what your feelings must be & how irritating of the Duke of Windsor to publish a letter of Alec's but I feel that any comment from someone as close to our private lives as you have been, & still are, would only do harm. We have suffered so much from Miss Crawford and the Duke of Windsor's indiscretions . . . [S]omehow this one subject of the abdication never seems to lose its anguish & misery for us. Of course, I have no idea what sort of thing you were thinking of writing, but if it is to be under your own name, I honestly think that it would be a great mistake. Do understand & agree with your old & affectionate friend.[2]*

Elizabeth too was discovering people's sensitivities. In April she went to Malta, followed by a two-week holiday with Philip in Italy, celebrating her twenty-fifth birthday in Rome. After much deliberation by the Foreign Office, it was decided Elizabeth should have an audience with the Pope: Margaret had done so in 1949. They also lunched with Italy's President and Prime Minister, but otherwise it was a private time. However, The Lord's Day Observance Society of Scotland was again upset, criticising the couple for attending a polo match on a Sunday, and for her audience: 'We feel "let down" as a Protestant country in the presence of a Roman Catholic community who have totally different traditions,' they said. Two Scottish churches also criticised both Princesses for having visited the Pope.[3]

Meanwhile, world events had been taking a dark turn once more. In June the previous year, North Korea had invaded South Korea. Prime Minister Attlee pledged Britain's support for the American proposal to the Security Council that members of the United Nations should provide support as necessary to check the North Korean invasion. The war had serious political repercussions in Britain, where the question of rearmament arose in the face of Russian aggression and Britain's difficult economic situation. Public feeling about the conflict ran high, of which the King was aware, as he was of the tension in Anglo-American relations.

'The incessant worries & crises through which we have to live got me down properly,' he wrote to a friend.[4]

On 3 May, he opened the Festival of Britain. A week later he received the King and Queen of Denmark on a State visit; and in Westminster Abbey on 24 May he installed the Duke of Gloucester as Great Master of the Order of the Bath. The King had a temperature, but he insisted on going through with the ceremony, then carried out an official engagement in the afternoon. That evening he went to bed with what he thought was influenza.

His doctors found inflammation on his left lung, indicating pneumonitis, and put him on a course of penicillin. Imminent engagements were cancelled but still he did not seem to be recovering fully, so they prescribed a prolonged period of convalescence. Elizabeth became his substitute on several occasions. For the first time, she took the salute at the Trooping of the Colour. 'Princess Elizabeth, a woman alone as the central figure of this almost overwhelmingly massive military occasion, acquitted herself extremely well,' said *The Times*. 'She showed throughout an exacting hour perfect poise and composure.' Helen Hardinge was deeply impressed, not only by the execution of the parade, but by the young Princess. She watched her ride slowly down the Mall and salute elegantly to the Queen and Queen Mary, who stood with King Haakon and Prince Charles; then she turned her horse to face 'the great panoply of troops'. Dressed in a scarlet coat and dark-blue riding habit skirt, and a tricorne hat with high white plume, 'she was the person on whom all the traditional ritual converged'.[5]

As his convalescence continued, the King felt optimistic about his progress. On 18 June, the Queen's lady-in-waiting told Helen: 'The King I hope is really on the mend now & the Queen is wonderful. She carried off the Ascot party as if she hadn't a care in the world.'[6] He had to miss the ceremony in St Paul's Cathedral on 4 July, in which General Eisenhower handed over to the Cathedral the Roll of Honour for those members of the US Forces who had died during wartime operations from the British Isles. He also missed the July Garden Party, at which the Queen pressed Queen Mary to join her, saying: 'I am rather horrified at the idea of being alone.'[7] At Balmoral, the King seemed to rally, but then he developed a chill and sore throat; in September, a biopsy confirmed his doctors' suspicion that it was lung cancer. Immediately, steps were taken to ensure that the constitutional functions of the Monarchy could continue. Lascelles arranged to have the Queen, both Princesses, the Duke of Gloucester and the Princess Royal designated Counsellors of State. Elizabeth agreed that it was the right thing to do, 'for it will relieve the King of so much of the ordinary routine things'.[8]

An operation to remove the tumour was carried out on 23 September. Messages came from all over the world, and outside the Palace thousands of people waited in silence. Churchill told Lascelles that he had done something he had not done for years: 'I went down on my knees by my bedside and prayed.'[9] Even the Duke of Windsor sent a kind note to the Queen. He also asked to see her but she declined politely, saying it was better to wait to see how Bertie progressed, as everything depended on that.

The operation went successfully and by mid-October the King was feeling much better. Margaret told Helen Hardinge, 'I can't tell you how much it helped us all to know that so many people are thinking of us – it was most encouraging and I am sure the King felt it too. He is getting on wonderfully well now, thank God, and beginning to get up a bit.'[10] Nevertheless, the Palace announced that he would not carry out his visit to Australia in 1952 and that Princess Elizabeth and the Duke of Edinburgh would go instead.

Elizabeth and Philip had been preparing themselves for further duties, and on 21 July Philip had come home from Malta on indefinite leave. Vice Admiral William-Powlett said, 'I am naturally sorry Prince Philip has left my command, because he is an outstanding officer in every way'.[11] At thirty, Philip hoped his naval service was merely suspended: he did not know he would never resume it. He soon found an outlet for his interest in science and technology and accepted the Presidency of the British Association for the Advancement of Science, making a considerable impact with his inaugural address in August.

Their main engagement as the King convalesced was a tour of Canada. Originally it had been proposed for three years earlier, and although Elizabeth was keen, Philip was not, saying he wanted to get a family started first. Now they had no reason to delay. However, the tour would be longer than originally anticipated, because Lord Halifax suggested it would be impolite not to visit the United States too. What was going to be a purely Commonwealth undertaking turned out to be a thirty-five-day tour in which they crossed North America twice and travelled ten thousand miles in Canada alone.

On 7 October, they flew to Newfoundland. Martin Charteris carried with him sealed envelopes containing the draft Accession documents, to be opened if the King died, and slept with them under his bed. At her address in Ottawa, dazzling in a gold and white lace evening dress and diamonds, Elizabeth said she had always 'cherished the dream' of coming to Canada. She spoke of her father's illness and their anxiety, and thanked them for their support.[12] Canada's Governor General, Viscount Alexander, told the King that in Ottawa the crowds were greater than those for the American and French presidents, and in Quebec the people were impressed by the Princess's French. Yet it did not stop criticism from the Canadian Press, who said she looked distracted and tired. They said she did not smile, although she told Charteris her face was 'aching with smiling'.[13]

Their programme was a packed one and they had to decline some requests. Mountbatten received one from Brigadier Wardell, whom he knew, in New Brunswick, and passed it to Boy Browning for consideration. The answer was necessarily negative. Mountbatten's answer to Wardell was doubtless meant to protect the couple, but had Elizabeth seen it, she may have objected to its condescension:

> *I do not believe that anybody who has not done a Royal Tour can have any idea of how exhausting it is to be driven day after day through cheering crowds to whom one has to smile and be nice. Even the Prince of Wales in his absolute heyday in 1920 in Australia collapsed physically and had to take a ten-day sick leave; and the Princess after all is a woman who cannot be expected to stand up to it in the same way as a man.[14]*

Nevertheless, Mountbatten was correct about the trials of a tour and, as in South Africa, much time was spent cooped up in a train. It was Philip's first experience of a lengthy royal tour and to relieve the monotony on the train, he developed a line in practical jokes, leaving a tin of fake nuts by his wife's breakfast table from where a toy snake jumped out, and chased her wearing a pair of false teeth. One morning he was heard calling her a 'bloody fool' but as Charteris said, probably others would have found it more shocking than she did: 'Although she was very young, she had a wise head on her shoulders. She always understood him – and his ways. And valued his contribution – which has been immense and is underestimated.'[15]

The Queen, writing to tell her that the King was getting stronger, reminded her to 'put a bit of <u>inflection</u> into your speeches, especially for coming over the radio, darling. They have been excellent so far, so clear too & good <u>pauses</u> – Philip came over splendidly'.[16] Indeed, Philip was much appreciated in Canada, where girls screamed as he waved and men shouted, 'Good old Phil!' Elizabeth was pleased by her husband's 'succès fou' and the growth of his 'legend'.[17] He made small gestures that were appreciated, such as donning a Stetson to watch a rodeo. They saw Philip as a man of action, Elizabeth rather shyer. However, she renewed the Canadians' sense of possession: 'Here at least is something the Americans have not got,' wrote one of them.[18]

When they crossed over into America, it was Elizabeth they loved. The *Washington Star* reported President Truman's comment: 'When I was a little boy I read about a fairy Princess, and there she is.' The British Ambassador said Truman was like a proud uncle presenting his favourite niece to his friends. He gave all federal employees time off work and they lined the streets of Washington to cheer the couple. The American visit may have been a brief 'stopover', but it was very successful. The Ambassador said their visit had had 'a very stimulating effect' on Anglo-American relations, and showed that there was 'a real and abiding bond' between the American people and the British.[19]

They arrived back in Britain on 17 November, having missed Charles's third birthday. The King was not well enough to meet them at the airport but Charles did, and although *The Times* reported the Princess bending down and hugging him affectionately, film footage shows the meeting as less demonstrative. While they were away there had been a General

Election, which put the Conservatives back in power and returned Churchill as Prime Minister, aged seventy-seven.

Soon the Duke of Windsor was back in England again for a publisher's lunch, and this time Queen Mary asked Bertie to persuade the Queen to see him, 'to bury the hatchet'; however, the Queen said that as the King was still frail, she did not feel she could. Shortly afterwards, on 30 November, he was able to go out for the first time, motoring to Royal Lodge and walking in the grounds of Windsor Castle. He was happy to be home and feeling better. A day of National Thanksgiving was held for his recovery and on 10 December, he revoked the warrant appointing the Counsellors of State and resumed his constitutional duties. Delighted with the way Elizabeth and Philip's tour of Canada had gone, the King appointed them members of the Privy Council.

However, he developed a troublesome cough which needed a second operation on 13 December; it left him hoarse but otherwise was successful. In a Christmas message that was pre-recorded to save him the strain, he gave thanks that 'by the grace of God and through the faithful skill of my doctors . . . have I come through my illness.' It was time to think of those 'now facing hardships and dangers in Malaya and Korea, "a band of brothers" drawn from all parts of my Dominions'. The King celebrated his fifty-sixth birthday and then went with the family to Sandringham.

In January 1952, as Elizabeth and Philip prepared for the tour of Australia and New Zealand, the King told Eisenhower confidently that he looked forward to a trip to South Africa that would mark the end of his convalescence, and plans were made for his and the Queen's departure on 10 March. He even felt able to resume shooting and went out several times in January, delighted to achieve his usually high standard.

On 31 January, Elizabeth and Philip flew from London Airport on the first stage of their journey, which would begin in East Africa. The King was there to see them off, with the Queen and Margaret. One of the dignitaries present was Oliver Lyttleton, Secretary of State for the Colonies. He was shocked by the King's appearance. 'He seemed much altered and strained,' he said. 'I had the feeling of doom which grew as the minutes before the time of departure ebbed away. . . . I felt with deep foreboding that this would be the last time he was to see his daughter, and that he thought so himself.'[20] On 5 February at Sandringham, with a group of twenty, he enjoyed another good day's shooting. It was his last.

Queen Mary, eighty-five, had outlived her husband and three sons[21] and was now paying her respects to the sixth monarch of her lifetime. Her lady-in-waiting told Helen Hardinge, 'The recent shock and strain have been considerable.'[22] But despite physical frailty she was not dimmed, and was alert to a threat that others had feared: the opportunity that the death of George VI might present to the Mountbattens.

At a time when the cold war with Russia had begun, the West was alert to the infiltration of communists into public life. An intelligence department in America, ISI,[23] investigated rumours that Philip might represent a threat to the new reign in Britain because of the socialist tendencies of the Mountbattens, over whom 'a red aura hangs'. However, the conclusion was that Philip 'has not influenced Elizabeth left-ward: rather Elizabeth has de-socialised Philip, and Philip is playing a wholly praiseworthy role as a public leader.' The influence of Mountbatten over his nephew was said to be brief: Philip's sister Theodora, the Markgrafin of Baden, said, 'Philip sees through his uncle and fully realises how great are the Mountbatten ambitions.'[24]

Those ambitions caused Mountbatten to take a view as to his proper place at the King's funeral. He told the Duke of Norfolk, in charge of state ceremonials, where he considered he should be placed in the funeral procession, as a personal ADC to the King but not a Royal Highness. Mountbatten said that he had asked the Admiralty to check where his father had been positioned at Edward VII's funeral, and they told him it was immediately behind the gun carriage, in front of the Royal Standard. The Duke of Norfolk checked and found it to be the case but said Mountbatten could not go there. However, he could walk 'as His Late Majesty's personal Naval ADC, exactly behind the three Royal Dukes'.[25] Mountbatten then discovered that the Queen, unexpectedly, was going to walk behind the coffin 'instead of driving in a carriage at the rear of the procession',[26] so he told Norfolk, 'I have naturally waived my claim to walk immediately behind the coffin as my father did. Before writing to accept this position [behind the Dukes] I consulted the Duke of Edinburgh at Sandringham and told him I proposed to accept this new position, in view of all the circumstances.'[27]

Days after the funeral, Queen Mary received alarming news. Prince Ernst August of Hanover told her he was at a dinner party at Broadlands where Mountbatten was heard to boast that 'the House of Mountbatten now reigns'. Queen Mary alerted Churchill, who urgently consulted the Cabinet; they shared the view that the family name of Windsor should be retained. Although Philip did not share his uncle's ambitions overall, he bitterly resented that his children would not bear his name. His stance did not help his relationship with senior royals or Churchill and was a source of sensitivity between him and Elizabeth.

A compromise would be reached before Prince Andrew's birth in 1960,[28] but meanwhile Elizabeth approved a declaration 'that I and My children shall be styled and known as the House and Family of Windsor and that my descendants who marry and their descendants shall bear the name of Windsor'. Philip was unhappy but had to accept it. Initially he was also reluctant to move from Clarence House, and as the Queen Mother, as she was now known, did not want to move out of Buckingham Palace, Philip suggested they all stay where they were and conduct the business of the monarchy from the Palace. His idea was not an acceptable one. Fortunately, most irksome issues were resolved before the Coronation in June 1953.

Clearly they reached a modus vivendi. 'Philip always remained his own man', says Myra Butter. 'That, I think, is extraordinary.'[29] Cousin Margaret said, 'Philip's been wonderful and he's mellowed tremendously in old age. They're delicious together.'[30]

ACKNOWLEDGEMENTS

I would like to give warm thanks to those who gave me their time and shared with me their memories of Princess Elizabeth and of Prince Philip: Lady Butter; Lady Penn; the Hon. Mrs Margaret Rhodes and subsequently Alan Gordon Walker of Umbria Press, as agent for her estate, for permission to use her photographs. I am also very grateful to His Royal Highness Crown Prince Alexander of Serbia, for permission to quote from the unpublished memoirs of his father, King Peter II of Yugoslavia; to Lord Hardinge of Penshurst, who allowed me to access his family archive and quote from documents; and to the University of Southampton for permission to quote from papers in the Mountbatten archive and to use photographs. Staff at the Hertfordshire Archive and Local Studies centre (HALS) were very helpful. Thanks also go to Anne Hodder for her kind assistance on aspects of the Bowes Lyon family; to my agent, Andrew Lownie; and to my husband for his patience and support.

Sources

Airlie, Countess of. *Thatched with Gold: The Memoirs of Mabell, Countess of Airlie*. Edited by Jennifer Ellis. London: Hutchinson, 1962.

Asquith, Lady Cynthia. *The Married Life of the Duchess of York*. London: Hutchinson, 1933.

Bradford, Sarah. *Elizabeth: A Biography of Her Majesty the Queen*. London: Penguin, 2002 (second edition).

Bradford, Sarah. *George VI*. London: Penguin, 2002 (reissued 2011).

Byrne, Paula. *Kick: The True Story of Kick Kennedy*. London: William Collins, 2016.

Campbell, Lady Colin. *The Untold Life of Queen Elizabeth the Queen Mother*. London: Dynasty Press, 2012.

Colville, Sir John. *Strange Inheritance*. Salisbury: Michael Russell, 1983.

Colville, Sir John. 'Working for a Lady'. *Minerva* Magazine, 1978.

Cooper, Lady Diana. *The Light of Common Day*. London: Rupert Hart-Davis, 1959.

Crawford, Marion. *The Little Princesses*. London: Orion Books, 2003.

Davenport-Hines, Richard. *Ettie: The Intimate Life and Dauntless Spirit of Lady Desborough*. London: Weidenfeld & Nicolson, 2008.

Davis, Jonathan M. 'Ministry of Economic Warfare: Anglo-American Relations from 1939–1941', thesis for Liberty University, April 2013.

Eade, Philip. *Young Prince Philip: His Turbulent Early Life*. London: Harper Press, 2012.

Edwards, Anne. *Royal Sisters*. London: Collins, 1990.

Forbes, Grania. *My Darling Buffy*. London: Richard Cohen Books, 1997.

Glamis, Lady. 'Glamis Castle' (feature), *Pall Mall Magazine*, March 1897.

Hardinge, Helen. *Loyal to Three Kings*. London: William Kimber, 1967.

Hardinge, Helen. *Path of Kings*. London: Blandford Press, 1952.

Hicks, Pamela. *Daughter of Empire: Life as a Mountbatten*. London: Weidenfeld & Nicolson, 2012.

King Peter II of Yugoslavia. *A King's Heritage: The Memoirs of King Peter II of Yugoslavia*. Unpublished.

Laird, Dorothy. *Queen Elizabeth, the Queen Mother*. London: Coronet Books, 1985.

Lascelles, Sir Alan. *King's Counsellor: Abdication and War, The Diaries of Sir Alan Lascelles*. Edited by Duff Hart-Davis. London: Weidenfeld & Nicolson, 2006.

Lascelles, Hon. Mrs Francis. *The Family Life of King George and Queen Mary*, pamphlet for Royal Jubilee Souvenir Series, 1935, presented with *Ideas and Town Talk*.

Lockhart, Sir Bruce. *The Diaries of Sir Bruce Lockhart, 1939–1965*. London: Macmillan, 1980.

Lovell, Mary S. *Straight on Till Morning: The Life of Beryl Markham*. USA: St Martin's Press, 1987.

Mead, Richard. *General 'Boy'*. Barnsley, South Yorkshire: Pen & Sword Military, 2010.

Morrah, Dermot. *Princess Elizabeth, Duchess of Edinburgh*. London: Odhams Press, 1950.

Peacock, Lady. *Her Majesty Queen Elizabeth II: Her Life of Service as Princess Elizabeth.*, London: Hutchinson, 1952.

Pimlott, Ben. *The Queen: Elizabeth and the Monarchy*. London: Harper Press, 2012.

Princess Elizabeth. 'The Coronation', in the Royal Collection.

Rhodes, Margaret. *The Final Curtsey.* London: Umbria Press, 2011.

Ridley, Jane. *Victoria: Queen, Matriarch, Empress.* London: Allen Lane, 2015.

Rose, Kenneth. *King George V.* London: Phoenix Press, 2000.

Shawcross, William. *Queen Elizabeth the Queen Mother.* London: Pan Books, 2010.

Shawcross, William, ed. *Counting One's Blessings: The Selected Letters of Queen Elizabeth the Queen Mother.* London: Macmillan, 2012.

Spencer Shew, Betty. *Royal Wedding.* London: Macdonald, 1947.

St Paul's Walden Bury Estate. *The Gardens at St Paul's Walden Bury.* Brochure, edition as at 2015.

Thornton, Michael. *Royal Feud.* London: Michael Joseph, 1985.

Vickers, Hugo. *Elizabeth, the Queen Mother.* London: Arrow Books, 2006.

Warwick, Christopher. *George and Marina, Duke and Duchess of Kent.* USA: Albert Bridge Books, 2016.

Wentworth Day, J. *Princess Marina Duchess of Kent.* London: Robert Hale, 1969.

Wheeler-Bennett, John W. *King George VI: His Life and Reign.* London: Macmillan, 1958.

Whitmore, Richard. *Hertfordshire's Queen.* Berkshire: Countryside Books, 1997.

Windsor, Duchess of. *The Heart Has Its Reasons.* London: Michael Joseph, 1956.

Ziegler, Philip. *King Edward VIII.* London: Collins, 1990.

ARCHIVES (DOCUMENT SOURCES)

National Archives, Kew

Churchill College, Cambridge

Durham County Records Office

Hertfordshire Archive and Local Studies

Jersey Local History Archives

Maidstone Local History Centre

Mountbatten archive, University of Southampton

National Records of Scotland

Royal Archives, Windsor

University of Glasgow

OTHER SOURCES

Author's interviews

Various articles and letters published online (as referred to in the endnotes)

Probate records of England and Wales

Desert Island Discs, BBC Radio 4, 23 January 1981

The Plot to Make a King, Channel 4 documentary, 2015

Elizabeth at 90: A Family Tribute, BBC 1 Documentary, April 2016.

The Times, The Daily Telegraph, New York Times, and many regional British newspapers which were an invaluable source; regrettably, many no longer exist.

ENDNOTES

Chapter 1: Suddenly a Queen (1952)

1 Duke of Windsor, on board the *Queen Mary* before it sailed, reading his prepared speech for television, 8 February 1952, reported in full in *Yorkshire Post and Leeds Intelligencer*, 9 February.

2 Speech in the Scottish Borders, 9 September 2015.

3 Author's interview, July 2015. Mrs Rhodes was born the Hon. Margaret Elphinstone in 1925. Her mother, Lady Elphinstone, born Mary (May) Bowes Lyon, was the eldest sister of Elizabeth Bowes Lyon, later Queen Elizabeth (consort to George VI), then the Queen Mother. Mrs Rhodes died on 25 November 2016.

4 Dermot Morrah, *Princess Elizabeth, Duchess of Edinburgh* (London: Odhams Press, 1950).

5 Mrs Rhodes to the author.

6 Ben Pimlott, *The Queen: Elizabeth and the Monarchy* (London: Harper Press, 2012).

7 Quoted in Pimlott, *The Queen*.

8 Daughter of Lord Mountbatten, Philip's uncle. At that time she was still Mountbatten. Quoted in Pimlott, *The Queen*.

9 Philip Eade, *Young Prince Philip: His Turbulent Early Life* (London: Harper Press, 2011).

10 Pamela Hicks, *Daughter of Empire: Life as a Mountbatten* (London: Weidenfeld & Nicolson, 2012).

11 Quoted in Pimlott, *The Queen*.

12 Hicks, *Daughter of Empire*.

13 Quoted in Eade, *Young Prince Philip*.

14 Lord Charteris of Amisfield in *The Spectator* interview, 7 January 1995.

15 Margaret Rhodes, *The Final Curtsey* (London: Umbria Press, 2011).

16 William Shawcross, ed., *Counting One's Blessings: The Selected Letters of Queen Elizabeth the Queen Mother* (London: Macmillan, 2012).

17 The others were Prince John and Prince George (Duke of Kent).

18 *Yorkshire Evening Post*, 6 February 1952.

19 Quoted in Pimlott, *The Queen*.

20 Margaret Saville for the *Portsmouth Evening News*, 31 January 1952.

21 Author's interview, one of several during 2015. Lady Butter, née Wernher, is a life-long friend of the Queen and a relation by marriage of Prince Philip. Her aunt, the Russian Countess Najada ('Nada'), was married to Philip's uncle, George Milford Haven, older brother of Louis Mountbatten.

22 *Washington Star*, 2 November 1951.

23 *The Times*, 11 February 1952.

24 Hugh Dalton quoted in Pimlott, *The Queen*.

25 Harold Macmillan quoted in Pimlott, *The Queen*.

26 Joe Illingworth, special correspondent for *Yorkshire Post and Leeds Intelligencer*, 16 February 1952.

27 Mrs Rhodes to the author.

28 Lady Butter to the author.
29 *The Times* and *Yorkshire Post and Leeds Intelligencer*, 11 February 1952.
30 Lady Butter to the author.
31 From the Queen's speech when unveiling her father's statue in The Mall on 21 October 1955, as reported in *The Times*, 22 October 1955.
32 Letter from Edward when Prince of Wales (David), to Lady Ettie Desborough, society hostess and friend of the royal family, 15 November 1929, Hertfordshire Archives and Local Studies (HALS).

Chapter 2: Into the World (1925–1926)

1 After the death of Prince John in 1919, there were five children.
2 Quoted by Hon. Mrs Francis Lascelles, *The Family Life of King George and Queen Mary*, pamphlet for Royal Jubilee Souvenir Series, 1935, presented with *Ideas and Town Talk*.
3 Letter from Sir Alec to his wife, 2 January 1925, Lord Hardinge archive, Kent Local History Centre, Maidstone.
4 Letter from Sir Alec to his wife, 18 January 1925, Lord Hardinge archive.
5 Letter from Sir Alec to his wife, 9 January 1925, Lord Hardinge archive.
6 Letter from Sir Alec to his wife, 3 December 1925, Lord Hardinge archive.
7 Quoted in John W. Wheeler-Bennett, *King George VI: His Life and Reign* (London: Macmillan, 1958).
8 Wheeler-Bennett, *King George VI*.
9 *Yorkshire Evening Post*, 26 April 1923.
10 Letter Sir Alec to wife, 30 January 1925, Lord Hardinge archive.
11 Letter Sir Alec to wife, 24 January 1925, Lord Hardinge archive.
12 *Dundee Evening Telegraph*, 4 June 1925.
13 *The Times*, 24 April 1924.
14 *Western Morning News and Mercury*, 16 July 1925.
15 *The Scotsman*, 16 July 1925.
16 Hugo Vickers, *Elizabeth the Queen Mother* (London: Arrow Books, 2006).
17 Letter Prince Albert to Lady Desborough, 2 February 1920, Desborough papers, HALS.
18 Wheeler-Bennett, *King George VI*.
19 *Dundee Courier*, 26 April 1923.
20 *Derby Daily Telegraph*, 4 May 1925.
21 Wheeler-Bennett, *King George VI*.
22 Letter Sir Alec to wife, 25 November 1925, Lord Hardinge archive.
23 Letter Sir Alec to wife, 3 March 1926, Lord Hardinge archive.
24 Letter Sir Alec to wife, 24 March 1926, Lord Hardinge archive.
25 Mrs Rhodes (née Elphinstone) to the author.
26 William Shawcross, ed., *Counting One's Blessings: The Selected Letters of Queen Elizabeth the Queen Mother* (London: Macmillan, 2012).
27 National Archives PC 8/1070.
28 *Hull Daily Mail*, 23 April 1926.
29 Wheeler-Bennett, *King George VI*.

30   Quoted in Philip Eade, *Young Prince Philip: His Turbulent Early Life* (London: Harper Press, 2012).

Chapter 3: A Hertfordshire Haven (1926)
 1   Quoted in Kenneth Rose, *King George V* (London: Phoenix Press, 2000).
 2   Countess of Airlie, *Thatched with Gold: The Memoirs of Mabell, Countess of Airlie*, ed. Jennifer Ellis (London: Hutchinson, 1962).
 3   Airlie, *Thatched with Gold*.
 4   *Dundee Courier*, 2 July 1928.
 5   *Dundee Courier*, 10 July 1926.
 6   *Western Morning News*, 16 June 1926.
 7   *Yorks Post and Leeds Intelligencer*, 10 April 1922.
 8   Gibside stayed in the family until the 1970s, when ownership was transferred to the National Trust.
 9   Née Grimstead.
10   *County Courts Chronicle*, 2 November 1863.
11   *The Gardens at St Paul's Walden Bury* Brochure given to visitors to St Paul's Walden Bury in 2015.
12   Dorothy Laird, *Queen Elizabeth the Queen Mother*, Coronet 1985, quoted in William Shawcross, *Queen Elizabeth the Queen Mother*, Macmillan 2009.
13   Mrs Rhodes, née Elphinstone, to author, July 2015.
14   Visitors' brochure.
15   Lord Hardinge archive, Kent Local History Centre, Maidstone.
16   Lady Cynthia Asquith, *The Married Life of the Duchess of York* (Hutchinson, 1933).
17   Asquith, *The Married Life of the Duchess of York*.

Chapter 4: Family Mysteries
 1   Richard Whitmore, *Hertfordshire's Queen* (Berkshire: Countryside Books, 1997).
 2   Registration of Births and Deaths Act 1874.
 3   Although the Act allowed penalties to be imposed, they were reserved for demeanours more serious than late registration, such as wilfully giving false information.
 4   Author of *Queen Elizabeth the Queen Mother* (London: Pan Books, 2010).
 5   In 1921 she was going to Paris for the first time. By then she and Bertie were good friends and his interest in her was clear.
 6   As at 16 December 2017.
 7   However, there seems to be no proof of Dr Thomas himself claiming this, and the identity of the woman he supposedly attended in childbirth has not been stated, although perhaps patient confidentiality precluded this.
 8   Quoted in Hugo Vickers, *Elizabeth, the Queen Mother* (London: Arrow Books, 2006).
 9   Lady Colin Campbell, *The Untold Life of Queen Elizabeth the Queen Mother* (London: Dynasty Press, 2012).
10   The Medical Register of 1903; also census of 1901.

11 Earl's death certificate, 7 November 1944.
12 Her operation is mentioned by Hugo Vickers.
13 *Taunton Courier and Western Advertiser*, 27 August 1930.
14 *Dundee Courier*, 1 August 1939.
15 Grania Forbes, *My Darling Buffy* (London: Richard Cohen Books, 1997).
16 Royal Archives, Windsor, informed the author that the register concerning that garden party states that 5,836 invitations were issued; 4,200 attended and 1,636 were absent, but there is no information as to who the absentees were.
17 Dorothy Laird, *Queen Elizabeth, the Queen Mother* (London: Coronet Books, 1985).
18 Forbes, *My Darling Buffy*.
19 The *Luton Times and Advertiser*.
20 Some authors have incorrectly stated that Elizabeth's birth was unannounced.
21 Violet's birthplace was announced as 79 Lexham Gardens (London); Mary's (May) as Fothringham, Forfar; Patrick's was St Paul's Walden Bury.
22 *Dundee Courier*, 1 September 1881 and 30 January 1895.
23 Hubert Ernest Malcolm Bowes Lyon.
24 Intriguingly, her middle name was Collie.
25 *The Times*, 12 July 1923. Angus was the son of Major Patrick Bowes Lyon, brother of Claude, 14th Earl of Strathmore.

Chapter 5: Early Years (1926–1929)

1 Letter to her mother 9 August 1926, from William Shawcross, ed., *Counting One's Blessings: The Selected Letters of Queen Elizabeth the Queen Mother* (London: Macmillan, 2012).
2 Countess of Airlie, *Thatched with Gold: The Memoirs of Mabell, Countess of Airlie*, ed. Jennifer Ellis (London: Hutchinson, 1962).
3 Electricity was introduced in 1929.
4 Quoted by Cecilia Bowes Lyon (then Lady Glamis) in the *Pall Mall Magazine*, March 1897.
5 Hugo Vickers, *Elizabeth, the Queen Mother* (London: Arrow Books, 2006).
6 Documentary, BBC1 April 2016, *Elizabeth at 90: A Family Tribute*, Producer/director John Bridcut.
7 Mrs Rhodes to the author, July 2015.
8 Mrs Rhodes to the author.
9 In 2011 they were the subject of a television documentary, which failed to mention that their father had died.
10 *Pall Mall Magazine*, 1897.
11 Mrs Rhodes to the author.
12 Margaret Rhodes, *The Final Curtsey* (London: Umbria Press, 2011).
13 Quoted by Hon. Mrs Francis Lascelles, *The Family Life of King George and Queen Mary*, pamphlet for Royal Jubilee Souvenir Series, 1935, presented with *Ideas and Town Talk*.
14 *Western Morning News*, 6 September 1926.
15 *Dundee Courier*, 12 August 1926.

16   *The Scotsman*, 30 August 1926.
17   *Dundee Courier*, 7 September 1926.
18   Letter to Nannie B. 5 October 1926, Shawcross letters.
19   *Lichfield Mercury*, 1 October 1926.
20   A type of bowl whose form originates from medieval times.
21   *The Times*, 21 December 1926.
22   Mrs Rhodes to the author.
23   Kenneth Rose, *King George V* (London: Phoenix Press, 2000).
24   Rose, *King George V*.
25   *The Scotsman*, 4 February 1927.
26   Letter 9 January 1927, Shawcross letters.
27   Quoted in John W. Wheeler-Bennett, *King George VI: His Life and Reign* (London: Macmillan, 1958).
28   *The Scotsman*, 30 March 1927.
29   *Western Morning News*, 7 April 1927.
30   Mrs Rhodes to the author.
31   Quoted in Rose, *King George V*.
32   Lady Butter to the author, July 2015.
33   Quoted in Anne Edwards, *Royal Sisters* (London: Collins, 1990).
34   *Portsmouth Evening News*, 7 June 1927.
35   Quoted in Wheeler-Bennett, *King George VI*.
36   Lady Cynthia Asquith, *The Married Life of the Duchess of York* (London: Hutchinson, 1933).
37   Edwards, *Royal Sisters*.
38   *Dundee Courier*, 2 July 1928.
39   Quoted in Rose, *King George V*.
40   Quoted in Asquith, *The Married Life of the Duchess of York*.
41   *Sunday Post*, 2 September 1928.
42   Quoted in Rose, *King George V*.
43   Quoted in Wheeler-Bennett, *King George VI*.
44   Letter 23 December 1928, Lord Hardinge archive.
45   Asquith, *The Married Life of the Duchess of York*.
46   Quoted in Richard Davenport-Hines, *Ettie: The Intimate Life and Dauntless Spirit of Lady Desborough* (London: Weidenfeld & Nicolson, 2008).
47   The children of Viscount Lascelles and Princess Mary were not royal.
48   *Dundee Courier*, 21 May 1929.

Chapter 6: New Playmates (1929–1932)

1   None of the three parties won sufficient seats in Parliament to call a majority. The Labour Party under Ramsay Macdonald held around 46 percent, Conservative under Stanley Baldwin 42 percent and Liberal under David Lloyd George 9 percent.
2   William Shawcross, *Queen Elizabeth the Queen Mother* (London: Pan Books, 2010).
3   Sir John Colville, *Strange Inheritance* (Salisbury: Michael Russell, 1983).

4 Letter 31 December 1929, William Shawcross, ed., *Counting One's Blessings: The Selected Letters of Queen Elizabeth the Queen Mother* (London: Macmillan, 2012).

5 Letter 8 June 1923, Lord Hardinge archive.

6 Letter 11 February 1930, Shawcross letters.

7 Interview by Andrew Alderson for the *Telegraph*, 23 April 2006 (online). On marriage Sonia became Berry. She died in 2012.

8 Article by Ian Lloyd, *Mail Online*, 25 July 2014.

9 *Dundee Evening Telegraph*, 30 January 1947.

10 *Derby Daily Telegraph*, 22 August 1930.

11 Quoted in John W. Wheeler-Bennett, *King George VI: His Life and Reign* (London: Macmillan, 1958).

12 *Derby Daily Telegraph*, 22 August 1930.

13 Letter 27 August 1930, Shawcross letters.

14 Letter 27 August 1930, Shawcross letters.

15 *Western Gazette*, 29 August 1930.

16 Quoted in Lady Cynthia Asquith, *The Married life of the Duchess of York* (London: Hutchinson, 1933).

17 Letter 10 September 1930, Shawcross letters.

18 Letter 6 September 1930, Shawcross letters.

19 Mrs Rhodes to the author.

20 Letter (as George VI) to Lady Desborough, 14 January 1949, Desborough papers, HALS.

21 Lady Butter to the author.

22 Letter 1 September 1931, Desborough papers, HALS.

23 Letter 16 September 1931, Shawcross letters.

24 Dermot Morrah, *Princess Elizabeth, Duchess of Edinburgh* (London: Odhams Press, 1950).

25 Lady Butter to the author.

26 Margaret Rhodes, *The Final Curtsey* (London: Umbria Press, 2011).

27 Lady Butter to the author.

28 22 March 1932.

Chapter 7: Seeds of Change (1933–1934)

1 Hon. Mrs Margaret Rhodes to the author.

2 Marion Crawford, *The Little Princesses* (London: Orion Books, 2003).

3 Countess of Airlie, *Thatched with Gold: The Memoirs of Mabell, Countess of Airlie*, ed. Jennifer Ellis (London: Hutchinson, 1962).

4 *Elizabeth at 90: A Family Tribute*, BBC1 documentary, April 2016.

5 Lady Butter to the author.

6 Mrs Rhodes to the author.

7 An anonymous courtier quoted in Sarah Bradford, *George VI* (London: Penguin, 2002, reissued 2011).

8 Lady Butter to the author.

9 Margaret Rhodes, *The Final Curtsey* (London: Umbria Press, 2011).

10 *Desert Island Discs*, BBC Radio 4, 17 January 1981.
11 Rhodes, *The Final Curtsey*.
12 Rhodes, *The Final Curtsey*.
13 23 June 1934. Mrs Lascelles was his aunt by marriage.
14 Quoted in Philip Ziegler, *King Edward VIII* (London: Collins, 1990).
15 The Prince of Wales was very much in love with Freda, who was already leading a separate life from her husband. She was liked by the Prince's staff and his friends and was considered to be very good for him in many ways. For some time she reciprocated his love but in 1923 told him he would have to settle for friendship. Although heartbroken, he did so, until Wallis Simpson made him give up his female confidantes.
16 Quoted in Ziegler, *King Edward VIII*.
17 Various letters came to light around 1998 and later, which were sold, and are referred to online by some newspapers, e.g. *The Telegraph* and *The New York Times*.
18 From Thelma's memoirs, quoted in Ziegler, *King Edward VIII*.
19 Ziegler, *King Edward VIII*.
20 Letter 11 February 1927, Lord Hardinge archives.
21 Letter from Balmoral, 7 September 1934, Desborough papers, HALS.
22 Philip Eade, *Young Prince Philip: His Turbulent Early Life* (London: Harper Press, 2012).
23 Lady Butter to the author.
24 Lady Butter to the author.
25 Lady Butter to the author.
26 Bessie C. Ritchie for *Dundee Courier*, 30 November 1934.
27 Bessie C. Ritchie for *Dundee Courier*, 30 November 1934.
28 Bessie C. Ritchie for *Dundee Courier*, 30 November 1934.

Chapter 8: Celebrations and Sadness (1935–1936)
 1 John W. Wheeler-Bennett, *King George VI: His Life and Reign* (London: Macmillan, 1958).
 2 *The Comet*, 6 June 2012.
 3 Cited in Sarah Bradford, *George VI* (London: Penguin, 2002, reissued 2011).
 4 Lady Butter to the author.
 5 *Sunday Daily Echo and Shipping Gazette*, 6 May 1935.
 6 Quoted in William Shawcross, *Queen Elizabeth the Queen Mother* (London: Pan Books, 2010).
 7 *The Times*, 7 May 1935.
 8 Helen Hardinge, *Loyal to Three Kings* (London: William Kimber, 1967).
 9 Philip Ziegler, *King Edward VIII* (London: Collins, 1990).
10 Quoted in Ben Pimlott, *The Queen: Elizabeth and the Monarchy* (London: Harper Press, 2012).
11 *Western Morning News*, 26 July 1935.
12 Margaret Rhodes, *The Final Curtsey* (London, Umbria Press, 2011).
13 Mary S. Lovell, *Straight on Till Morning: The Life of Beryl Markham* (USA: St Martin's Press, 1987).

14 Quoted in Shawcross, *Queen Elizabeth the Queen Mother*.
15 Quoted in Kenneth Rose, *King George V* (London: Phoenix Press, 2000).
16 Letter 29 December 1935, William Shawcross, ed., *Counting One's Blessings: The Selected Letters of Queen Elizabeth the Queen Mother* (London: Macmillan, 2012).
17 Quoted in Rose, *King George V*.
18 Blanche Lennox to Mabell Airlie, quoted in Countess of Airlie, *Thatched with Gold: The Memoirs of Mabell, Countess of Airlie*, ed. Jennifer Ellis (London: Hutchinson, 1962).
19 Lascelles, letter to his wife, 17 January 1936, Lascelles papers, Churchill College, Cambridge, LASL 4/2.
20 Lascelles, letter to his wife, 18 January 1936, Lascelles papers.
21 Lascelles, letter to his wife, 18 January 1936, Lascelles papers.
22 Edward was David's first name.

Chapter 9: An Early Annus Horribilis (1936)

1 Bingham became US Ambassador to Britain in 1933. The Society was founded on 16 July 1902. It is a British-American society whose aims are 'to promote goodwill, good-fellowship, and everlasting peace between the United States and Great Britain'. Its current President is the Queen.
2 Quoted in Countess of Airlie, *Thatched with Gold: The Memoirs of Mabell, Countess of Airlie*, ed. Jennifer Ellis (London: Hutchinson, 1962).
3 Halsey, quoted in Philip Ziegler, *King Edward VIII* (London: Collins, 1990).
4 Letter 20 March 1921, Desborough papers, HALS.
5 Quoted in William Shawcross, *Queen Elizabeth the Queen Mother* (London: Pan Books, 2010).
6 Letter 11 March 1936, William Shawcross, ed., *Counting One's Blessings: The Selected Letters of Queen Elizabeth the Queen Mother* (London: Macmillan, 2012).
7 *Western Morning News*, 30 March 1936.
8 Quoted in Ziegler, *King Edward VIII*.
9 The Prince of Wales always bears the title of Duke of Cornwall.
10 Ziegler, *King Edward VIII*.
11 Quoted in Shawcross, *Queen Elizabeth the Queen Mother*.
12 Quoted in Helen Hardinge, *Loyal to Three Kings* (London: William Kimber, 1967).
13 Helen Hardinge, *The Path of Kings* (London: Blandford Press, 1952).
14 Letter Lady Diana Cooper to Conrad Russell, July 1935, quoted in her book *The Light of Common Day* (London: Rupert Hart-Davis, 1959).
15 Cooper, *The Light of Common Day*.
16 Cooper, *The Light of Common Day*.
17 The Duchess of Windsor, *The Heart Has Its Reasons* (London: Michael Joseph, 1956).
18 Windsor, *The Heart Has Its Reasons*.
19 Windsor, *The Heart Has Its Reasons*.
20 Marion Crawford, *The Little Princesses* (London: Orion Books, 2003).
21 Quoted in Shawcross, *Queen Elizabeth the Queen Mother*.
22 Countess of Airlie, *Thatched with Gold*.

23 Windsor, *The Heart Has Its Reasons*.
24 Hardinge, *Loyal to Three Kings*.
25 *Sunderland Echo and Shipping Gazette*, 18 June 1936.
26 Letter to Conrad Russell, 20 July 1938, Lady Diana Cooper papers, Churchill College, Cambridge.
27 Letter 19 September 1936, Shawcross letters.
28 Letter 19 September 1936, Shawcross letters.
29 Quoted in Shawcross, *Queen Elizabeth the Queen Mother*.
30 Hardinge, *Loyal to Three Kings*.
31 Mrs Rhodes to the author.
32 From 'The Britannicus Letter' 15 October 1936, quoted in Hardinge, *Loyal to Three Kings*.
33 Letter 13 November 1936, quoted in John W. Wheeler-Bennett, *King George VI: His Life and Reign* (London: Macmillan, 1958).
34 Letter to May Elphinstone, 6 December 1936, Shawcross letters.
35 From the Duke's chronicle, quoted in Wheeler-Bennett, *King George VI*.
36 From the Duke's chronicle, quoted in Wheeler-Bennett, *King George VI*.
37 From the Duke's chronicle, quoted in Wheeler-Bennett, *King George VI*.
38 Letter from Duchess of York to Viscountess Milner, 7 December 1936, Lord Hardinge papers. Viscountess Milner was the mother of Helen Hardinge.
39 From the Duke's chronicle, quoted in Wheeler-Bennett, *King George VI*.
40 From the Duke's chronicle, quoted in Wheeler-Bennett, *King George VI*.
41 From the Duke's chronicle, quoted in Wheeler-Bennett, *King George VI*.
42 *The Times*, 12 December 1936.
43 Letter from Elizabeth R to Cosmo Lang, 12 December 1936, Shawcross letters.
44 *The Times*, 14 December 1936.
45 *The Times*, 12 December 1936.
46 Margaret Rhodes, *The Final Curtsey* (London: Umbria Press, 2011).
47 Dermot Morrah, *Princess Elizabeth, Duchess of Edinburgh* (London: Odhams Press, 1950).
48 Morrah, *Princess Elizabeth, Duchess of Edinburgh*.

Chapter 10: Everything Changes (1936–1937)

1 Lady Butter to the author.
2 Quoted in Hugo Vickers, *Elizabeth, the Queen Mother* (London: Arrow Books, 2006).
3 Quoted in William Shawcross, *Queen Elizabeth the Queen Mother* (London: Pan Books, 2010).
4 Countess of Airlie, *Thatched with Gold: The Memoirs of Mabell, Countess of Airlie*, ed. Jennifer Ellis (London: Hutchinson, 1962).
5 Mrs Rhodes to the author.
6 Quoted in John W. Wheeler-Bennett, *King George VI: His Life and Reign* (London: Macmillan, 1958).
7 The friend was a family doctor, Sir John Weir, quoted in Shawcross, *Queen Elizabeth the Queen Mother*.

8   Quoted by Sarah Bradford, *George VI* (London: Penguin, 2002, reissued 2011).
9   Letter from Lady Elizabeth Bowes Lyon to Helen Hardinge, undated except 'Friday' but clearly after their wedding, which was in February 1921. Lord Hardinge archives.
10 *The Scotsman*, 2 January 1937.
11 Countess of Airlie, *Thatched with Gold*.
12 Sonia Berry, interview by Andrew Alderson, *Telegraph* online, 23 April 2006.
13 Exhibited at the Royal Childhood Exhibition at Buckingham Palace, July 2014.
14 Marion Crawford, *The Little Princesses* (London: Orion Books, 2003).
15 *The Coronation* by Princess Elizabeth, in the Royal Collection.
16 Margaret Rhodes, *The Final Curtsey* (London: Umbria Press, 2011).
17 *The Coronation* by Princess Elizabeth.
18 Marion Crawford, *The Little Princesses*.
19 *The Coronation* by Princess Elizabeth.
20 *The Coronation* by Princess Elizabeth.
21 *The Coronation* by Princess Elizabeth.
22 Rhodes, *The Final Curtsey*.
23 *The Coronation* by Princess Elizabeth.
24 *The Coronation* by Princess Elizabeth.
25 *Yorkshire Post and Leeds Intelligencer*, 10 May 1937.
26 Quoted in Shawcross, *Queen Elizabeth the Queen Mother*.
27 Queen Mary to the Duke of Windsor, from Marlborough House, 5 July 1938, quoted in Philip Ziegler, *King Edward VIII* (London: Collins, 1990).
28 Letter signed 'Edward', 19 May 1927, from Chateau de Condé; the present was an old Sèvres china inkstand that he had admired at Panshanger. Desborough papers, HALS.
29 Letter 13 June 1937, from Schloss Wasserleonburg in Austria, Desborough papers, HALS.
30 Quoted in Ziegler, *King Edward VIII*.
31 Discussed in Ziegler, *King Edward VIII*.
32 Lady Bowes Lyon, quoted by Richard Whitmore, *Hertfordshire's Queen* (Berkshire: Countryside Books, 1997).
33 Lady Butter to the author.
34 Quoted in Ben Pimlott, *The Queen: Elizabeth and the Monarchy* (London: Harper Press, 2012). The Hon. Patricia Mountbatten became Lady Brabourne on marriage (and after her father's death, Countess Mountbatten).
35 *The Times*, 17 November 1937.
36 *New York Times*, 23 November 1937.
37 Lady Butter to the author.
38 Quoted in Philip Eade, *Young Prince Philip: His Turbulent Early Life* (London: Harper Press, 2012).
39 Eade, *Young Prince Philip*.
40 Lady Butter to the author.
41 *Aberdeen Journal*, 17 December 1937.
42 *The Scotsman*, 22 December 1937.

Chapter 11: Before the Storm (1938)

1 Letter 5 January 1938, William Shawcross, ed., *Counting One's Blessings: The Selected Letters of Queen Elizabeth the Queen Mother* (London: Macmillan, 2012).
2 Mrs Rhodes to the author.
3 Lady Butter to the author.
4 From Rose Kennedy papers, quoted by Paula Byrne, *Kick: The True Story of Kick Kennedy* (London: William Collins, 2016).
5 *Arbroath Herald and Advertiser*, 24 June 1938.
6 Letter 23 June 1938, Shawcross letters.
7 Lady Diana Cooper, *The Light of Common Day* (London: Rupert Hart-Davis, 1959).
8 Marion Crawford, *The Little Princesses* (London: Orion Books, 2003).
9 William Shawcross, *Queen Elizabeth the Queen Mother* (London: Pan Books, 2010).
10 *The Scotsman*, 9 September 1938.
11 *Yorkshire Evening Post*, 27 September 1938.
12 Pamela Hicks, *Daughter of Empire: Life as a Mountbatten* (London: Weidenfeld & Nicolson, 2012).
13 Quoted in Philip Eade, *Young Prince Philip: His Turbulent Early Life* (London: Harper Press, 2012).

Chapter 12: Love and War (1939)

1 Mrs Rhodes to the author.
2 Marion Crawford, *The Little Princesses* (London: Orion Books, 2003).
3 Dermot Morrah, *Princess Elizabeth, Duchess of Edinburgh* (London: Odhams Press, 1950).
4 Crawford, *The Little Princesses*.
5 Mrs Rhodes to the author.
6 *Nottingham Evening Post*, 14 August 1939.
7 Quoted in Paula Byrne, *Kick: The True Story of Kick Kennedy* (London: William Collins, 2016).
8 As Queen, she and the Duke of Edinburgh were staying at Luton Hoo in Bedfordshire, an estate in Myra's family, where they often used to shoot. At the time of President Kennedy's assassination, Myra and her husband were with them and all heard the news.
9 Hannen Swaffer for *Daily Herald*, 22 March 1939.
10 *The Times*, 1 April 1939.
11 *Daily Record and Mail*, 22 April 1939.
12 *Newcastle Evening Chronicle*, 18 April 1939.
13 Crawford, *The Little Princesses*.
14 Crawford, *The Little Princesses*.
15 Quoted in Hugo Vickers, *Elizabeth, the Queen Mother* (London: Arrow Books, 2006).
16 Vickers, *Elizabeth*.
17 *The Scotsman*, 8 May 1939.

18 Letter from the Queen, on RMS *Empress of Australia*, to Queen Mary, 8 May 1939, William Shawcross, ed., *Counting One's Blessings: The Selected Letters of Queen Elizabeth the Queen Mother* (London: Macmillan, 2012).

19 Sir Alan Lascelles, *King's Counsellor: Abdication and War, The Diaries of Sir Alan Lascelles*, ed. Duff Hart-Davis (London: Weidenfeld & Nicolson, 2006).

20 Lascelles, *King's Counsellor*.

21 Quoted in John W. Wheeler-Bennett, *King George VI: His Life and Reign* (London: Macmillan, 1958).

22 Quoted in Philip Eade, *Young Prince Philip: His Turbulent Early Life* (London: Harper Press, 2012).

23 Crawford, *The Little Princesses*.

24 Quoted in Eade, *Young Prince Philip*.

25 Lady Butter to the author.

26 Mrs Rhodes to the author.

27 From her official website. She died in 2011.

28 Eade, *Young Prince Philip*.

29 Lady Butter to the author. With Prince Philip, she and her siblings share Tsar Nicholas I as their great-great-grandfather.

30 Jane Ridley, *Victoria: Queen, Matriarch, Empress* (London: Allen Lane, 2015).

31 *The Scotsman*, 8 August 1939.

32 Letter from the Queen to Queen Mary, 31 August 1939, Shawcross letters.

33 *The Times*, 4 September 1939.

34 Letter Rose Leverson-Gower to the Queen, 6 September 1939, Shawcross letters.

35 Margaret Rhodes, *The Final Curtsey* (London: Umbria Press, 2011).

36 Memo dated 30 October 1939, from the Queen at Buckingham Palace to 'Alec', Lord Hardinge papers. Her comment on his 'beauty' is interesting; the Duke of Windsor once said that when she was Elizabeth Bowes Lyon, she had been in love with him before Bertie.

37 *The Times*, 13 November 1939.

38 Letter to Lord Louis Mountbatten, 27 November 1939, Mountbatten papers MB1/A111, University of Southampton.

39 Quoted in Eade, *Young Prince Philip*.

Chapter 13: A Symbol of the Future (1940)

1 *The Scotsman*, 13 January 1940. The moss was used for surgical dressings.

2 19 November 1939.

3 Quoted in William Shawcross, *Queen Elizabeth the Queen Mother* (London: Pan Books, 2010).

4 This record of the captain's meeting was shown to Channel 4 for its documentary, *Prince Philip: The Plot to Make a King*, 2015.

5 Lady Butter to the author.

6 Sarah Baring, quoted by Philip Eade, *The Daily Telegraph*, 4 June 2011.

7 Janie Spring, quoted by Eade, *The Daily Telegraph*.

8   Letter from the Queen at Buckingham Palace to Neville Chamberlain, 17 May 1940, William Shawcross, ed., *Counting One's Blessings: The Selected Letters of Queen Elizabeth the Queen Mother* (London: Macmillan, 2012).
9   Winston Churchill, quoted in Shawcross, *Queen Elizabeth the Queen Mother*.
10 Jonathan M. Davis, 'Ministry of Economic Warfare: Anglo-American Relations from 1939–1941', thesis for Liberty University, April 2013.
11 Letter 7 July 1940 from 'S of S' (?) to the Hon. Sir Alexander Cadogan, Permanent Under-Secretary at the Foreign Office. National Archives, FO/1093/23.
12 Letter 19 July 1940 from 'S of S' (?) to the Hon. Sir Alexander Cadogan. National Archives, FO/1093/23.
13 Memo to the Prime Minister from D. Morton, 4 August 1940, National Archives, FO/1093/23.
14 Undated and unheaded report, National Archives, FO/1093/23.
15 Quoted in John W. Wheeler-Bennett, *King George VI: His Life and Reign* (London: Macmillan, 1958).
16 Wheeler-Bennett, *King George VI*.
17 Quoted in Wheeler-Bennett, *King George VI*.
18 Letter from the Queen at Windsor Castle to May Elphinstone, October 25, 1940, Shawcross letters.
19 *The Times*, 14 October 1940.
20 Sarah Gertrude Millin, quoted in Dermot Morrah, *Princess Elizabeth, Duchess of Edinburgh* (London: Odhams Press, 1950).
21 Telegram sent on behalf of the Duke of Windsor in the Bahamas, 14 December 1940. National Archives, FO/1093/23.
22 Quoted in Shawcross, *Queen Elizabeth the Queen Mother*.
23 Letter from Princess Elizabeth at Windsor Castle to Helen Hardinge, 27 December 1940, Lord Hardinge archive.
24 Letter from Princess Margaret to Helen Hardinge, 28 December 1940, Lord Hardinge archive. On Windsor Castle notepaper but probably sent from Sandringham. Lord Hardinge archive.
25 From *The King's Daughters in Wartime*, by Ann Ring, published in *Strand* magazine and quoted in *Rochdale Observer*, 7 December 1940.

Chapter 14: Allies at Last (1941)
1   Letter from the Queen at Sandringham to Queen Mary, 7 January 1941, William Shawcross, ed., *Counting One's Blessings: The Selected Letters of Queen Elizabeth the Queen Mother* (London: Macmillan, 2012).
2   Quoted in Philip Eade, *Young Prince Philip: His Turbulent Early Life* (London: Harper Press, 2012).
3   Interview with Philip's sister, whose title by marriage was the Markgrafin of Baden, quoted in newsletter of the International Services of Information (ISI), March 1952. Mountbatten archives, University of Southampton.
4   Eade, *Young Prince Philip*.
5   Eden replaced Lord Halifax, who was now British Ambassador to the United States.

6   Ronald Tree, in whose house in the United States David Bowes Lyon's children were staying during the war, was Parliamentary Private Secretary to the Minister of Warfare. His letter was to the Rt. Hon. Anthony Eden in the Foreign Office, 15 March 1941. National Archives, FO 954/29 US/41/3b.

7   Sir Bruce Lockhart, *The Diaries of Sir Bruce Lockhart, 1939–1965* (London: Macmillan, 1980). Lockhart was Director-General of the PWE.

8   Interview reported in *The Sunday Dispatch*, 16 March 1941.

9   Letter from RH Brand in British Embassy, Washington, to Lord Halifax, 7 April 1941, National Archives, FO/1093/23.

10 Letter from 'Norman' on Rhode Island, to 'Darling', 12 April 1941. National Archives, FO/1093/23.

11 Margaret Rhodes, *The Final Curtsey* (London: Umbria Press, 2011).

12 Rhodes, *The Final Curtsey*.

13 Lady Butter to the author.

14 Extracted from *A King's Heritage: The Memoirs of King Peter II of Yugoslavia*, unpublished, reproduced by kind permission of his son, HRH Crown Prince Alexander.

15 Quoted in William Shawcross, *Queen Elizabeth the Queen Mother* (London: Pan Books, 2010).

16 Quoted in Eade, *Young Prince Philip*.

17 Anne Edwards, *Royal Sisters* (London: Collins, 1990).

Chapter 15: Growing Up (1942)

1   Ben Pimlott, *The Queen: Elizabeth and the Monarchy* (London: Harper Press, 2012), 67.

2   *Newcastle Journal*, 22 April 1942.

3   Quoted in Anne Edwards, *Royal Sisters* (London: Collins, 1990). Sheridan's visit was in 1940.

4   Marion Crawford, *The Little Princesses* (London: Orion Books, 2003).

5   J. Wentworth Day, *Princess Marina Duchess of Kent* (London: Robert Hale, 1969).

6   Letter from George, Duke of Kent, at Badminton, to Lady Desborough, 13 July 1942, Desborough papers, HALS.

7   Letter from the King at Buckingham Palace to Helen Hardinge, 4 September 1942, Lord Hardinge archive.

8   *Daily Herald*, 27 October 1942.

9   Quoted in William Shawcross, *Queen Elizabeth the Queen Mother* (London: Pan Books, 2010).

10 Pamela Hicks, *Daughter of Empire: Life as a Mountbatten* (London: Weidenfeld & Nicolson, 2012).

11 Lady Butter to the author.

12 Quoted in Philip Eade, *Young Prince Philip: His Turbulent Early Life* (London: Harper Press, 2012).

13 Sir Alan Lascelles, *King's Counsellor: Abdication and War, The Diaries of Sir Alan Lascelles*, ed. Duff Hart-Davis (London: Weidenfeld & Nicolson, 2006).

14 *Sunday Post*, 13 December 1942.

Chapter 16: All the Young Men (1943)

1 Mrs Rhodes to the author.
2 Mrs Rhodes to the author.
3 The Duke of Grafton to Graham Turner, quoted by Philip Eade in *Duke of Edinburgh: Right Man for the Job*, online article for *Telegraph*, 6 June 2012.
4 Martin Charteris, quoted by Eade in *Duke of Edinburgh*, 6 June 2012.
5 Earl of Carnarvon to Gyles Brandreth, quoted by Eade in *Duke of Edinburgh*, 6 June 2012.
6 Quoted by Eade in *Duke of Edinburgh*, 6 June 2012.
7 Unnamed lady-in-waiting to Graham Turner, quoted by Eade in *Duke of Edinburgh*, 6 June 2012.
8 Hugo Vickers, *Elizabeth, the Queen Mother* (London: Arrow Books, 2006).
9 *The Scotsman*, 13 May 1943.
10 Memo from Washington to the Foreign Office, 17 April 1943, National Archives, FO 954/23.
11 Diary entry for Wednesday, 23 June 1943, Lascelles.
12 Letter from the Queen at Buckingham Palace to Helen Hardinge, 7 July 1943, Lord Hardinge archives.
13 Quoted in William Shawcross, *Queen Elizabeth the Queen Mother* (London: Pan Books, 2010).
14 Gwen Robinson of Calne, Wiltshire, in a letter to her grandfather Mr A. Ruddle of Trowbridge, published in *Wiltshire Times and Trowbridge Advertiser*, 24 July 1943.
15 The Queen at Buckingham Palace to David Bowes Lyon, 17 October 1943, William Shawcross, ed., *Counting One's Blessings: The Selected Letters of Queen Elizabeth the Queen Mother* (London: Macmillan, 2012).
16 Quoted in Philip Eade, *Young Prince Philip: His Turbulent Early Life* (London: Harper Press, 2012).
17 Prince Philip, quoted in Eade, *Young Prince Philip*.
18 Marion Crawford, *The Little Princesses* (London: Orion Books, 2003).
19 Letter from the Queen at Buckingham Palace to Osbert Sitwell, 30 November 1943, Shawcross letters.
20 Cecil Beaton, quoted in Anne Edwards, *Royal Sisters* (London: Collins, 1990).
21 *Gloucester Citizen*, 18 December 1943.
22 Crawford, *The Little Princesses*.
23 Sir Alan Lascelles, *King's Counsellor: Abdication and War, The Diaries of Sir Alan Lascelles*, ed. Duff Hart-Davis (London: Weidenfeld & Nicolson, 2006).
24 Lascelles, *King's Counsellor*.
25 John W. Wheeler-Bennett, *King George VI: His Life and Reign* (London: Macmillan, 1958).
26 Quoted in Shawcross, *Queen Elizabeth the Queen Mother*.

Chapter 17: Rumours (1944)

1 Quoted in Philip Eade, *Young Prince Philip: His Turbulent Early Life* (London: Harper Press, 2012).

2 Quoted in Countess of Airlie, *Thatched with Gold: The Memoirs of Mabell, Countess of Airlie*, ed. Jennifer Ellis (London: Hutchinson, 1962).

3 Quoted in William Shawcross, *Queen Elizabeth the Queen Mother* (London: Pan Books, 2010).

4 Quoted in Shawcross, *Queen Elizabeth the Queen Mother.*

5 Diary entry 24 January 1944, Sir Alan Lascelles, *King's Counsellor: Abdication and War, The Diaries of Sir Alan Lascelles*, ed. Duff Hart-Davis (London: Weidenfeld & Nicolson, 2006).

6 Lascelles, diary entry 27 January 1944.

7 Quoted in John W. Wheeler-Bennett, *King George VI: His Life and Reign* (London: Macmillan, 1958).

8 Lascelles, diary entries 23 and 24 February 1944.

9 Quoted in Wheeler-Bennett, *King George VI.*

10 Letter from the Queen at Sandringham to Queen Mary, 11 April 1944, William Shawcross, ed., *Counting One's Blessings: The Selected Letters of Queen Elizabeth the Queen Mother* (London: Macmillan, 2012).

11 *Liverpool Daily Post*, 21 April 1944.

12 *The Times*, 17 April 1944.

13 *Daily Record*, 21 April 1944.

14 'Uncle Charlie' in *Gloucester Journal*, 22 April 1944.

15 Quoted in Wheeler-Bennett, *King George VI.*

16 Letter from Princess Elizabeth at Buckingham Palace to Lady Desborough, 25 April 1944, Desborough papers, HALS.

17 Quoted in Eade, *Young Prince Philip.*

18 Pamela Hicks, *Daughter of Empire: Life as a Mountbatten* (London: Weidenfeld & Nicolson, 2012).

19 Olga Franklin in *Newcastle Journal*, 17 April 1944. She also said that he had been interviewed once before, after he was spotted by a correspondent in the House of Commons, when he had gone to see how Parliament operated. The reporting must have been very local and limited.

20 From a letter to her sister Beryl, quoted in a feature about the late Olga Franklin in *Mail Online*, 14 May 2015.

21 Quoted in Eade, *Young Prince Philip.*

22 *The Times*, 7 June 1944.

23 Letter from the Queen at Buckingham Palace, 27 June 1944, Shawcross letters. Mrs Ronnie Greville was a long-time friend of the King and Queen who died in 1942, leaving the Queen her jewellery, including a diamond necklace said to have belonged to Marie Antoinette. She also left £20,000 to Princess Margaret.

24 Marion Crawford, *The Little Princesses* (London: Orion Books, 2003).

25 In November 1944 Lady Mary married Major the Hon. Anthony Strachey and served with Princess Elizabeth until 1947. In December 1955 her husband killed himself by a shot in the head. In 1981 she became the second wife of St John Gore.

26 Letter from the Queen at Buckingham Palace to Queen Mary, 17 July 1944, Shawcross letters.

27 Letter from the Queen at Buckingham Palace to the King, 26 July 1944, Shawcross letters.
28 Letter from Princess Elizabeth at Balmoral Castle to Betty Shew, 1947, part-published online, *PeopleRoyals*, 23 September 2016.
29 Letter from Sir Michael Duff to Lady Desborough, 12 July, no year but clearly 1944, ref. D/ERV C711/12 Desborough docs, HALS.
30 Letter from the Queen at Balmoral Castle to Queen Mary, 19 August 1944, Shawcross letters.
31 Letter 28 July 1944 from Helen Hardinge to Alec Hardinge, Lord Hardinge archive.
32 Letter from the Queen at Buckingham Palace to Queen Mary, 6 November 1944, Shawcross letters.
33 Letter from the Queen at Buckingham Palace to David Bowes Lyon, 14 November 1944, Shawcross letters.
34 Lascelles, diary entry 23 December 1944.
35 *The Scotsman*, 26 December 1944.

Chapter 18: Freedom (1945)

1   *The Times*, 31 January 1945.
2   Letter from the Queen at Appleton to Queen Mary, 26 January 1945, William Shawcross, ed., *Counting One's Blessings: The Selected Letters of Queen Elizabeth the Queen Mother* (London: Macmillan, 2012).
3   Marion Crawford, *The Little Princesses* (London: Orion Books, 2003).
4   Quoted in Dermot Morrah, *Princess Elizabeth, Duchess of Edinburgh* (London: Odhams Press, 1950).
5   Morrah, *Princess Elizabeth*.
6   Letter from Princess Elizabeth to Winifred, née Hardinge, undated but later in 1945, Lord Hardinge archive.
7   Jean was born into the Hambro banking dynasty.
8   Mrs Rhodes to the author.
9   Margaret Rhodes, *The Final Curtsey* (London: Umbria Press, 2011).
10 Princess Elizabeth's diary entry, 7 May 1945, quoted in Rhodes, *The Final Curtsey*.
11 Quoted in William Shawcross, *Queen Elizabeth the Queen Mother* (London: Pan Books, 2010).
12 Diary entry, 14 April 1945, Sir Alan Lascelles, *King's Counsellor: Abdication and War, The Diaries of Sir Alan Lascelles*, ed. Duff Hart-Davis (London: Weidenfeld & Nicolson, 2006).
13 Quoted in John W. Wheeler-Bennett, *King George VI: His Life and Reign* (London: Macmillan, 1958).
14 Rhodes, *The Final Curtsey*.
15 Rhodes, *The Final Curtsey*.
16 Lord Porchester talking to Sarah Bradford in 1989, recounted in her feature for *The Telegraph* online, 20 April 2015. A film came out in 2015 called *A Royal Night Out*, which did not mention Porchey.

17 Letter sent in 1945 by Diana Carnegie to her husband James, in Germany with the Royal Artillery, quoted in feature by agencies, *The Telegraph* online, 17 March 2014.

18 Princess Elizabeth's diary entry, 9 May 1945, quoted in Rhodes, *The Final Curtsey*.

19 Lascelles, diary entry, 17 May 1945.

20 *Sunday Mirror*, 3 June 1945.

21 Letter from Princess Elizabeth to Winifred, Murray, née Hardinge, undated but clearly 1945, Lord Hardinge archives.

22 A statue of a urinating boy.

23 Princess Elizabeth's diary entry, 15 August 1945, quoted in Rhodes, *The Final Curtsey*.

24 Gyles Brandreth, 'Portrait of a Marriage', *The Telegraph* online, 5 September 2004.

25 *Aberdeen Press and Journal*, 8 July 1941.

26 Quoted by Brandreth, 'Portrait of a Marriage'.

27 Quoted by Philip Eade, *Young Prince Philip: His Turbulent Early Life* (London: Harper Press, 2012).

28 Quoted by Brandreth, 'Portrait of a Marriage'.

29 Crawford, *The Little Princesses*.

30 Clifford Webb for the *Daily Herald*, 16 April 1945.

Chapter 19: Courting at Last (1946)

1 Letter from Princess Elizabeth at Sandringham to Lady Desborough, 6 January 1946, Desborough papers, HALS.

2 Countess of Airlie, *Thatched with Gold: The Memoirs of Mabell, Countess of Airlie*, ed. Jennifer Ellis (London: Hutchinson, 1962).

3 Letter from Alice Bruce at Windsor Castle to Lady Desborough, 6 January 1946, Desborough papers, HALS.

4 Quoted in Philip Eade, *Young Prince Philip: His Turbulent Early Life* (London: Harper Press, 2012).

5 Quoted in Betty Spencer Shew, *Royal Wedding* (London: Macdonald, 1947).

6 Marion Crawford, *The Little Princesses* (London: Orion Books, 2003).

7 Letter from Princess Elizabeth at Balmoral to Betty Shew, 1947.

8 Quoted in William Shawcross, *Queen Elizabeth the Queen Mother* (London: Pan Books, 2010).

9 Dermot Morrah, *Princess Elizabeth, Duchess of Edinburgh* (London: Odhams Press, 1950).

10 Lady Butter to the author.

11 Quoted in Eade, *Young Prince Philip*.

12 Quoted in Crawford, *The Little Princesses*. Lady Margaret later married Sir Jock Colville.

13 Letter Prince Philip to the Queen, 12 June 1946, quoted in Shawcross, *Queen Elizabeth the Queen Mother*.

14 Crawford, *The Little Princesses*.

15 Crawford, *The Little Princesses*.

16 Lady Butter to the author.

17 Lady Penn to the author, 4 May 2016. In 2016 she and HM Queen Elizabeth II both reached ninety and they attended each other's celebrations.
18 *Dundee Evening Telegraph*, 9 September 1946.
19 Airlie, *Thatched with Gold*.
20 Letter from Prince Philip to the Queen, 14 September 1946, quoted in Shawcross, *Queen Elizabeth the Queen Mother*.
21 Lady Butter to the author.
22 Letter from Prince Philip to the Queen, 3 December 1946, quoted in Shawcross, *Queen Elizabeth the Queen Mother*.
23 Obituary, *The Times*, 29 February 2016.
24 Pamela Hicks, *Daughter of Empire: Life as a Mountbatten* (London: Weidenfeld & Nicolson, 2012).
25 She was born in March 1925.
26 Lady Butter to the author.
27 Quoted in Eade, *Young Prince Philip*.
28 Defence (Armed Services) Regulations 1939.
29 *Yorkshire Post*, 6 December 1946.
30 Letter from Mountbatten to Tom Driberg, 4 December 1946, programme on Channel 4, 2015, *Prince Philip: The Plot to Make a King*.

Chapter 20: A Royal Announcement (1947)

1   Lady Penn to the author.
2   Quoted in Philip Eade, *Young Prince Philip: His Turbulent Early Life* (London: Harper Press, 2012).
3   Quoted in Eade, *Young Prince Philip*.
4   Letter Mountbatten to Boy Browning, early February 1947, MB1/E23, Mountbatten papers, Southampton University. Browning had been Mountbatten's Chief of Staff in SE Asia Command and was now Military Secretary of the War Office.
5   Pamela Hicks, *Daughter of Empire: Life as a Mountbatten* (London: Weidenfeld & Nicolson, 2012).
6   Letter from Princess Elizabeth at Balmoral Castle to Betty Spencer Shew, 1947.
7   Betty Spencer Shew, *Royal Wedding* (London: Macdonald, 1947).
8   Quoted in Dermot Morrah, *Princess Elizabeth, Duchess of Edinburgh* (London: Odhams Press, 1950).
9   Quoted in Ben Pimlott, *The Queen: Elizabeth and the Monarchy* (London: Harper Press, 2012).
10 Quoted in William Shawcross, *Queen Elizabeth the Queen Mother* (London: Pan Books, 2010).
11 Betty Spencer Shew, *Royal Wedding* (London: Macdonald, 1947).
12 Princess Elizabeth to Queen Mary, 28 March 1947, quoted in Shawcross, *Queen Elizabeth the Queen Mother*.
13 Quoted in Spencer Shew, *Royal Wedding*.

14 Quoted in Hugo Vickers, *Elizabeth the Queen Mother* (London: Arrow Books, 2006).

15 Quoted in Vickers, *Elizabeth the Queen Mother.*

16 *The Times*, 22 April 1947.

17 Pimlott, *The Queen.*

18 *The Times*, 22 April 1947.

19 Quoted in Morrah, *Princess Elizabeth.*

20 Quoted in Pimlott, *The Queen.*

21 Marion Crawford, *The Little Princesses* (London: Orion Books, 2003).

22 Eade, *Young Prince Philip.*

23 Letter from Princess Elizabeth at Balmoral, 1947.

24 Quoted by Gyles Brandreth when she was Lady Gina Kennard, article, *Portrait of a Marriage, The Telegraph* online, 5 September 2004.

25 Admiral Sir William O'Brien, from his memoirs, quoted in his obituary, *The Times*, 29 February 2016.

26 7 July 1947, quoted in Shawcross, *Queen Elizabeth the Queen Mother.* Shawcross says it was in draft form and probably not sent.

27 Letter from the Queen at Buckingham Palace to May Elphinstone, 7 July 1947, William Shawcross, ed., *Counting One's Blessings: The Selected Letters of Queen Elizabeth the Queen Mother* (London: Macmillan, 2012).

28 Letter from the Queen at Buckingham Palace to Philip, 9 July 1947, Shawcross letters.

29 Crawford, *The Little Princesses.*

30 Quoted by Morrah, *Princess Elizabeth.*

31 Letter from Princess Elizabeth at Balmoral to Betty Spencer Shew, 1947.

32 *The Scotsman*, 10 July 1947.

33 Lady Penn to the author.

34 Spencer Shew, *Royal Wedding.*

35 Letter from Sir Michael Duff to Lady Desborough, 14 July, no year but clearly 1947, Desborough papers, HALS.

36 Letter from Sir Michael Duff to Lady Desborough, 14 July, no year but clearly 1947, Desborough papers, HALS.

37 Countess of Airlie, *Thatched with Gold: The Memoirs of Mabell, Countess of Airlie*, ed. Jennifer Ellis (London: Hutchinson, 1962).

38 Quoted in Eade, *Young Prince Philip.*

39 Crawford, *The Little Princesses.*

40 Quoted in Eade, *Young Prince Philip.*

41 Note 15 July 1947, INF 12/180, Central Office of Information, National Archives.

42 Letter to Miss Fell, 31 July 1947, INF 12/180, Central Office of Information, National Archives.

43 INF 12/180 Letter from 'BJF', 31 July (?) 1947, Central Office of Information, National Archives. Black and white photographs were to be handled by *Planet* and *Daily Sketch.*

44 Quoted by Brandreth, *Portrait of a Marriage*.
45 Lady Penn to the author.
46 Quoted in Pimlott, *The Queen*.
47 Lady Penn to the author.
48 Letter Lady Hamilton at Balmoral to Helen Hardinge, 8 October 1947, Lord Hardinge archive.

Chapter 21: Light and Hope (1947)

1 Quoted in Ben Pimlott, *The Queen: Elizabeth and the Monarchy* (London: Harper Press, 2012).
2 Letter 19 September 1947 in Home Office file HO/144/23365, National Archives.
3 Letter 19 September 1947 in Home Office file HO/144/23365, National Archives.
4 Quoted in Betty Spencer Shew, *Royal Wedding* (London: Macdonald, 1947).
5 Quoted in Pimlott, *The Queen*.
6 Mrs Rhodes to the author.
7 Pamela Hicks, *Daughter of Empire: Life as a Mountbatten* (London: Weidenfeld & Nicolson, 2012).
8 Lord Chamberlain reported in the *Daily Telegraph*, 16 September 1947.
9 Pimlott, *The Queen*.
10 Quoted in Philip Eade, *Young Prince Philip: His Turbulent Early Life* (London: Harper Press, 2012).
11 Home Office file HO/144/23365, National Archives.
12 Countess of Airlie, *Thatched with Gold: The Memoirs of Mabell, Countess of Airlie*, ed. Jennifer Ellis (London: Hutchinson, 1962).
13 Sally Bedell Smith, *Vanity Fair* online, January 2012.
14 John W. Wheeler-Bennett, *King George VI: His Life and Reign* (London: Macmillan, 1958). Philip was not created a Prince at that stage, even though he was HRH; the Queen would create him a Prince of the United Kingdom in February 1957 in recognition of the services he had rendered to the country and the life of the Commonwealth.
15 Lady Brabourne, Channel 4 documentary, *Prince Philip: The Plot to Make a King*, 2015.
16 Hicks, *Daughter of Empire*.
17 Mrs Rhodes to the author.
18 Lady Longford in *The Times*, 15 November 1997.
19 Quoted in Spencer Shew, *Royal Wedding*.
20 Hicks, *Daughter of Empire*.
21 Marion Crawford, *The Little Princesses* (London: Orion Books, 2003).
22 Princess Elizabeth to the Queen, 22 November 1947, quoted in William Shawcross, *Queen Elizabeth the Queen Mother* (London: Pan Books, 2010).
23 The Queen at Buckingham Palace to Princess Elizabeth, 24 November 1947, William Shawcross, ed., *Counting One's Blessings: The Selected Letters of Queen Elizabeth the Queen Mother* (London: Macmillan, 2012).
24 Quoted in Wheeler-Bennett, *King George VI*.

25 Princess Elizabeth to the Queen, 30 November 1947, quoted in Shawcross, *Queen Elizabeth the Queen Mother*.
26 The Queen at Buckingham Palace to Philip, 1 December 1947, Shawcross letters.
27 Philip to the Queen, 3 December 1947, quoted in Shawcross, *Queen Elizabeth the Queen Mother*.

Chapter 22: Getting Settled (1948)

1   Colville's diary, quoted in Ben Pimlott, *The Queen: Elizabeth and the Monarchy* (London: Harper Press, 2012).
2   Mrs Rhodes to the author.
3   Lady Butter to the author.
4   *The Times*, 14 May 1948.
5   Sir John (Jock) Colville, 'Working for a Lady', *Minerva* Magazine, 1978.
6   Lady Butter to the author.
7   Quoted in Pimlott, *The Queen*.
8   Duke of Edinburgh in Foreword to *General 'Boy'* by Richard Mead, Pen & Sword Military, 2010.
9   Letter from the Queen at Buckingham Palace to Philip, 1 December 1947, William Shawcross, ed., *Counting One's Blessings: The Selected Letters of Queen Elizabeth the Queen Mother* (London: Macmillan, 2012).
10 Marion Crawford, *The Little Princesses* (London: Orion Books, 2003).
11 Lady Butter to the author.
12 Quoted in Philip Eade, *Young Prince Philip: His Turbulent Early Life* (London: Harper Press, 2012).
13 Quoted in Anne Edwards, *Royal Sisters* (London: Collins, 1990).
14 *The Times*, 24 April 1948.
15 *The Times*, 14 May 1948.
16 Dermot Morrah, *Princess Elizabeth, Duchess of Edinburgh* (London: Odhams Press, 1950).
17 Quoted in Edwards, *Royal Sisters*.
18 Colville, *Working for a Lady*.
19 *Aberdeen Press and Journal*, 20 May 1948.
20 *The Times*, 20 May 1948.
21 Quoted in Pimlott, *The Queen*.
22 Pimlott, *The Queen*.
23 Crawford, *The Little Princesses*.
24 *Western Daily Press*, 9 June 1948.
25 Philip remained a member until the reforms of 1999 but never spoke, due to his proximity to the Queen, who must remain politically neutral.
26 2 July 1948.
27 Macmillan diaries.
28 Eade, *Young Prince Philip*.
29 Interview with Lord Hardinge of Penshurst, 22 March 1988, quoted in Sarah Bradford, *George VI* (London: Penguin, 2002, reissued 2011).

Chapter 23: Princess, Wife, Mother (1949– 1950)

1 Letter from Princess Elizabeth at Sandringham to Lady Desborough, 11 February 1949, Desborough papers, HALS.
2 The King at Sandringham to Lady Desborough, 14 January 1949, Desborough papers, HALS.
3 The Queen from Royal Lodge to Sir D'Arcy Osborne, 5 March 1949, William Shawcross, ed., *Counting One's Blessings: The Selected Letters of Queen Elizabeth the Queen Mother* (London: Macmillan, 2012).
4 Letter from Princess Elizabeth at Buckingham Palace to Helen Hardinge, 30 May 1949, Lord Hardinge archive.
5 Ben Pimlott, *The Queen: Elizabeth and the Monarchy* (London: Harper Press, 2012).
6 Pimlott, *The Queen*.
7 Quoted in Philip Eade, *Young Prince Philip: His Turbulent Early Life* (London: Harper Press, 2012).
8 Quoted in Eade, *Young Prince Philip*.
9 Eade, *Young Prince Philip*.
10 *Dundee Evening Telegraph*, 13 July 1949.
11 Letter from the Queen at Sandringham to Queen Mary, 13 February 1949, Shawcross letters.
12 Letter from the Queen at Balmoral to Helen Hardinge, 4 October 1949, Lord Hardinge archives.
13 *Western Morning News*, 8 November 1949.
14 Mrs Rhodes to the author.
15 Quoted in Eade, *Young Prince Philip*.
16 Quoted in Pimlott, *The Queen*.
17 Pamela Hicks, *Daughter of Empire: Life as a Mountbatten* (London: Weidenfeld & Nicolson, 2012).
18 The Queen at Buckingham Palace to Princess Elizabeth, 21 December 1949, Shawcross letters.
19 Letter 18 April 1949, quoted in Philip Ziegler, *King Edward VIII* (London: Collins, 1990).
20 Draft of letter 16 December 1949, quoted in Ziegler, *King Edward VIII*.
21 Christopher Wilson, 'The Duke and Duchess of Windsor's Secret Plot to Deny the Queen the Throne,' *Telegraph* online, 22 November 2009.
22 Hicks, *Daughter of Empire*.
23 Colville in *Minerva*, 1978.
24 *Hull Daily Mail*, 18 October 1949.
25 Letter from the Queen at Buckingham Palace to Helen Hardinge, 21 February 1950, Lord Hardinge archive.
26 Letter from Cynthia Colville, lady-in-waiting, at Marlborough House, to Helen Hardinge, 7 March 1952, Lord Hardinge archive.
27 Letter from the Queen at Buckingham Palace to Helen Hardinge, 21 February 1950, Lord Hardinge archive.
28 Hicks, *Daughter of Empire*.

29 Quoted in Valentine Low, 'Queen Walks Malta's Memory Lane', *The Times*, 27 November 2015.
30 Letter from the Queen at Buckingham Palace, 24 April 1950, Shawcross letters.
31 Letter from the Queen at Buckingham Palace, 21 July 1950, Shawcross letters.
32 Letter from Princess Elizabeth at Clarence House to Helen Hardinge, 5 September 1950, Lord Hardinge archive.
33 Quoted in Eade, *Young Prince Philip*.

Chapter 24: Rehearsing the Future (1951–1952)

1 Lord Charteris of Amisfield, *Saying What Everyone Thinks*, *Spectator* archive, 7 January 1995.
2 Letter from the Queen at Sandringham to Helen Hardinge, 18 January 1951, Lord Hardinge archive. Helen proceeded with the book, *Loyal to Three Kings*, in 1967, after Sir Alec's death.
3 *Yorkshire Post and Leeds Intelligencer*, 25 May 1951.
4 Quoted in John W. Wheeler-Bennett, *King George VI: His Life and Reign* (London: Macmillan, 1958).
5 Helen Hardinge, *The Path of Kings*.
6 Letter from Lady Olivia Mulholland at Buckingham Palace to Helen Hardinge, 18 June 1951, Lord Hardinge archive.
7 Quoted in William Shawcross, *Queen Elizabeth the Queen Mother* (London: Pan Books, 2010).
8 Letter from Princess Elizabeth, quoted in Shawcross, *Queen Elizabeth the Queen Mother*.
9 Quoted in Shawcross, *Queen Elizabeth the Queen Mother*.
10 Letter from Princess Margaret at Buckingham Palace to Helen Hardinge, 11 October 1951.
11 *Portsmouth Evening News*, 21 July 1951. He was the Flag Officer of Destroyers in the Mediterranean Fleet.
12 From Ottawa, reported in the *Yorkshire Post*, 11 October 1951.
13 Quoted in Ben Pimlott, *The Queen: Elizabeth and the Monarchy* (London: Harper Press, 2012).
14 Letter from Mountbatten to Brigadier M. Wardell, 19 October 1951, Mountbatten archive, University of Southampton.
15 Charteris, quoted in Philip Eade, *Young Prince Philip: His Turbulent Early Life* (London: Harper Press, 2012).
16 Letter from the Queen at Buckingham Palace to Princess Elizabeth, 15 October 1951, William Shawcross, ed., *Counting One's Blessings: The Selected Letters of Queen Elizabeth the Queen Mother* (London: Macmillan, 2012).
17 Letter 4 November 1951, mentioned in Shawcross letters.
18 Quoted in Wheeler-Bennett, *King George VI*.
19 Wheeler-Bennett, *King George VI*.
20 Quoted in Hugo Vickers, *Elizabeth, the Queen Mother* (London: Arrow Books, 2006).

21 The first was Prince John.

22 Letter 7 March 1952 from Marlborough House, Lord Hardinge archives.

23 International Services of Information.

24 From memorandum of the ISI, March 1952, ME1/H260 f1, Mountbatten archive, University of Southampton.

25 Letter from the Duke of Norfolk, 9 February 1952. The Dukes were Windsor, Gloucester and the young Kent. The Duke of Edinburgh also walked with them. Mountbatten archive, University of Southampton.

26 On the day itself, the Queen rode in a carriage behind the coffin with the Queen Mother, Princess Margaret and the Princess Royal.

27 Note to the Duke of Norfolk, dictated by Mountbatten on 11 February 1952. Mountbatten archive, University of Southampton.

28 The Queen agreed that the surname of Mountbatten-Windsor should be used by those members of the royal family who were no longer entitled to be called Prince or Princess but would have to use a surname.

29 Lady Butter to the author.

30 Mrs Rhodes to the author.

Index

About the Author

After graduating from the University of Cambridge, Jane Dismore taught English and Drama and began writing articles for national magazines. A complete change of lifestyle saw her running private yachts in the Mediterranean, which she combined with writing features and presenting for the British Forces Broadcasting Service. She re-qualified as a Solicitor of the Supreme Court of England and Wales and worked in private practice but continued to write in her free time, focusing on biographical subjects. Her first non-fiction book, *The Voice from the Garden* (2012), was longlisted for the New Angle Prize for Literature. Her most recent book is *Duchesses: Living in 21st Century Britain* (2014), which examines the lives of Britain's non-royal duchesses and their dukes. She now writes full time, contributing to history websites and magazines such as *History Today* and has also been published in newspapers, including *The Times* and *The Daily Telegraph*. She lives in England.